Bristol-Avonmouth

Zinkhütte „Imperial Smelting Corp. Ltd."

Länge (westl. Greenw.): 2° 41′ 45″   Breite: 51° 29′ 50″

Mißweisung: — 11° 34′ (Mitte 1941)   Zielhöhe über NN 6 m

Maßstab etwa 1 : 14 500

Genst. 5. Abt.   Mai 1941

Karte 1 : 100 000

GB/E 32

Mouth of the Severn

River Avon

1. Schmelzöfen, Kessel- und Maschinenhäuser, massiv, verschiedene Dacharten, hohe Schornsteine etwa 18 000 qm
2. Fabrikations- und Lagerhallen, massiv, verschiedene Dacharten etwa 6 000 qm
3. Nebenproduktengewinnung (Benzol, Schwefelsäure) mit mehreren Fertigungs- und Fabrikationsgebäuden sowie Wäschern und Behältern, ein hoher und mehrere kleine Schornsteine etwa 24 800 qm
4. Kühltürme
5. Verwaltungs- und Nebengebäude, massiv, versch. Dacharten etwa 3 200 qm
6. Rundbehälter, ⌀ etwa 15 m

7. Lagerplatz mit mehreren Aufbereitungs-, Fabrikations- und Nebengebäuden etwa 2 800 qm
8. Kläranlage
9. Schlacken und Kohlenhalden

○ a) Sperrballone
   Gleisanschluß vorhanden.

Bebaute Fläche etwa 54 800 qm
Gesamtausdehnung etwa 835 000 qm

GB 14 31 Barackenlager
GB 45 55 Hafenanlagen
GB 56 56 Getreidemühle und -lager am Avonmouth Dock
GB 56 64 Transitgetreidesilo und Großmühle „Cooperative Wholesale"

1   AVONMOUTH. Aerial view taken by the Luftwaffe en route to bomb Filton 27 September 1940. German Intelligence locate Imperial Smelting Corporation Ltd Works, C.W.S. Flour Mills, Provender Mills, Docks, Port Installations, Army Barracks on Penpole Point, and barrage balloons (sperrballone) etc.

WAR STORY

ETHEL THOMAS

Ettiel Thomas

Published by
Mrs. Ethel Thomas
55 Cook Street
Avonmouth
Bristol BS11 9JY

Phototypeset in Bembo and Printed by Burleigh Press Ltd., Bristol

2 JACKET PICTURE:

Hospital Ship *Oranje* arriving at Royal Edward Dock, Avonmouth 14 March 1944. *Foreground:* Bomb-damaged armed merchant ship.

The largest of the Hospital Ships to put into Avonmouth Docks during the Second World War, was the 20,017 gross registered tonnage (g.r.t.) oil engine, three screw Dutch luxury liner *Oranje* – a very beautiful ship with three swimming pools. Built in 1938 by Nederland Scheepsbouw Maatshappij for Owners Nederland Stoomvaart Maatschappij, *Oranje* was specially designed to operate in shallow waters, for high speed and greatest stability. These factors, together with maximum passenger outboard staterooms gave her sides a great bulge, which led to some difficulties in manoeuvring her safely into the Dry Dock at Avonmouth for repairs, with only a few inches to spare either side!

Oranje was intended to cruise between Holland and the Dutch East Indies, and sailed on her maiden voyage in September 1939. Due to the war breaking out she remained at Java, and was converted into a Hospital Ship. In March 1941 she was given to Australia by the Netherland East Indies.

After the war, *Oranje* was handed back to her Owners, and refitted. In 1964 she was sold to an Italian firm, renamed *Angelina Lauro*, and thence operated a round-the-world service from Europe (calling at Southampton) to Australia and New Zealand.

Due to strict censorship pertaining to all events taking place in Avonmouth during the war, the above is one of the rare photographs now in existence taken in the Parish during that time.

ACKNOWLEDGEMENTS

The Author wishes to express her grateful thanks to the many people who have kindly offered information or photographs which have been so helpful in the preparation of this book, particularly Captain Kenneth Leslie, Mr. Ian James, Mr. John Penny, Mr. Bill Thomas and Mr. Frederick Hooper, and also special thanks to Mrs. Olive Guinn (née Webb) and her husband Bob for their meticulous proof reading.

ILLUSTRATIONS

The photographs in this book form part of the Ethel Thomas 'AVONMOUTH COLLECTION', and emanate from the following contributors to whom the Author is most grateful:

AeroFilms Ltd. Hendon, B.B.C. Hulton Picture Library, Bristol Records Office, Bristol United Press, J. H. Bromhead of Clifton, Mrs. Ethel Brown, Mr. Leonard Brown, Jeff. Brownhut Promotions Ltd. Leeds, Mr. W. Butcher, Mrs. Ada Cummings, Mrs. Barbara Davis, Evening Post, Evening World, Mrs. N. E. Franklin, Gloucestershire Gazette Series of Newspapers, Mr. R. E. Hadlow, Hutchinson & Co. (Publishers) Ltd., Illustrated Magazine, Imperial War Museum, Mr. David Ireland, Mr. I. James, Mrs. Joyce Lait, Captain Kenneth J. Leslie, S. Loxton (Sketches), Mr. A. H. May, The Mariners Museum, Newport News, Virginia, U.S.A., Mr. N. J. Martin, Midland Region of British Rail, Ministry of Information, Mr. Colin Momber, Odhams Press Ltd., Kenneth I. Oldroyd, F.R.P.S., Mrs. G. Pinnock, Port of Bristol Authority Photograph Library, Mr. W. W. Powell, Mr. Bert Rice, Mr. John Rich, Mrs. Edith Room, Mr. E. F. Rowley, Mrs. Marjorie Simmonds, Messrs. Spillers-French Ltd., Mrs. Kay Stark, Mr. Alexander Taylor, Mrs. Mavis Thomas, Mrs. R. Walter, Mr. R. F. Warne, Mr. F. G. Warne, Mr. R. Waters, Western Daily Press, Mr. Howard Westlake, Mr. J. T. Williams, Mr. Reece Winstone and Mr. Rowland Woodall.

Forty-four photographs were taken by the Author.

LIST OF ILLUSTRATIONS

PREFACE

By Edwin J. Thomas, Husband of the Author.

This book, 'War Story', completes the trilogy on the parishes of Avonmouth and Shirehampton. Many readers of the first two books, 'Down the 'Mouth' and 'Shirehampton Story', have asked for a book telling the story of the two parishes through two World Wars, hence this volume.

Many books written about the Second World War, explain in vivid detail great battles on land, sea and in the air. These pages, on the other hand, tell the story of the dangers, excitements and sadness of two Wars, as seen through the eyes of local folk, who endured the bombing and destruction of their own homes, and of the grief suffered with the deaths of so many unsung heroes.

After many hours and eight years of heartrending research in writing this book, it is hoped the reader will recall many personal memories of those terrible war years. There is a saying which goes, 'Time is a great healer'. How true this is.

Many of us can now look back at those dark war years recalling sadnesses on so many occasions, but can also have a chuckle at the comical moments and events. Like my father, who just finished work one night, was walking home in the black-out, when he bumped into a pillar-box, and said, 'Sorry missus – my fault'. When we pointed out to him it was only a pillar-box, he declared, 'I'll go back in a minute and kick it!'

Sadly, we didn't see much of our Dad during the War. He worked at Jefferies Dry Dock at Avonmouth repairing ships, and when he left home on Monday mornings we had no idea when we would see him again. He often sent a messenger round home to get some more cheese sandwiches, as he wouldn't be home till Wednesday, or Thursday, then back on Friday to work till Saturday.

Is there anyone who cannot relate a funny story of the black-out, or a brave deed performed by someone 'just passing by', or even a story of rationing and under-the-counter activities?

It is hoped that readers will enjoy the nostalgic events related in 'War Story', and look back at those times with pride and affection.

25 March 1988   EDWIN J. THOMAS

CONTENTS

3   NEWSPAPER BOY. Sunday 3 September 1939. Placards and special newspaper editions published the official Declaration of War.

I. WAR IS DECLARED . . . AGAIN!

At 11.0 a.m. on Sunday 3 September 1939 Great Britain declared war against Germany. Thus started the Second World War. It lasted six years until 15 August 1945 when the Allied Forces had finally achieved complete victory.

The news that a state of war existed between Britain and Germany was announced at 11.15 a.m. on that fateful September morning in 1939 in a broadcast over B.B.C. Radio by the then Prime Minister, Mr. Neville Chamberlain. Those who heard his broken and disappointed voice would never forget it as long as they lived. Many folk to this very day still remember the Prime Minister's words quite vividly, and almost by heart when he said:

'I am speaking to you from the Cabinet Room at No. 10 Downing Street. This morning, the British Ambassador in Berlin handed the German Government a final note stating that unless we heard from them by 11 o'clock that they were prepared at once to withdraw their troops from Poland, a state of war would exist between us. I have to tell you now that no such undertaking has been received, and that consequently this Country is at war with Germany. . . .'

This was the second time in living memory that Britain had been at war with Germany. It was somewhat ironic that the nation should have been asked to stand by for a pronouncement by the Prime Minister on a Sunday morning whilst Church Services were in progress throughout the land, and at a time when the faithful were on their knees earnestly praying for peace! Many priests like the Revd. William Kingsley Martin at St. Paul's, Bedminster took their wireless receivers into their Churches that morning so that the congregations there gathered might hear for themselves Mr. Chamberlain's grave announcement.

Britain neither wanted war nor was prepared for it. The Prime Minister had done his utmost to try and prevent another war, but the time had now come for Britain to make a firm stand against Hitler's outrageous acts of aggression in Europe, and his fanatical dreams of world domination. That same evening His Majesty King George VI made an historic broadcast, in which he said:

'It is unthinkable that we should refuse to meet the challenge. It is to this high purpose that I now call my people at home and my peoples across the seas who will make our cause their own. I ask them to stand calm, firm and united. . . .'

and the King's call found a ready response in the hearts of his loyal subjects.

Upon the declaration of war Avonmouth became a place of National and International importance, and all that took place here was subject to the censor's blue pencil for the duration of hostilities.

II. THE GREAT WAR 1914–1918

(Sometimes referred to as
'THE FIRST WORLD WAR' or 'WORLD WAR I')

Britain took up arms in 1939 in a sober spirit. There were no cheering crowds in the streets singing patriotic songs and waving Union Jacks, or the blasting from ships' sirens at Avonmouth as had been the case when Britain declared war against Germany in August 1914. On the contrary, the memory was still too fresh in the minds of people of the loss of a whole generation of young men in the carnage of bloody trenches in France during the Great War for there to be any patriotic demonstrations this time. There had been hardly a family throughout the land who had not lost a loved one during that terrible conflict.

Had not the Great War been 'The war to end wars' and 'Never again!' been the hope and belief of everyone in November 1918? The League of Nations had been born in 1920 specifically to ensure International Peace and Security and to prevent another war. Little wonder then that in 1939 Bristolians went about their business quietly with a feeling of great foreboding.

In hindsight many historians maintain that the Second World War was a mere continuation of the Great War which had not been brought to a satisfactory conclusion. In 1939 much was said of the Germans not having experienced battles being fought on their own soil, that Berlin had not undergone air-raids as had many other European Cities, including London and our own Eastern Counties and Midlands. It was therefore resolved by the British Government, and Mr. Winston Churchill in particular, that under no circumstances would Britain consider any peace treaty this time except on 'unconditional surrender' terms by Germany, and that the armies of the Allies would fight all the way to Berlin itself.

Some historians attribute the rise of the evil Nazi Party and Herr Hitler to the harsh Peace Treaties imposed upon Germany following the Armistice in 1918. Germany was ultimately blamed for having caused that terrible war, and in consequence had to pay a huge sum in reparation for the damage caused. Besides which Germany's Colonies were taken from her, the size of her army, navy and manufacture of munitions was limited, and British troops occupied German territory west of the Rhine from 1918 until 1929. Hitler's rise to power (he became German Chancellor in 1933) was the result of Germany wishing to re-arm to take her revenge.

Be that as it may, Avonmouth and Shirehampton played an important part in the Great War in three particulars, namely: Avonmouth's activities as a port, Shirehampton's Remount Depot and the Mustard Gas Factory at Chittening.

AVONMOUTH PORT

Port installations in wartime are the vital starting points of the life-lines to the fighting Forces abroad. Upon the outbreak of war, dock-workers and seamen overnight become essential members of the war effort.

The Boer War (1899–1902) was Avonmouth Dock's first experience of wartime activities in the loading of guns and munitions for the Imperial Yeomanry, and the soldiers of Queen Victoria. The advantages which Avonmouth could offer the War Department were greatly increased with the opening of the Royal Edward Dock in 1908.

These were at once recognised by Lord Kitchener, who, soon after the start of the Great War visited Avonmouth in order to judge its capabilities. Some little time previously, a mysterious meeting had taken place with the Military personnel on a Sunday morning on the Downs. There followed at the Avonmouth Docks a never-to-be explained embarkation/disembarkation exercise of guns and transports, carefully timed by the watching brass-hats. As it turned out this was probably a rehearsal for the 1914–1918 war which had been anticipated.

The Parishioners of Avonmouth never forgot the first week in August 1914 when motor vehicles of all descriptions were rushed to the Docks to be shipped to France with the First Expeditionary Force. During the four years of strife Avonmouth proved an important centre from which supplies of men and materials were despatched to the armies at the Fronts. In January 1915 it was reported that some 2,000 motor transport wagons had already gone from Avonmouth during the first five months of the war, whilst thousands more were to follow.

Men, lorries and motor 'buses arrived in Bristol from all parts of the country and passed through the City in a continual stream. Day after day one could stand at a window of an office overlooking the route to Avonmouth and watch the interminable lines of war vehicles on their way to France. Motor-cars fitted as ambulances went by in hundreds, and even more numerous at a later stage were the London omnibuses, sent out to assist in the quick movement of our soldiers at the Fronts. Great guns drawn by powerful caterpillar tractors rumbled through the Bristol thoroughfares, and adjoining buildings vibrated with the weight of this unprecedented heavy traffic.

Many drivers, being strangers to the district, lost their way, and found themselves at various points where they were not wanted. The only route to Avonmouth was via Durdham Downs, Stoke Bishop and Shirehampton

Park, at that time nothing more than a narrow, winding country lane, and not too easy a route for a stranger to follow. This problem was remedied by the erection of large sign-posts, some at points scores of miles away from Bristol, stating 'TO AVONMOUTH', which were intended as a temporary measure, but many remained 'in situ' long after the war was over. This situation highlighted the miserable lack of a decent road link between Bristol and its port of Avonmouth seven miles away on the City outskirts, and led to the construction of the Portway. The new road was actually planned during the Great War and work was begun in May 1919 at the Avonmouth end, only six months after Armistice.

In the days before the present roll-on-roll-off method of shipping motor vehicles, each one had to be driven alongside the ship and then lifted on board individually by cranes. This was a slow and arduous business, and caused long queues of waiting vehicles. They spilled over from the dockside into Avonmouth Village, and many times queues reached along Avonmouth Road as far back as St. Mary's Church in High Street Shirehampton.

Much of the happenings of those days was top secret, and contemporary records of military movements and preparations was forbidden by the Authorities. The use of cameras was strictly prohibited, and of the many interesting sights witnessed at Avonmouth during the Great War *not a single photograph exists,* as far as is known! It is now therefore very interesting to recall that the first ever tank was shipped to France from Avonmouth under great secrecy.

4   FIRST TANK seen on active service in France/Flanders during the Great War. First photograph released for publication. Initially used at Battle of Somme 15 September 1916.

The stevedoring firm of C. J. King & Sons took charge at Avonmouth during the Great War, and handled much of the 13 million tons of materials which passed through the Port. They also sent trained foremen and stevedores to assist elsewhere. At Portsmouth the staff of King's helped in loading tanks for France, and have memories of a certain exuberant Cabinet Minister who insisted on helping to drive one of the new fangled tank machines himself.

Footnote:

The first tanks were designed by the Navy, and bore the initials H.M.L.S. (His Majesty's Land Ships). They were not named at first, merely given numbers. The engine was in the middle of the vehicle, with guns on each side, and although they only had a speed of 'walking pace', and were very uncomfortable to ride in, their potential performance has never been equalled. The first tanks required a crew of eight – needing four to drive them. The name 'Tank' was coined due to the factories making them being told they were making 'water carriers', and because of the Army's use of initials, the name 'Tank' was officially adopted. Tanks were first used on the Somme on 15 September 1916.

5   HOLT CATERPILLAR TRACTORS on active service in France/Flanders during the Great War.

Tractor Depot

In addition to the embarkation, landing of troops and stores, etc., Avonmouth Docks were also used for other purposes during the Great War. A Base Supply and Mechanical Transport Depot was established at the Dock Passenger Station, and a Tractor Depot at Avonmouth Farm.

The latter had been brought about by the extensive use of caterpillar tractors, and had a large staff occupying about 50 acres of land. Avonmouth Farm, which was part of the King's Weston estate, was owned by Squire Philip Napier Miles, and was adjoining St. Andrew's Road to the east. Mr. Miles leased part of Avonmouth Farm to the Government to be used as a tractor training ground, on which 'Holt' caterpillar tractors were used. Lorries also were parked at Avonmouth Farm, and in consequence the tenant-farmer, Mr. George Lait, had to reduce his head of cattle for the duration of the war.

Ships

From August 1914 to the signing of the Peace Treaty in 1919, a total of 2,282 ships on war service were dealt with at Avonmouth Docks – many being troopships. In the year 1915 alone some 118 troopships were dealt with here. Local Clergy conducted services on board all the troopships before they left port, and St. Andrew's Church was filled Sunday by Sunday for parade services.

6   R.M.S. *Royal Edward* sunk in Mediterranean with loss of 935 lives on 13 August 1915.

The sinking of the troopship *Royal Edward* in the Mediterranean in August 1915 after having set sail from Avonmouth (see 'Other Memorials') with deplorable loss of life, was keenly felt locally.

From February 1917 to July 1918 Avonmouth Docks was regularly used by hospital ships, either bringing the wounded from the theatres of war, or returning convalescent servicemen home to their own countries. Altogether 24,048 patients were disembarked at Avonmouth, and conveyed directly from the ships by ambulance trains to military hospitals in various parts of the country. In addition 13,000 convalescent Canadians, Australians, New Zealanders and South Africans sailed for home from Avonmouth. A total of 64 hospital ships and 250 ambulance trains were dealt with at Avonmouth during the Great War.

Despite the fact that in accordance with convention hospital ships were always painted white, with large red crosses on their sides, and at night brightly lit up, the Germans had no qualms about attacking them! The wanton attacks by German submarines upon hospital ships caused a world-wide revulsion, and was just another example of the barbaric methods of warfare adopted by the German Government.

The first hospital ship to come into Avonmouth was the *Rewa* in February 1917, after which she made two further calls. On 4 January 1918, whilst carrying sick and wounded, she was nearing Avonmouth when, without warning, she was torpedoed and sank very quickly 19 miles west of Hartland Point. The patients were all saved and landed at Swansea, but four crew members were killed.

A little later the hospital ship *Glenart Castle,* after calling at Avonmouth, was outward bound from Newport when she was torpedoed 10 miles off Lundy at the entrance to the Bristol Channel, resulting in the loss of 153 lives. The hospital ship *Guildford Castle* was bound for Avonmouth when she too was attacked by a submarine in the same vicinity. When she safely berthed in the Royal Edward Dock various scars on her hull confirmed the ship had been struck by a torpedo which failed to explode.

The fine R.M.S. *Asturias,* whilst on hospital service was attacked twice. The first occasion was on 1 February 1915 by a submarine when 15 miles off Havre Light Vessel, and the torpedo missed her. On 21 March 1917, when 5 miles south of Start Point making her way to Southampton after calling at Avonmouth she was torpedoed a second time with the loss of 50 lives. As the damage was slight *Asturias* was beached on the Cornish coast, and later towed into Plymouth.

After taking home Canadian wounded from Avonmouth the hospital ship *Llandovery Castle* was returning to Liverpool, when she was torpedoed without warning 100 miles west of Ireland. Some 234 members of crew and nursing staff lost their lives.

The Avonmouth dry docks and ship repairing establishments were very largely used during the Great War for the repairs of both transports and fighting ships. Fifty vessels carrying the white ensign passed through the docks for repairs, whilst a number of armed merchant ships also made use of Avonmouth Docks as a base for victualling and refitting.

7 *Englishman (5257 g.r.t.).* Regular trader Avonmouth/Canada (Dominion Line) from 1908. Torpedoed by submarine 30 miles N.E. of Malin Head, Northern Ireland 24 March 1916. Ten crew lost.

St. Andrew's Soldiers' Home

Avonmouth in 1914 was still very much a rural area, surrounded by farms and fields, and could then quite well have been described as 'a village with a dock'. The Parish population had hardly begun to expand, so little wonder that Parishioners never forgot the first week in August 1914 when motor vehicles of all descriptions were rushed to the Docks to be shipped to France. (A similar situation occurred in September 1939 – see 'St. Mary's Canteen'.)

The question arose of feeding and housing the drivers arriving with the vehicles, as no adequate arrangements had been made by the Army authorities. The people of Avonmouth were quickly on the scene to do what they could to meet the needs of the men who were arriving at all hours of the day and night.

The few shops that were in existence did a brisk trade in supplying cups of tea and light refreshments, and made their fortune, but being totally unprepared for such an emergency, were very soon cleared of their stocks.

The plight of the men had become really serious when the Revd. Harold Gibson (Vicar of Shirehampton, and later the first Vicar of Avonmouth) and Mr. Napier Miles (the Squire of King's Weston) stepped in with a remedy, and were helped as far as possible by the residents in Avonmouth and Shirehampton. They very soon established St. Andrew's Soldiers' Home, using St. Andrew's Parish Room, the wooden hut beside St. Andrew's Church. Friends in Clifton who owned motorcars also helped by driving down to Avonmouth with food supplies and provisions of all kinds which they had collected in Bristol. The Parish Room was opened for the accommodation of the lorry drivers, where food was distributed, and the men were only too glad to sleep in the building, lying on the floor!

The capacity of the Home was soon over-taxed, and a relief building in Meadow Street was taken. The Public Hall in Station Road, Shirehampton was also used as a recreation room for the men, where entertainments and special concerts were held.

With an increase of transport through Avonmouth, the need for further development was recognised, so another hut was built adjoining St. Andrew's Parish Room, and the whole building was converted into a canteen and recreation room where the men could read, write, play billiards and otherwise amuse themselves. In the early days the Revd. Harold Gibson was in charge of the Soldiers' Home, and when he joined H.M. Forces, his place was taken by Mr. Philip Napier Miles.

At the end of May 1919 St. Andrew's Soldiers' Home was handed over by the Committee to the Revd. E. Cousins (the second Vicar of Avonmouth)

8   316900 PRIVATE LEONARD BROWN (Author's Father) aged 18 in 1917. Served with 15 Tank Battalion – demobbed 5 December 1919.

as a social centre for the use of the Parish. The building continued as such, and gave excellent service to the Parish until 1963 when it was demolished in favour of the present permanent St. Andrew's Church Hall.

The ceaseless passage of men and arms made such an impression on the parish, that when the war was over a memorial tablet was placed in St. Andrew's Church to the memory of those who had passed through Avonmouth, to meet the enemy on land, in the air, on the sea and under the seas. The memorial of bronze was erected on the interior south wall of the Church. It was unveiled by the Chairman of the Docks Committee (deputising for the Lord Mayor of Bristol) and dedicated by the Bishop of Bristol on Sunday, 28 May 1922. The embosses on the side of the memorial show tanks, army transport vehicles, aeroplanes and naval vessels, indicating the wartime activities of the Port, and reads:

'TO THE GLORY OF GOD
AND THE IMMORTAL MEMORY OF THE MEN
WHO PASSED THROUGH THIS PORT
DURING THE GREAT WAR 1914–1918,
AND MET AND DEFEATED THE ENEMY
ON SEA AND LAND AND IN THE AIR,
AND BY THEIR SACRIFICE PRESERVED OUR
FREEDOM AND UPHELD THE CAUSE OF
JUSTICE AND TRUE CHRISTIAN CHIVALRY.

"Ye that live on mid England's pasture green,
Remember them, and think what might have been"

Erected by the St. Andrew's Soldiers' Home.'

Fortunately, the bronze memorial tablet survived Hitler's blitz on Avonmouth in January 1941, when St. Andrew's Church was burnt out, and it can still be seen where it was originally placed.

9 BRONZE PLAQUE. Erected by St. Andrew's Soldiers Home on south interior wall, St. Andrew's Parish Church, Avonmouth. Unveiled 28 May 1922.

SHIREHAMPTON REMOUNT DEPOT

Horses and mules still had an important role to play in the Great War, despite the already arrival on the scene of motor vehicles. In the early days of the war horses throughout the United Kingdom were requisitioned for military use, but due to high casualties other sources had to be found quickly. They were duly imported through Avonmouth Docks from Ireland, Canada and the United States in their tens of thousands for the British Forces at home and abroad. So many remounts and mules went through Avonmouth Docks during the war period that the stevedores who handled them earned the nickname of 'The horse-gang', and they worked under Commander Dobbin!

10   VIEW FROM PENPOLE *c* 1918. *Centre:* Huts of Shirehampton Remount Military Unit. *Foreground:* New houses in King's Weston Avenue.

In September 1914 the Shirehampton Remount Depot was opened to accommodate some 5,000 animals. The main object of the Depot was to quarantine the animals from 14 to 21 days, test with mallein for glanders, get them fit and clean before sending them by rail to reserve units in Britain for further training before being sent overseas.

The Remount Depot was divided into ten squadrons and occupied a huge expanse of ground in the regions of Barrow Hill and Penpole. It was also a large hospital base, having a veterinary hospital for 500 horses, and isolation ward for 100 infectious cases. It was reported that the 'extreme value of the climate of the district and the healthful properties of the water supply' were beneficial for the quick and lasting recovery of the animals after their long voyages. When mange was discovered amongst the overseas horses disinfecting baths were installed, and the treatment was remarkably successful in checking the disease. The fact that so little mange occurred in the British Army animals at the Front speaks for the care taken of the horses and mules.

11   REMOUNT DEPOT. Sketch by S. Loxton entitled *Huts at Veterinary Hospital, Penpole Point, Shirehampton*, dated 1919.

During the five years of its activity a total of 347,045 horses and mules passed through the Remount Depot. The first consignment arrived on 24 October 1914 and from that date ships arrived at Avonmouth with varying regularity up to 25 November 1918. The largest number of animals landed in a single day was 2,958, and the largest accommodated at one time was 7,244. After being put ashore they were taken in droves through the streets from the Docks to the Remount Depot, and the clatter of hooves became a very familiar sound in Avonmouth and Shirehampton. Mr. John Cross recalled seeing convoys of mules headed by a cowboy clad in sheepskin-fronted trousers, whilst one or more cowboys brought up the rear.

The Depot started with a civilian staff of 1,380 men under army officers, but was made a Military Unit in 1915. Colonel D. C. Carter, C.B., C.M.G., D.S.O., was the Commandant of the Remount Depot for the whole period of its existence. He proved very popular with all his staff, and he paid great attention to the care and training of the animals by methods in every way humane and considerate.

The importance of the work of the Depot was fully appreciated by people in higher circles, and it was honoured by two V.I.P. visits. On 7 September 1915 King George V and Queen Mary came to inspect the Depot (see Chapter

'Royal Events') and on 23 February 1916 the Commander of the Home Forces, Field-Marshal Viscount French (hero of Mons and Ypres) followed their example.

The Remount Depot was closed and dismantled in October 1919, when the Bristol Corporation purchased a number of huts to relieve the extreme shortage of houses in the neighbourhood. One of the huts ended its days at Patchway.

After the Great War it was decided that a recreation centre was required at Patchway especially for the men who had recently returned from the Armed Forces. A big effort was made there to raise the money, and in 1921 one of the remount huts at Shirehampton was purchased for £95. It was transported to Patchway in sections by horses and wagons, and officially opened on 2 November 1921 in the presence of some 270 people as 'The Patchway Club Room'. Nevertheless it has always been referred to as 'The Hut'. The Patchway local historian, Mr. John Agate, wrote in 1979, 'The Hut still stands and serves as a valued meeting place for numerous local organisations'.

As regards Shirehampton, the name 'Barracks Lane' is a lasting reminder of the Remount Depot here during the Great War.

12 BARRACKS LANE NAME-PLATE. Shirehampton's lasting reminder of the Great War Remount Depot. Photo: September 1987.

CHITTENING GAS FACTORY

The use of poisonous gases in warfare has been universally considered highly immoral. It was first suggested during the Crimean War by burning Flowers of Sulphur to produce Sulphur Dioxide. This suggestion was vetoed by the British Government on the grounds of it being inhumane. The American Government took the same view when it was suggested that Chlorine shells should be used during the American Civil War.

The first country to resort to gas warfare was Germany when she used Chlorine shells on the Russian Front in 1915. It was Germany again who first introduced the use of Mustard Gas when attacking British troops at Ypres on the Western Front in 1917. The results were so terrible and the casualties so devastating that Britain's leaders decided to retaliate. Whereupon the Government sent some 30 chemists to a factory at Chittening to deal with the problem. The required Mustard Gas was being produced in large quantities at the end of a six week experimental work period, and the number of chemists was then reduced to half-a-dozen.

Officially the factory was called 'His Majesty's Factory, St. Andrew's Road, Avonmouth' but locally it was just referred to as 'Chittening Gas Factory'. Before commencing work there everyone was obliged to take an oath before a Magistrate on the Official Secrets Act.

13 AERIAL VIEW, CHITTENING GAS FACTORY. Official name 'H.M. Factory, St. Andrew's Road, Avonmouth'. Erected during the Great War, and engaged in the manufacture of Mustard Gas 1917/1918.

Around the factory hung an unpleasant smell not unlike a sickly wild garlic. This was Dichlorethyl Sulphide, the deadly Mustard Gas. The dangers of producing such a highly toxic chemical was only too evident by the warning notices ringed around the factory forbidding the public to pick blackberries within a mile for fear of contamination. Having first been used at Ypres in France, the French called Mustard Gas 'Yperite', but the workers at the Chittening factory, like our troops on the Western Front called it 'H.S.' meaning Hun Stuff. The Germans called it 'Lost', on account of its deadly effects.

At Chittening the shells were filled by a large workforce of women and girls, who proved just as courageous as the men in sticking to the work. There was sometimes a quite considerable number of workers affected by the gas. According to Mr. Reginald Tayler (who worked at the factory as an errand boy) three French scientists were in a laboratory about 100 yards away when there was a terrific explosion and debris came raining down on the wooden office building where he was at the time. Sadly all three were killed.

Leaks from the gas tanks and during manufacture were not uncommon. Again Mr. Tayler recalls the day some men were digging a trench when one of the tanks leaked into the trench. Their legs were badly burnt. Some injuries were self-induced. One of the ingredients used was 100% proof whisky spirit. Some reckless workmen attempted to drink the potent brew, only to suffer badly burnt throats and stomachs. On a single day, it is recorded, there were 140 cases for hospital treatment, and during the entire period of the work nearly 1,300 persons were more or less seriously gassed.

It must have cheered the Avonmouth workers in so dangerous an occupation to know that the first experiment with Mustard Gas shells proved most disastrous to the enemy. A report came from the Western Front that the British Artillery first used gas against the Hindenburg Line on 30 September 1918 most effectively. The enemy suffered great losses, and the Line was broken on a wide front. Shells filled at Chittening were instrumental in winning a decisive battle. By the end of the war 50% of German shells were filled with such materials, and the British were prepared to load 25% of their shells with gas chemicals. At the time of the Armistice it was estimated some 1,100 workers were producing up to 20 tons of Mustard Gas each day for shells of about 100 lbs. at the Chittening Gas Factory.

A succession of conventions have tried to ban gas warfare, it being rightly considered uncivilised, or even its manufacture, but regrettably without success so far.

SPELTER WORKS

Spelter is the name given to the commercial form of metallic zinc. Today, the spelter works is such a well-known and familiar part of the Avonmouth scene, one cannot imagine the parish without that industry. Yet, had it not been for the Great War, Avonmouth might never have attracted the spelter works here, which over the ensuing years has provided so much employment for many inhabitants of Avonmouth and Shirehampton.

Britain found herself at a distinct disadvantage at the outbreak of the Great War, having at that time to import from Germany the materials required in the manufacture of munitions. This bizarre position arose through Germany having some years earlier obtained the franchise on purchase of the residues containing zinc from the lead and silver mines at Broken Hill in Australia. After this the whole of the spelter requirements of this country could only reach the U.K. as zinc metal by the good offices of the German smelters. With this source now cut off, of course, alternative supplies could only be obtained from the U.S.A.

At the outbreak of the war the Australian Government stepped in and cancelled the German contracts. At the same time, the Prime Minister of Australia, the Rt. Hon. W. M. Hughes, came to this country with the object of selling the raw materials from Broken Hill to any smelting works which might be erected in Britain for the purpose of treating it. A number of experts were accordingly employed to examine and report upon sites near ports in Britain, as suitable for a new smelting works. Eventually it was decided Avonmouth was the most favourable place, and a site near the Royal Edward Dock covering an area of about 400 acres, adjoining the St. Andrew's Road Railway Station was acquired from the King's Weston estate, owned by Squire Philip Napier Miles. The Ministry of Munitions acquired a portion of the site to erect a large plant for the production of sulphuric acid for munition purposes.

The stone required to build this new works was obtained from a quarry in Penpole Hill, where also an excellent clay for brick-making was discovered. A brickworks was erected near the quarry, which, with the exception of the first few months, was able to supply all the bricks needed for building the spelter works. In addition over 3,000 tons of stone and 1,500,000 bricks were supplied for building the new Shirehampton housing estate which provided homes for the employees of this new Industry. Arrangements were made with the University Women's Settlement in Bristol to open a branch here, and the wonderful social work undertaken by the late Miss Rotha Mary Clay is now a well-known and remembered fact, and part of Shirehampton's history.

In 1917 a long-term Agreement was signed by the British Government for the purchase of Australian concentrates, and in the same year the National Smelting Company was formed to produce zinc and sulphuric acid. The Company acquired from the Ministry of Munitions the sulphuric acid plant at Avonmouth, together with a partly built distillation zinc smelter. In 1929 the National Smelting Company passed into control of the newly-formed Imperial Smelting Corporation Ltd.

The Germans were fully aware of the vital importance of the smelting industry to the war effort. During the Second World War they specially marked out on their reconnaissance aerial photograph of Avonmouth the area occupied by the Imperial Smelting Corporation Ltd. as being the main target area 'zinc spelter foundry', etc. It may not be a coincidence therefore, that the first German bombs to be dropped on Avonmouth Parish (3 July 1940) landed in a field adjoining Cowley Farm, near the Imperial Smelting Corporation works, but caused no damage. The British Government too realised the importance of these works, and due to the defences they provided only a very few German bombs actually reached the Imperial Smelting Corporation Ltd. 'target area'.

WOMEN WAR WORKERS

Any chronicle of the Great War would be quite incomplete without mention of the role played by women. Following in the steps of Florence Nightingale it was then the accepted thing for women to enrol as nurses to care for wounded and sick servicemen. The great revolution as far as the fair sex was concerned was brought about during the Great War when they turned their hands to every and any kind of job.

For the first time in our history women were enrolled in the Army, Navy and Air Force, either in the Queen Mary Army Auxiliary Corps, Women's Royal Naval Service or Women's Royal Air Force. WAACS (Women's Auxiliary Army Corps) worked as cooks, domestics and clerks at the Shirehampton Remount Depot and at the Motor Transport Depot at Avonmouth.

As the young men joined the Forces, women volunteered to take their places in munition workshops and factories, to do jobs hitherto not before undertaken by the so-called 'weaker sex', and any who doubted their efficiency for such tasks were speedily converted. There were few jobs the women did not tackle, and themselves being unskilled they mainly did labouring jobs, such as carting bricks and making concrete, as happened when the female labour force helped to build the new spelter works at Avonmouth. A large part of the workforce at H.M. Gas Factory at Chittening was also made up by women and girls, and they seemingly relished their new found emancipation. In keeping up with the men they formed themselves into a football team, and many happy hours have since been recalled when the ladies' team at the National Smelting Co. played football games against the ladies' team at the Chittening Gas Factory.

Some ladies became postwomen, and even in some places firewomen too.

In March 1917 women Police first took up their duties. On the Railways women were employed as porters, ticket-collectors and cleaners in the grimy locomotive sheds keeping the steam-engines spruce and shining – certainly no picnic! During the Second World War women were also employed on the Railways as guards and signalwomen.

December 1916 saw the first introduction of women conductors on the Bristol tramcars and 'buses, and they did their work well until the men returned once more. During the Second World War women conductors on the Bristol 'buses was the norm rather than the exception. Altogether 4,055 female conductors were recruited during the Second World War in Bristol, of whom 20 women were trained as bus drivers.

The movement in favour of votes for women had started in the second half of the 19th century, and grew rapidly. Having gained no success at all by 1906 its members became impatient and aggressive, and resorted to violence to advertise their Cause. Several Bills had been placed before Parliament between 1906 and 1912 for women's suffrage, but all had been thrown out by that all-male political establishment. The great change was brought about by women themselves during the Great War in demonstrating their ability to do men's jobs, and causing a profound impression. Without further ado Parliament conceded votes to women in 1917 and in 1918 they gave the right of women to stand for Parliament. The Armistice was soon followed by a General Election in which for the first time women took part both as voters and candidates. History was made on 1 December 1919 when Nancy Astor took her seat as Member of the House of Commons, and was the first woman to do so.

ROYAL EVENTS

During the Great War two noteworthy local Royal events took place. Firstly, Shirehampton was honoured by a visit by King George V and Queen Mary on Tuesday 7 September 1915. Two years later on 20 July 1917, the separate Parish of Avonmouth, which had hitherto been part of the parish of Shirehampton, was formed by King George V by Order in Council. (Squire Napier Miles made this possible by his gift of £2,000 towards its endowment.)

When the King and Queen came to Shirehampton it was in effect the parish's second Royal Visit, the first having taken place on 5 September 1690 when William III (Prince of Orange) landed at the Lamplighters and spent the night at King's Weston – see 'Shirehampton Story'.

The Royal Visit of 1915 was an unofficial affair, and took place under profound secrecy. Their Majesties came to Bristol principally to visit wounded and convalescent soldiers in the Military Hospitals. The King and

14 KING GEORGE V & QUEEN MARY.
Pictured on the occasion of their Silver
Wedding Anniversary 6 July 1918.

Queen arrived in Bristol by special train, but first came to Shirehampton where they were received at the Remount Depot by the Officer-in-Charge. After spending an hour inspecting the Depot, the Royal visitors returned to the train which was moved to a quiet and picturesque spot near Horseshoe Bend for lunch. Afterwards the train returned to Shirehampton Station where motor vehicles were waiting to take the Royal party on to Southmead Hospital and the Beaufort Military Hospital (now Glenside Hospital) at Fishponds. In all Their Majesties saw nearly 1,000 men that day.

Despite being a semi-private visit, the fact that the King and Queen were in Bristol became generally known, with the result that crowds of people lined the Royal route. The newspapers at the time reported that there was little demonstration, the citizens receiving Their majesties with respectful *SILENCE!* At that time public passions and feelings were running very high against everything German, due to the unrestricted U-boat attacks on British shipping, Zeppelin air-raids and the high casualty lists coming from the Western Front. Unfortunately, the Royal Family then possessed a German name inherited from Queen Victoria's husband, that of Saxe-Coburg and Gotha. Furthermore, King George V was actually first cousin to the German Kaiser (Emperor Wilhelm II) who was now Britain's bitterest enemy.

On 17 July 1917, because of public opinion, the King decreed a change of family name, and the House of Windsor was established by Royal

Proclamation. At the same time Queen Mary's family name of Teck became Cambridge, and the Battenburg family name was changed to Mountbatten. By Act of Parliament enemy Princes who held British titles were deprived of them, and all enemy members of British Orders of Chivalry were expelled from them. The British Royal House was now segregated from its previous Continental entanglements, and this proved a wise and popular move by the King. It endeared him to the hearts of his people, and helped him to keep his throne at the time when many European Monarchs were losing theirs.

A second Royal visit to Bristol by King George V and Queen Mary took place on 8 November 1917. It was a two-day visit by Their Majesties this time, and the Royal train which was used as a residence by the Royal Party, remained in a siding at Henbury overnight.

LOCAL AUXILIARY HOSPITALS

There was a drastic shortage of hospital beds in 1915, when in common with dozens of aristocratic families throughout Britain who owned large mansion houses, Mr. Philip Napier Miles and his wife, Sybil Marguerite, converted their home King's Weston House into a hospital for wounded and convalescent servicemen.

The War Office labelled it Bristol / 10 King's Weston Auxiliary Hospital. It was organised and controlled by Mr. and Mrs. Miles, and Mrs. Miles became the Matron. As a lasting memento of the period when King's Weston House was an Auxiliary Hospital a plaque was erected above the south door of the house, which remains still, and reads:

'1915   TO THE HAPPY MEMORY OF THE WOUNDED   1919
FROM EVERY LAND OF THE BRITISH EMPIRE WHO
WERE GATHERED IN THIS HOUSE IN THE GREAT WAR'

In January 1920 Mrs. Miles was appointed an Officer of the Order of the British Empire (O.B.E.) for her meritorious service.

After the war Squire Miles (as he was affectionately called) presented a plot of land in his Shirehampton Park for the erection of Shirehampton's War Memorial (see Chapter 'War Heroes'). Again in 1930 he gave a further two acre plot in Westbury Lane for the erection of the Douglas Haig Memorial Homes for ex-servicemen and their families, now Haig Close. Field-Marshal Earl Haig (1861–1928) commanded the British Forces in France from 1915, was educated at Clifton College, a Freeman of the City of Bristol and was founder of the British Legion.

At nearby Stoke Bishop Mr. Robert Bush converted his beautiful house, Bishop's Knoll on the edge of Avon Gorge into a hospital for 100 beds at his own expense. Mr. Bush had been a sheep farmer in Australia for 35 years and

15   AUXILIARY HOSPITAL, KING'S WESTON HOUSE between 1915 and 1919. Patients
pictured in the grounds.

16   KING'S WESTON AUXILIARY HOSPITAL. Group of patients receiving Therapy in one
of the Wards.

17   HAIG CLOSE, Westbury Lane, Sea Mills. Two acre plot – gift in 1930 of Squire Napier Miles for homes for ex-servicemen and their families. *Inset:* Earl Haig depicted on plaque above entrances to No's 8 & 9.   Photo: September 1988.

18   BISHOP'S KNOLL, STOKE BISHOP. Converted into hospital for Australian soldiers by owner Robert Bush at his own expense. House demolished in 1973 in favour of modern flats.

his Red Cross hospital was especially for Australian soldiers. It became the only privately owned hospital in the country to receive wounded straight from the Front Line.

Mr. Bush acted as Commandant of the Bishop's Knoll Hospital, and his wife, Margery, O.B.E., was Quartermaster. By 1918 it was estimated some 2,000 Australians had passed through Bishop's Knoll.

Unfortunately this large house is no longer with us. Having been demolished in 1973 blocks of modern flats and garages now occupy that most desirable site. However, a Preservation Order covers a section of the grounds of former Bishop's Knoll to preserve a rare wild plant which still only grows in the Avon Gorge.

WAR HEROES

In a sense every soldier taking up arms during war-time is a hero. To build a land 'fit for heroes to live in' was the unanimous resolve following the Armistice, when British soldiers were returning home from the battlefields. To some, however, is given an inner courage to perform supreme acts of bravery in times of extreme personal danger.

Britain's highest decoration, the Victoria Cross *'FOR VALOUR'* was established by Queen Victoria in 1856. During the Great War there were 570 Victoria Crosses awarded, of which at least six stand to the credit of Bristol.

The Distinguished Conduct Medal is awarded for exceptional service, and in winning this medal Lance-Corporal W. J. Redmore brought the first Military Honour to Avonmouth, and became Avonmouth's first hero of the Great War, the second was Sergeant (then Corporal) T. Hatcliffe.

Lance-Corporal W. J. Redmore, D.C.M.

Born in Bath in 1892, Bill Redmore came to Avonmouth when only a few months old. His father was an Avonmouth man who lived in Richmond Terrace, and worked for the Docks Committee (P.B.A.). Bill attended Avonmouth School, and on leaving also went to work for the Docks Committee, first as a messenger-boy, then as a shunter, before joining 'C' Company 1/6th Gloucestershire Regiment, and going to France in March 1915.

During the night of 25 November 1915, Private Redmore was one of a party of 20 volunteers who went into the German trenches. After highly successful hand-to-hand fighting he was about to return to his lines, when he discovered Corporal Verrier lying in a trench severely wounded in the knee, and unable to stand. Finding all his comrades gone, with no help available,

19 LANCE-CORPORAL W. J. REDMORE, D.C.M. ('C' Coy. 1/6th Glo'sters). Recipient of Avonmouth's first Military Honour.

and without thought for his own safety, Bill Redmore picked up the wounded Corporal and carried him back under fire some 700 yards, through three lines of enemy barbed-wire entanglements to safety.

Corporal Verrier, co-incidentally also a Bristolian, probably owed his life to Private Redmore, and for this extreme act of bravery King George V conferred on Private Redmore the Distinguished Conduct Medal. It also earned him a Lance-Corporal's stripe!

Saturday 1 April 1916, a day of lovely Spring sunshine, was a red letter day for Avonmouth. Lance-Corporal Redmore home on leave received his Decoration in Avonmouth Park, before a crowd of hundreds of enthusiastic spectators and well-wishers. Prior to the ceremony, which was conducted by the Lord and Lady Mayoress of Bristol, there had been a grand procession through the village made up of detachments of the Dorset and Devon Regiments, Army Service Corps, Friendly Societies, Boy Scouts, school-children and a band. At the same time, as a tangible tribute to his heroism, the Parish presented Bill Redmore with a handsome clock and £100 in Exchequer Bonds.

When the war was over Bill Redmore went to seek his fortune in Africa, where he died.

The person who seconded a vote of thanks to the Lord Mayor on that memorable occasion was a certain Mr. Ernest Bevin. No one could have foreseen on that day in 1916 what a vital contribution Mr. Bevin was destined to make during the Second World War in his role as Minister of Labour and National Service in Mr. Churchill's war-time Cabinet.

Sergeant T. Hatcliffe, D.C.M.

Sergeant T. Hatcliffe of 5 Police Cottages, Green Lane, Avonmouth, served with the 479th (S Mid) Field Company 61st (S.M.) Division of the Corps of Royal Engineers, and was awarded the Distinguished Conduct Medal.

The citation for Sergeant (then Corporal) Hatcliffe reads, 'For conspicuous gallantry and devotion to duty when working on the defence of a captured strong-point at Somme Farm, on the night of 23/24 August 1917. On ground completely dominated by the enemy he reconnoitred the position with a view to wiring. While reconnoitring he saw several of the enemy in shell holes, and immediately went forward alone, cleared the enemy from the shell holes, capturing six prisoners. The whole operation was carried out under heavy shell and machine gun fire!'

Sergeant Hatcliffe was presented with his D.C.M. at a special ceremony held in Avonmouth National School. He survived the Great War, and some time afterwards the Hatcliffe family moved to King's Weston Avenue, Shirehampton to live.

LEST WE FORGET

The Great War exhibited an amount of effort, suffering and sacrifice without parallel in the world's history. Bristol took no mean part in the struggle, and her contribution was a generous one both in mechanics of war and lives. The City enlisted something like 60,000 men and women for H.M. Forces, of whom 4,000 lost their lives.

Two National Memorials were raised to commemorate all the valour and losses of the war. On 11 November 1920, the second anniversary of Armistice, King George V unveiled the Cenotaph in Whitehall. On the same occasion, an Unknown Warrior was interred in Westminster Abbey, with Admirals, Field Marshals and Generals as pall-bearers. The idea of an Unknown Warrior originated in Britain, and very soon other Countries followed our example.

Scarcely a family throughout the land had not lost a loved one during the war, and in the years that followed every Parish raised its own memorial to their sons who did not return. Some Parishes, like Shirehampton and Avonmouth raised more than one.

20 SHIREHAMPTON
WAR MEMORIAL. Pic-
tured on day of unveil-
ing and dedication,
4 September 1921.

Shirehampton War Memorials

Shirehampton's war memorial was erected on a piece of land in Shirehampton Park, given for the purpose by Mr. Philip Napier Miles. It is in the form of a cross of York stone, with bronze finial, which bears the inscription, 'TO THE HONOURED MEMORY OF THE MEN OF SHIREHAMPTON WHO FELL IN THE GREAT WAR 1914–1918', and lists 58 names, as follows:

Bell W.	Gould W. G.	Quayle J.
Bleaken A.	Hack L.	Rae T. W.
Bodger W.	Hack W. J.	Rice C.
Booth W.	Hall G. W.	Robinson J. O.
Boulton F.	Hatherall F.	Sansum C. N. S
Brooks A.	Hatherall R.	Sansum H. R. A.
Broomsgrove A.	Head R. J.	Sealey T.
Brown T.	Hill J.	Smith S.
Burton W.	Hill S	Smith W. V.
Chapman W.	Hill W. T.	Tanner T.
Chidgey D.	Jefferies F.	Taylor J.
Codrington J. H.	Jones R.	Treverton S.
Cole T.	Kingsbury W. F.	Webber F. G.
Collins F. B.	Marks G. D.	Webb H.
Cox-Buck J.	Matthews W. H.	White L.
Davis L.	May W.	Whitehead W.
Edwards G. T.	Miles C.	Wilkins A.
Edwards W.	Parfitt W. R.	Williams W.
Evans E.	Pike H.	
Gard C.	Pinner F. G.	

The memorial was unveiled by General the Hon. C. G. Bruce, D.S.O., and dedicated by the Archdeacon of Bristol at an Ecumenical Service on 4 September 1921. (General Bruce had known Shirehampton since boyhood days, and he had been a patient at King's Weston Auxiliary Hospital). The memorial was designed by Mr. Ernest Newton, R.A., and cost £460. The plot was later laid out as a garden, and surrounded by a little wooden fence.

Shirehampton's other memorial took the form of a stained-glass window which was installed in the south aisle of the Parish Church of St. Mary in the High Street. Unfortunately a great fire occurred at the Church on 15 January 1928 which gutted the building, and totally destroyed the memorial window. Some of the melted remains from it were later placed under a stone in the chancel of the present church during the rebuilding operations.

The then Vicar of Shirehampton, the Revd. C. W. Dixon, replaced the memorial window in the new church at the east end at his own expense. It depicts Our Lord on the Cross, with Roman soldiers below casting lots for His raiment, and the names of the fallen were inscribed on the glass at the bottom. The window was designed by Mr. Arnold Robinson, R.W.A., of Messrs. Joseph Bell & Son, and dedicated by the Archdeacon of Bristol on 9 February 1930.

In 1961 an entirely new east window was a gift to St. Mary's by the widow of the Revd. Dixon, Mrs. D. M. Dixon. This necessitated the memorial window being moved to the west end of the church where it can still be seen. At the time of the window's transfer Mr. Geoffrey Robinson of Joseph Bell & Son re-arranged the names of the fallen. The 58 of the 1914–1918 Great War

21   WAR MEMORIAL WEST WINDOW, St. Mary's Parish Church, Shirehampton – listing fifty-eight Servicemen killed in 1914/1918 War, and forty-one fallen in 1939/1945 War. Photo: July 1987.

he placed on the left hand panel, and added the names of the 41 fallen of Shirehampton during the 1939–1945 Second World War on the right hand panel, viz:

Andrews R.	Domaille W.	Newman J. L.
Barclay R. H.	Early S.	Oliver D. F. A.
Beacham R.	Eynon L.	Patterson W. J.
Bowd D. M.	Fowles A. T.	Redwood F. W.
Boyce J.	Furber J.	Robson J. A.
Brinton R. J. H.	Hadley I.	Sainsbury A.
Brown F. G.	Hadley R.	Spence M. C.
Chard L. C.	Hallett, R. D.	Storer I. L.
Cheeseman F. W.	Horton R.	White W. L.
Chubb J. E.	Lewis A. R.	Whitlock A.
Collins H.	Lisle R.	Wills G.
Cook C. C.	Lukins W. S.	Wooller G. W.
Crichton A.	Marsh P. C.	
Davies R. C.	Milsom, G.	Wright P. B. *D.F.C.*

Avonmouth War Memorials

At Avonmouth two memorials were raised following the Great War to perpetuate the memory of her sons who did not return. One was at St. Andrew's Parish Church, the other at the Congregational Church in Portview Road. Both were funded by public subscription and were inscribed with the same honours list of 44 names, viz:

Bennett F.	Gould W. J.	Parsons E. M.
Berry G.	Hammond S.	Payne H.
Berry W.	Hawker H.	Pearce A.
Brown G.	Hood F. J.	Piper S.
Bugler L. H.	Jennings G. F.	Poston H.
Bullock W. E.	Lister W.	Sanger F. G.
Clark T.	Lumbard H. J.	Sanger W.
Clegg H.	Maggs E. F.	Saunders W.
Dungey H. W. T.	May W. E.	Sims G.
Edwards W. J.	Mears E. E.	Sims H.
England W. E.	Mears T.	Tanner T. G.
Foden H. R.	Noyes A. J.	Thomas E.
Gale J. J.	Oliver G. H.	Williams H.
Gibbs J. A.	Page C.	Williams W.
Gould E. L.	Page H.	

St. Andrew's memorial was unveiled by Mrs. Parsons and dedicated by the Archdeacon of Bristol on 20 December 1921. Mrs. Parsons was the widow of Edward M. Parsons, a former sidesman at the church and whose name was included on the Memorial.

The Memorial took the form of an oak tablet erected on the centre pillar of the church, and was made by Messrs. Harry Hems & Sons of Exeter. The design was in keeping with the architecture of the church with traceries to conform with the church windows. It was described as having . . . 'carved gables to support a canopy of pierced tracery, in the midst of which was a Crown of Victory', and above a carved paterae of crockets terminating in a trefoil cross. The inscriptions and honours list were inscribed in raised and gilded letters. Underneath the Tablet was a carved pedestal for the purpose of placing flowers, which bore the words, 'LIFT UP YOUR HEARTS IN CHRIST 1914–1918'.

Associated with the Memorial Tablet was the installation of an electric lighting system, replacing the church's original gas lamps. Sadly, nothing remains of St. Andrew's War Memorial, it having been lost in the Second World War when the church was hit by numerous German incendiary bombs 16/17 January 1941 reducing the building to a burnt out shell. The only reminder today of the War Memorial is a brass plaque, which having been erected in the church vestry escaped the fire. It reads: 'The installing of the electric lighting system in this Church in October 1921 was associated with the placing of the oaken Tablet to commemorate the men of the Parish who gave their lives in the Great War 1914–1918. *Eternal Rest grant unto them O Lord, and let Perpetual Light shine upon them'*.

The War Memorial at the Congregational Church was unveiled on 25 February 1921 by the Lord Mayor of Bristol, Mr. C. B. Britton, M.P. Also associated with the Memorial was the installation of a new organ and electric lighting at the church, both of which had previously been dedicated on 5 January 1921 at an Ecumenical Service.

The War Memorial took the form of three brass panels arranged within a stone surround in the south aisle. The names of the fallen were inscribed on the two outside panels, whilst the wording on the middle panel read: 'THE ORGAN IN THIS CHURCH WAS ERECTED TO THE GLORY OF GOD TO COMMEMORATE PEACE AND TO PERPETUATE THE MEMORY OF THE MEN OF AVONMOUTH WHO FELL IN THE GREAT EUROPEAN WAR 1914–1918. *Greater love hath no man than this, that a man lay down his life for his friends. John XV 13.'*

The Avonmouth Congregational Church is, alas, no longer in existence, having been closed in March 1972. Before being demolished in 1974, however, the three Memorial Brasses were handed to the Parish Church of St. Andrew for safe keeping. These are now not only Avonmouth's remaining war memorial, but also the only reminder in existence of the once thriving Avonmouth Congregational Church. One day, perhaps, we shall see the Memorial Brasses re-erected once again.

22 AVONMOUTH CONGREGATIONAL WAR MEMORIAL. Unveiled by Lord Mayor of Bristol, Mr. C. B. Britton, M.P., 25 February 1921. Photo: July 1970.

Other Memorials

A brass plaque with 35 names was erected at the Missions to Seamen Chapel at 124 Portview Road, Avonmouth by the members of the Royal Edward Athletic & Social Club, which reads:

'IN MEMORY OF OUR FALLEN COMRADES
(of the Catering Dept)
WHO WERE DROWNED 13 AUGUST 1915
IN HIS MAJESTY'S TRANSPORT s.s. "ROYAL EDWARD"
THEY DIED FOR KING & COUNTRY.'

In June 1982 the Missions to Seamen became part of the Avonmouth International Seafarers Centre, and moved premises to Gloucester Road, Avonmouth, which is where the *Royal Edward* memorial plaque can now be seen.

The *RMS Royal Edward* was sister ship to the *RMS Royal George* of the Canadian Northern Royal Line. Both ships 12,000 tons and 18,000 horse power. From May 1910 until September 1914 they maintained a fortnightly passenger and emigration service from Avonmouth to Canada, and were advertised as being the fastest from Bristol to Canada. At the outbreak of the Great War they were requisitioned, and both used as troopships.

The *Royal Edward,* as the plaque records, met a tragic end. She sailed from Avonmouth on 30 July 1915 with 12,000 people on board to take

23   *Royal Edward & Royal George.* Pictured in Royal Edward Dock, Avonmouth between April 1910 and August 1914.

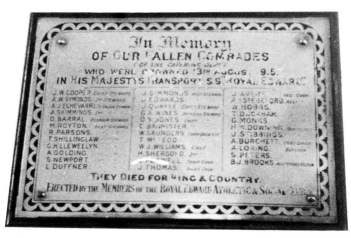

24 *Royal Edward* MEMORIAL PLAQUE at Mission to Seamen Chapel, Portview Road, Avonmouth, 5 March 1971.

reinforcements to the Dardanelles. When in the Mediterranean at the entrance to the Aegean Sea on 13 August 1915 she was torpedoed, and sank with the loss of 935 lives. The *Royal George* survived the war, and under Cunard Line was afterwards sold as scrap . . . ironically enough to the Germans!

Some large firms and Companies raised memorials of their own in remembrance of employees who gave their lives in the Great War. One such is the Midland Railway Company War Memorial at Derby, unveiled 15 December 1921, on which the following four local names are inscribed:

Baber A. W.	Avonmouth Station	Page W.	Avonmouth Dock
Gough C. H.	Avonmouth Dock	Shipway S. D. B.	Shirehampton Station

There was a 14-year time-lag before Bristol erected the City's War Memorial to vindicate the honour of her 4,000 citizens who fell in the Great War. Bristol was the last major city in the Country to build a shrine in memory of her war dead, and newspaper headlines like 'Bristol has honoured her dead at last!' were justifiable.

The delay, we are led to believe, was due to disagreements over the most suitable site and also design. These problems were resolved in the end with Colston Avenue in the centre of Bristol as the site, and a Memorial similar to the Cenotaph in Whitehall (which had been designed by Sir Edwin Lutyens) with the main inscription, 'SACRED TO THE MEMORY OF BRISTOL'S SONS AND DAUGHTERS WHO MADE THE SUPREME SACRIFICE'.

It was a fine sunny Sunday afternoon on 26 June 1932 when Bristol's War Memorial was duly unveiled. The ceremony was performed by Field Marshal Sir William Birdwood (an Old Cliftonian), in the presence of the Lord Mayor of Bristol, Mr. John H. Inskip, and a vast crowd estimated to be in the region of some 50,000.

In hindsight, the quotation also inscribed on the Memorial, *'THEY DIED THAT MANKIND MIGHT LEARN TO LIVE IN PEACE'* was somewhat ominous. In less years than it had taken Bristol to erect her War Memorial, Britain was for the second time plunged into the great abyss of war with the old enemy, Germany!

FROM WAR TO PEACE

At 11.0 a.m. on 11 November 1918 (the eleventh hour, eleventh day and the eleventh month) an Armistice was granted to the German armies, now utterly defeated after four years of bloody fighting on the Western Front.

Just a few days previously, when defeat was seen to be inevitable, a revolution had broken out in Germany and a Republic established. The Kaiser fled to Holland, and remained there in exile for the rest of his days. His ambition to gain German domination in Europe had brought about the most destructive war in the history of the world. Due to him a greatly increased savagery of war was introduced to add to the horrors of warfare. He died in 1941 during the Second World War in complete obscurity, little heard of and unmourned.

As the special editions of the newspapers spread the good news of the Armistice (no radio or T.V. at that time) there was a great and overwhelming sense of relief throughout the land. At last there was an end to the bloodshed, and wild rejoicings broke out in all the big cities. In Bristol the whole day was one of public jubilations, church bells rang out and all thought of business was abandoned. The main streets soon became gay with flags, thoroughfares thronged with excited people dancing in the streets, and on the tramcars and buses it was free rides for all.

Before the close of 1918 Bristol Council had conferred the Freedom of the City on three of Britain's war leaders who had engineered the victory, Admiral of the Fleet Earl Beatty, Field-Marshal Earl Haig and the Prime Minister, the Rt. Hon. David Lloyd George.

In February the following year a peace conference was held at Versailles, near Paris, to decide on terms of peace, and in June the Peace Treaty was signed. The nineteenth of July 1919 was the day officially appointed for national peace celebrations. The festivities in Bristol began with the Lord Mayor reading the proclamation of peace on the steps of the Council House (then in Broad Street) before a vast crowd, followed by a military procession

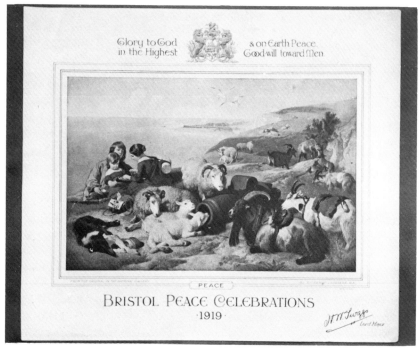

25 PEACE SOUVENIR CARD. Specially designed showing painting by Sir Edwin Landseer, R.A. entitled 'Peace', presented to all Bristol school children.

26 GERMAN PRISONERS OF WAR pictured at Penpole Camp, Shirehampton on 20 September 1919. *N.B.* Camouflaged hut, barbed wire fencing, and wide variety of uniforms. (Two pet kittens included!)

of returned soldiers and veterans, the Lord Mayor taking the salute outside the Victoria Rooms. The treats for the children and old folk were deferred until 24 July. Every child in Bristol received suitable refreshments and a specially designed souvenir card signed by the Lord Mayor, Alderman H. W. Twiggs. The subject 'Peace' was the painting of Sir Edwin Landseer, R.A. from the original in the National Gallery portraying Isaiah's prophecy in the Bible of the Peaceful Kingdom.

On Peace Celebration Day Avonmouth did the children proud. We know this through the Franklin family, who carefully saved their young son's programme of events. Written in a childish hand, with the teacher's corrections marked in red ink, it gives a clear indication of the festivities which took place on 24 July 1919. Activities commenced at 2.00 p.m. with a special cinema performance for the children. After which they assembled at the School for a procession to the park for tea, followed by a fancy dress parade. From 5.00 to 7.00 p.m. there were sports activities, and then chocolates were distributed. No doubt at this stage in the proceedings the Lord Mayor's souvenir cards were also distributed. The day ended with a band concert and dancing on The Green.

Feelings and hopes on that day in 1919 were very strong that the children would never again know another war. Alas, as history has unfolded, these hopes and feelings – though unwavering – were idealistic. The feelings have never varied, but the hopes have proved illusionary. Even the birth of the League of Nations in 1920, specifically formed to promote International Peace and Security, did not prevent another war breaking out in 1939.

Prisoner of War Camp

It is not generally known that German Prisoners of War were at some time during the Great War housed on Penpole, confirmed by a photograph in my History Collection.

The photograph is entitled 'Shirehampton, 20 September 1919', and shows 55 men wearing a wide variety of uniforms. The camouflaged roof to the hut in the background, and barbed wire at the windows makes this a sinister picture. However, the broad smiles worn by all the prisoners implies, perhaps, that repatriation was not too far off. Also included in the picture are two pet kittens!

The signature on the reverse side is that of Otto Müller, presumably included, who gave the photograph to a Shirehampton girl. That it has survived the years, and been handed down to my Collection suggests that despite the very strong anti-German feelings prevalent during the Great War, some kind of friendly relations existed between the prisoners of war on Penpole and the local inhabitants.

27 GREAT WAR GAS-DRIVEN 'BUS (No. 28 route: Tramways Centre/Avonmouth).
Due to petrol shortage, gas was utilised and stored in large bag over roof of Bristol's fleet of
'buses. *N.B.* Solid tyres and 12 m.p.h. speed restriction. Women conductors introduced in
December 1916.

28 TEMPORARY DWELLINGS at Barrow Hill, Shirehampton. Sketch by S. Loxton dated
1920.

III. THE YEARS BETWEEN

There is no doubt that the Great War brought about an immense change in the order of things, and it was a different Britain to which the men of the Forces returned after fighting in the trenches. Old beliefs and restraints had vanished – especially among the younger generation. The position of women had changed too, they now had the vote, and were being accepted in Industry, the Universities and in the professions. Class snobbery started to break down, and wealth was no longer confined to the few.

As far as Shirehampton was concerned there was to be a great change in the Parish scene. Avonmouth had become a separate and independent parish in 1917, and the picturesque rural village image which Shirehampton had enjoyed for centuries past quickly disappeared. Within the next ten years Shirehampton became a built-up area, accommodating a large council house estate, with the Portway cutting through the Parish, as an ever-present reminder of the new-found speed in life. The building of the Portway was amongst the projects put into motion by Bristol Corporation to provide employment for servicemen returning from the war. Work began at the Avonmouth end in May 1919, and the road was officially opened by Lieut-Colonel Wilfred Ashley, the then Minister of Transport, on 2 July 1926.

The Remount Depot at Shirehampton was dismantled in October 1919, and Bristol Corporation purchased the huts to relieve a shortage of houses in the neighbourhood. According to the artist, Mr. S. Loxton, writing in 1920, the Corporation purchased 72 huts to make 144 dwellings. He described them as being iron built with asbestos lining, water and electricity laid on, and a garden of about 300 square yards to each. He estimated the life of these houses would be about twenty-five years under suitable conditions. When he sketched them in 1920 ten houses were ready for occupation, and a further ten a week or so later. The huts in the Officers' quarters, wrote Mr. Loxton, were better than these, and had larger rooms, with two bedrooms, a sitting room, kitchen, scullery, pantry, store-room, wash-house and an outside w.c. What life was like living in the Remount huts is recorded by Mr. Ralph Hunt of Pensford, who wrote his memories in December 1975, as follows:

'My aunt lived in one of the old Remount huts at Shirehampton. This was No. 52 at the top of Barrow Hill. The huts were built on stilts (presumably to stop the rats burrowing underneath them). One hut served as a bath-house, and we used to pay 4d for a hot bath in 1926 – take your own towel and soap. No. 52 had a large garden, and we could sell cabbages at 2d each to Messrs. Wise & Co. who sold them to the ships docking at Avonmouth.'

Just before the Great War started in 1914, housing the people had become a serious question for Bristol Corporation, and complaints were being heard of overcrowding in certain districts of the City. When the war was over 'Never again!' became the watchword of the Prime Minister. 'Never again', he said, 'must it be permitted to perpetuate this overcrowding. Homes fit for heroes to live in must be made, if our race were to recover from the terrible loss sustained by the slaughter of the pick of our youth.'

In consequence, Bristol proposed to erect 5,000 new houses on the Garden City Association lines (later the Town and Country Planning Association) with modern conveniences, not more than ten houses to the acre, and so arranged that each tenant could have his own small allotment adjoining his cottage, gardens front and back. This system shows new thinking on housing, providing semi-detached so unlike the Victorian terraced dwellings.

A start was made at Shirehampton in 1919 with the first 150 houses. The whole plan was to erect 2,000 new council houses at Shirehampton, but in effect Shirehampton had 1,000 built during the 1920's, with twenty or more new roads coming into existence, such as Groveleaze, St: Mary's Road and St. Bernard's Road. The other 1,000 new houses were accommodated in open fields to the east between Shirehampton Park and Stoke Bishop, when Sea Mills was established. At the same time new housing estates sprang up at Southmead, Knowle West and Bedminster Down which made up the balance of 5,000 new homes. According to the estimate of the Revd. C. W. Dixon, Vicar of Shirehampton, the population of his parish of 4,009 souls in 1920 escalated sharply to 11,000 in 1928.

The whole plan for Bristol's new housing schemes were so arranged that the amenities associated with Garden Cities should be secured with spaces for cricket, football, tennis and bowls, with playgrounds for the children, as well as a hall for social activities like concerts and entertainments, educational lectures and public meetings. Shirehampton missed out on some of this side of the planning, but nevertheless was provided with brand new Schools, Portway Senior Girls' and Portway Senior Boys' opened in 1932, besides Shirehampton Junior and Infants Schools. Entertainment was provided by The Savoy modern cinema which had its grand opening on 2 October 1933. The palatial new indoor Swimming Baths, the last word in modern swimming baths, was opened on 20 May 1935.

PRELUDE TO WAR . . . THE MUNICH CRISIS

Hitler first embarked on his bid to rule the world in March 1938, when his storm-troopers invaded Austria, and seized control without a shot being fired. The Nazi's found Austria easy prey, and within six months Hitler

29 AERIAL VIEW OF PORTWAY in 1927 – the year after its opening, showing Barrow Hill houses being built, whilst St. Mary's Road and Groveleaze are not yet developed. *Foreground:* West Town Road and Lane showing Crown Terrace at West Town.

turned his aggression towards the next country on his list, namely, Czecho-Slovakia. Both Britain and France were allied by Treaty to Czecho-Slovakia, and war was perilously close.

In 1938 the German Reich was greater than ever before, whereas during the 1920's and 30's Britain, in company with many world powers having agreed on reducing their naval forces, had been busily engaged in a disarmament policy, scrapping her warships and the like. Britain was certainly not prepared for war when Hitler set his sights on Czecho-Slovakia in September 1938. In order, therefore, to try to find a peaceful settlement to Germany's claims Mr. Chamberlain flew out from Heston Aerodrome London to Munich to meet Adolf Hitler, and not *once*, but *three* times in as many weeks! On the first two occasions the Prime Minister returned having miserably failed in his mission, but on the third occasion (30 September 1938), he came back to Heston triumphantly waving a Treaty Document signed by Hitler, and exclaiming, 'I believe it is peace for our time . . . peace with honour. . . .'

That a British Prime Minister should actually travel by air was in itself something of a sensation, as aeroplanes were not used by V.I.P.'s as readily in those days as they are today. Also, that a British Prime Minister being obliged to go to Germany (Britain's former enemy) to meet their upstart Leader was unprecedented. This showed the urgency of the situation, and to what lengths Neville Chamberlain was prepared to go to ensure the peace. It was expected that Hitler would honourably keep his word, but it soon transpired the Fuehrer was a ruthless Dictator whose word meant nothing. He had intended by 1 October 1938 to invade Czecho-Slovakia in any case.

On 15 March 1939 Hitler ritually installed himself in the Hradschin Castle overlooking Prague, the historic home of Bohemian Kings and Czecho-Slovakian Presidents. Czecho-Slovakia had been deserted by her Allies, and Neville Chamberlain has since been severely criticised for his appeasement policies. This may have been the case, but knowing just how unprepared Britain was for war in 1938 the Prime Minister had parlied with Hitler to buy time for Britain to prepare for the war which would inevitably come. For Britain the Munich Crisis was a blessing in disguise.

Avonmouth in 1938 was celebrating the 21st anniversary of the Parish having been formed, and the then Vicar of Avonmouth (the Revd. R. W. Philipson) wrote in the Parish magazine:

'Strife at the birth of the Parish, and the nearness of war at maturity, with troops, guns and trenches. During the recent Munich Crisis we discovered that Avonmouth is of National Importance. In times of peace this is not considered, but the imminence of war opened all eyes in this our coming-of-age year. . . .'

Following the Munich Crisis, Avonmouth and Bristol, together with the rest of Great Britain, lost no time at all in preparing for war. Meanwhile

30 H.M.S. *Birmingham* at Royal Edward Dock, Avonmouth *c* 1920. *Second-class Cruiser*, built 1913 and fought at Battle of Jutland. Fell victim to the Government's disarmament policy between the wars. Scrapped in 1931.

31 MUNICH CRISIS 29 September 1938. On the day Prime Minister Chamberlain flew to Munich in a third bid for peace, work of assembling gas masks for Bristolians was watched by the Lord Mayor.

Hitler kept screaming that he wanted peace. Unfortunately he spelt the word 'piece' and he wanted a piece of every country he could get his hands on. By June 1939 he wanted a piece of Poland, the Dantzig Corridor. On 1 September 1939 the German army invaded Poland without having declared war on that unhappy country. On 2 September Mr. Chamberlain sent Hitler an ultimatum that 'If Germany did not withdraw her troops immediately from Poland she must consider herself at war with Britain. . . .' Hitler chose to ignore the British ultimatum, thus Britain was at war with Germany. In only 36 days the German army completely over-ran Poland, and the swiftness with which that country fell not only surprised the poor Poles, but the Nazi's themselves!

IV. FROM PEACE TO WAR

The Second World War lasted nearly six years, and proved to be the most violent and prolonged injury which mankind has ever inflicted upon itself.

The two World Wars have often been compared, especially by those who experienced them both. In the case of the First War, battles were in the main lost or won in the trenches on the Western Front, and because of the horrors of the fighting there when a generation of young men were wiped out, it is not always realised that the Second World War was immeasurably the more destructive of the two. The Second World War involved everyone, men, women and children, who were put in the Front Line through the air raids. And not only the civilians in Britain, but also those in other European Countries, including Japan. It cost over 50 million lives.

The Second World War eventually became world-wide, involving 56 Nations. It ended with the utter defeat of Germany and all her Allies. Although Japan fought on for three months after the collapse of Germany, she too was brought to complete surrender after the atom bombs (mankind's latest and most terrible weapon of destruction) had been dropped on that country. When the war was all over great cities and towns were left in ruins, with millions of starving and destitute peoples.

The good which came out of the evil of the Second World War was its assisting and accelerating advances in medical knowledge and surgical techniques. It caused so many appalling casualties and created such widespread conditions where disease could flourish as to confront the

32 ADOLF HITLER whose fanatical
dreams of world domination plunged
Europe into the abyss of war in 1939.
Graffiti discovered on wall of forgotten underground air raid shelter at
South Street Primary School, Bedminster, Bristol in 1987.

medical profession with an enormous challenge. The doctors of the world
rose to this challenge magnificently, especially two British doctors, Sir
Alexander Fleming, the pioneer of Penicillin, and 'Archie' McIndoe, the
great plastic surgeon. Of paramount importance to the fighting services was
the Blood Transfusion Service, one of the main depots for which was at
Southmead Hospital.

   In September 1939 Avonmouth was designated a place of national
importance, and a curtain of security descended upon the Parish and all its
activities for the duration. So stringent was the security that even today the
Imperial War Museum do not list in their records Avonmouth or
Shirehampton for either war. The first step security-wise was taken by the
Army who mounted armed sentries on all the Dock entrances. From thence,
and for the rest of the war, only persons having legitimate business inside the
Docks were allowed through the gates, and only then on showing their
special passes. At the same time the seaward entrance to Avonmouth was
guarded by a heavy ring-mail torpedo net, strung from side to side of the lock
gates. This had to be lowered to the sea bed each time shipping wished to
enter or leave Avonmouth Docks during the war.

   Having Military guards at the Docks entrances was no new experience for
Avonmouth. Similar circumstances had arisen in August 1914 at the

33 TORPEDO NET protecting entrance to Royal Edward Dock, Avonmouth. Photo: March 1944

outbreak of the Great War. But there was one important difference this time. After the Armistice in 1918 Avonmouth Docks were again 'opened' so that anyone who wished could go into the Docks as they pleased. It was the local custom to take a pleasant stroll out on to the Docks to watch the banana ships arrive, especially after Church on Sunday evenings. Following the Second World War the Avonmouth Docks, unlike Docks elsewhere, were not 'opened' again, and remain 'closed' to the general public to this very day. Even Avonmouth's local historian is not allowed entry into the Docks by the Docks Police without having first obtained a special pass!

THE BLACK-OUT

The news on that fine Sunday morning in September 1939 that Britain was at war was black indeed, but at the time it seemed not half so black as the darkness into which Britain was instantly plunged that same evening. The Emergency Powers Act brought Black-out Regulations into immediate operation. No longer were lights of any description allowed. No street lights or shop lights. It was a terrifying darkness, and the suddenness of it made it even more so.

At first there was a total ban on car headlights and torches, so that for pedestrians, crossing the streets became a dangerous and hazardous business, a game of chance no less. Even though drivers painted the mud-guards and running-boards of their vehicles with white paint, the total black-out led to so many road accidents that a Movement arose in favour of some modification in the total black-out ruling. This seemed justifiable, and early in January 1940 it was agreed that a modified form of street lighting should be authorised. The experts now revealed that light of an intensity of 0.00025 foot candles on the ground could safely be left burning during an air raid.

From then on car headlights were permitted with the use of masks which threw a very narrow beam of light directly downwards on to the road. Masks for torches were also allowed, but, not surprisingly, batteries for torches became very scarce and hard to come by. There was a particular hue and cry over the disappearance of No. 8 batteries, which was the size required for the most popular pocket torch.

To assist in the black-out the edges of pavement curbs and steps were daubed with white paint, and trees growing in pavements had white bands painted on them. Eventually masked signs were allowed to indicate that such and such a public house or shop was open. The times of Church Services, choir practices, and other public meetings which had hither-to been held during the evenings were now re-timed and held during the afternoons to enable folk to return to their homes in safety during the hours of daylight. In any case the majority of Churches proved too difficult and too expensive a task to black-out them satisfactorily.

Black-out Regulations meant that windows in all our homes had to be blacked out to make quite sure that indoor lights could not be seen from the outside. Even a mere glimmer of light which could be seen from a chink in the black-out curtains always brought loud shouts of 'Put that light out!!' from Air-raid Wardens or Police – the safety of everyone depended upon it. Not many houses were lucky enough to have shutters to their windows, but fortunately some shops soon stocked suitable materials with which to make black-out curtains and/or frames. Needless to say those shops did a roaring trade in aids to black-out.

The following incident might seem to us now to be very far fetched, but it is nevertheless a true story, and bears witness to just how dense the black-out at times proved to be, especially on moonless nights. Mr. John of Chelwood Road, Shirehampton was an Air-raid Warden, and with his co-Warden named Jack was patrolling the streets of Shirehampton during the heavy raid on Friday, 4 April 1941. They were walking along the Portway near Shirehampton Railway Station, when Mr. John became aware that he was walking alone! He began to look for Jack, but with difficulty due to the minute beam of light showing from his torch. Mr. John called out, 'Where are you, Jack?' to which a voice from the deep replied, 'Here I am! For Heaven's sake help me!' In the darkness Jack had walked right into a bomb crater which had burst a water mains pipe, and the poor man was up to his neck in water. Mr. John was soon able to drag Jack out of the bomb crater to safety.

Of all the Emergency Regulations there is no doubt that the Black-out was the one most generally hated. It had a more depressing effect on people than anything else, and everyone became heartily sick of it. Nevertheless it had to be endured until the tides of war had sufficiently turned in favour of the Allies for it to be considered safe enough to relax some of the strict Regulations.

Double Summer Time and Dim-Out

Britain first introduced Summer Time in May 1916 during the Great War by advancing Greenwich Mean Time (G.M.T.) by one hour during the summer months. By prolonging the use of daylight the Act proved a beneficial fuel saving measure and it was made permanent in 1925.

During the Second World War Britain put the clocks forward yet another hour with the introduction of Double Summer Time on 2 April 1944. The previous winter had passed with the use of Summer Time, and now the clocks were two hours ahead of G.M.T., led to some curious experiences. For instance, it was most pleasant to be able to play tennis in daylight in June until 11.00 p.m., especially when one's partner happened to be an attractive member of the opposite sex. It was not so enjoyable in mid-winter having to cycle to work at 8.30 a.m. in complete darkness or even by moonlight.

Double Summer Time was ended on 16 September 1944 when the clocks were put back one hour, again leaving Summer Time for the winter months. The opportunity was taken at the same time to replace black-out with dim-out, which meant that lights could be a little brighter, and only a drawn curtain would suffice at a lighted window. Even though this lighting was in a very modified form, after five long years of strict black-out it seemed to have flood-lighting effect, and people were attracted to the streets to enjoy having some light in the darkness of night once again.

Dim-out was abolished when Peace returned in 1945, but due to severe fuel shortages in the years immediately following the war, there continued to be restrictions on the uses of flood-lighting, illuminated and neon signs, etc. In the event it was March 1949 before, in the words of the wartime song '. . . the lights went up in London' again, and City centres could return to their former peace-time glitter. Britain, in fact, underwent nearly ten long years of darkness and gloom.

34 IDENTITY CARD issued in the Great War in 1915.

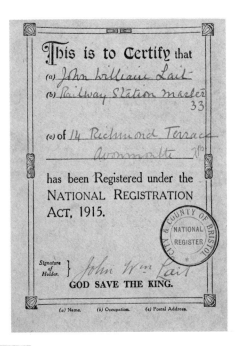

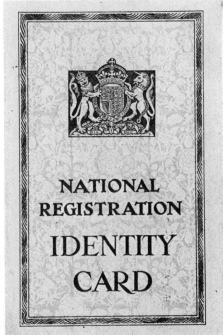

35 IDENTITY CARD issued September 1939. Had to be carried on person and shown on demand. Remained in force until February 1952.

IDENTITY CARDS

The Great War had entered its second year, when an enumeration of Britain's population took place. Under the provisions of the National Registration Act, 1915, all persons between the ages of 16 and 65 years on the night of 15 August 1915, were required to furnish various particulars, from which statistics were compiled for the guidance of Government Departments in formulating schemes for the administration of the war.

When Bristol's Register was compiled 218,768 persons were listed, and the task of keeping it up to date was quite involved. On attaining the age of 16 years people were entered on the Register, and on reaching 65 names were withdrawn. Males were issued with blue cards, and females with cream coloured cards.

The Second World War was barely a month old, when a census of Britain's civil population took place. Registration was compulsory irrespective of age or sex, and Friday 29 September 1939 was deemed Registration Day.

Schedules were filled in by every householder in Great Britain and Northern Ireland giving details in order of precedence of everyone living under their roof on that night. Within a few days the Enumerators called personally to collect the schedules, when they then issued Identity Cards. Everyone was given an Identity number (my own being OAVI 234 3) and people were encouraged to learn their Identity number by heart. Throughout the war every citizen was compelled to carry their Identity Card with them at all times, to be shown on demand by Police or Military. This time there was no differentiation between the sexes, as all Cards were coloured blue.

Even the King and Queen were included in the National Registration, and were recorded on the appropriate forms in London. As it so happened, our present Queen, then Princess Elizabeth, was staying at Balmoral Castle on Registration Day, so that her Identity Card started with the letter 'S', denoting that the holder was registered in Scotland.

The National Registration Returns formed the basis of Britain's food rationing scheme, and a few weeks later householders received the first issue of Ration Books through the Post.

After the war, many people considered the carrying of Identity Cards in peace-time an infringement of personal freedom, and from January 1946 there was a campaign for their abolition. Nevertheless, Identity Cards remained in force until 21 February 1952, when the then Minister of Health, Mr. H. Crookshank, announced to the House of Commons that the Government had decided it was no longer necessary for the public to possess and produce an Identity Card, or to notify change of address for National Registration purposes. Understandably this statement was greeted with loud

Ministerial cheers. The Identity numbers, however, continued to be used in respect of the Naional Health Service.

CENSORSHIP

The newspapers during the war were subject to strict censorship because Germany was always able to obtain copies of British newspapers through neutral countries. One such was Eire which remained 'neutral' for the duration of the war, and another was Portugal.

It was not until 1971 that some of the West Country's store of secrets from World War II could be published, and it was then disclosed for the first time that Whitchurch Civilian Airport at Bristol was the British end of the famous Lisbon line. Even in wartime, seemingly, civilian flying had to continue, and as far as Whitchurch was concerned, the aircraft was unarmed, and flights restricted to the hours of darkness.

The Luftwaffe turned a blind eye to the Lisbon line because it served the Germans a useful purpose. It was a two-way spy line. Enemy agents in the guise of businessmen arrived here, and the Allies used the same route for under-cover men. Furthermore, bundles of British newspapers fresh from the presses were loaded into Lisbon-bound aircraft at Whitchurch Airport, many of them due to be eagerly purchased on arrival by Axis agents.

In view of this the Editors of our newspapers were quite adamant in not publishing a single word which could be of use to the enemy. This rigorous censorship certainly helped win the war, and was for our own good, but it has nevertheless made the historian's subsequent task extremely difficult and frustrating, especially as far as Avonmouth is concerned. Not once during the war was Avonmouth mentioned by name in any of the newspapers! When reporting news of Avonmouth it was disguised as a 'South West Town', which could have meant anywhere in the South West. Mostly, events taking place in Avonmouth during the war were not mentioned at all in the newspapers.

A typical example of newspaper censorship in regard to Avonmouth is the Royal Visit which King George VI and Queen Elizabeth paid to Bristol and Avonmouth on 8 February 1940. The local newpapers described in full Their Majesties visit to Bristol mentioning by name the Downs, Kellaway Avenue, Horfield, Bristol University, Clifton College and even the Bristol Aeroplane Co.'s works at Filton. When it came to reporting the Avonmouth part of the Royal Visit, the newspapers referred to it merely as the 'Dock Area'. This could now be interpreted as having been the Bristol City Docks, but that the King and Queen actually came to Avonmouth is confirmed by the many eye-witnesses on that day who actually saw them in Avonmouth, and also by the event having been recorded in Avonmouth School log book.

Keeping Records

The keeping of records, compiling and collating information (especially concerning damage caused by air raids) was a contravention of a Defence Regulation because of possible value to the enemy. Fortunately for future generations three people undoubtedly broke the Law by keeping diaries, in which they jotted down war-time events. Their diaries, which have since been published, not only make fascinating reading forty years later, but also provide local war-time information which would not have otherwise been recorded.

The job of a newspaper journalist was a particularly frustrating one during the war, being debarred from writing about many aspects of the local war-time scene. Bombs fell, aircraft crashed, factories and shops destroyed, yet nothing of this could be reported. One such journalist was the editor of the Gazette Series of Newspapers at Dursley, Glos., Mr. A. W. Hughes, who found himself in the unusual position of having to suppress news information rather than reporting it. Mr. Hughes' war-time diary was his personal rebuff to censorship, and posterity has been given authentic observations of the local scene at that time. The book 'Gloucestershire at War 1939–1945' edited by Derek Archer published in 1979 by F. Bailey & Sons Ltd. at Dursley consists mainly of pages from Mr Hughes' war-time diaries.

Mr. George H. Gibbs was the Lord Mayor of Bristol's Secretary during the war. He was also deputy to Mr. H. M. Webb, the City's A.R.P. Controller. Being at the centre of things, Mr. Gibbs was in a position to collate all the facts at first hand about Bristol's air raids, which he kept in a diary. When the war was over the Western Daily Press published twice weekly from 7 June 1946 to 16 August 1946 very valuable accounts of Bristol's air raids taken from Mr. Gibbs' diaries. These articles are not only unique but are the only record in existence to give the story of the Battle of Bristol.

Mrs. Violet A. Maund describes herself as just a very ordinary Bristol housewife in her book 'The Diary of a Bristol Woman 1938–1945' published in 1950 by Arthur H. Stockwell Ltd., Ilfracombe, Devon. During the war Mrs. Maund lived with her husband, a Government Official (also doing obligatory fire watching duties) in Arley Hill, Redland. They had a daughter attending Redland High School. In her personal diaries Mrs. Maund noted the impact of the war on the City and its people. The book is especially unique in having wartime experiences in Bristol written from a woman's point of view, i.e. having to cope with shortages of all kinds of commodities, besides rationing of food and clothing, and herself also having to do war work.

It is doubtful whether either Mr. Hughes, Mr. Gibbs or Mrs. Maund realised when they were chronicling their diaries how important they would one day become. Local historians owe to them a profound debt of gratitude for the invaluable contribution to local history they have provided.

War Artists

It was in order to some extent to combat censorship, and to ensure that future generations might have some idea what the war was like, that the Ministry of Information commissioned various artists of the day to depict war-time scenes of their own choice. The 'War Artists Scheme' as it was called was organised by Sir Kenneth Clark, and was based on the National Gallery in London. Official War Artist was a reserved occupation, and they were sent on assignments all over Britain, as well as to the fighting Services to illustrate the war's progress.

Under this scheme, Mr. Harry Morley came to Avonmouth in 1940. He made an oil-painting of the Miles Arms Hotel as it was on the morning of 2 September 1940, having received a direct hit by a German bomb during the previous night. Mr. Morley entitled his work 'The Miles Arms Hotel, West Coast', and it has now become a unique and very special link in the record of war-time Avonmouth. The picture belongs to the Nation, having been given by the War Artist's Advisory Committee in 1946 to the Ministry of Works. For the last forty years the oil-painting has been at the Miles Arms Hotel, appreciated and enjoyed by the Parish.

War artists were also employed in the art of camouflage on both ships and aircraft. One out-standing example of this was clearly remembered by the late Mr. Wallace Tucker, a retired employee of the Port of Bristol Authority, who saw a merchant ship docked in Avonmouth during the war which had a painting of a Naval Destroyer on her side, perfect in every detail. From a distance it was hoped the enemy might mistake this piece of art for a real destroyer escorting the merchantman in a convoy or whatever. Unfortunately, there is no knowing whether or not this ingenious deception was successful in keeping the ship and her precious cargo afloat. We can only hope that it did succeed at the time when Britain was so desperately short of escort ships. In the main, camouflage was to distract enemy submarines from their target, by making it difficult for them to set their range-finder on straight up-right lines.

Footnote:

HARRY MORLEY, A.R.A. (1881–1943) was a distinguished and gifted artist. He first studied for an architect, but subsequently turned painter. From 1909 he was a regular exhibitor at the Royal Academy, his works having versatility in subject, style and medium. His 'Apollo & Marsayas' is in the Tate Gallery, and other works of his are in permanent collections at Leeds, Manchester, Bradford, Leicester, Bath,

Reading and Durham. In 1911 he married Lilian Helen Swain, and had two daughters, one of whom (Mrs. Beryl Castle) in 1985 wrote, 'I remember my father being sent off to a mystery destination – for security reasons he wasn't allowed to say where it was – and him returning about a week later with several water-colour sketches, from which he painted the Miles Arms Hotel, and another painting called "The Bombed Tascalusa" '. The latter painting depicts the oil-tanker *s.s. Tascalusa* (6,499 g.r.t.) beside a burnt wooden quay, after having been bombed by enemy 'planes in Falmouth Harbour on 10 July 1940. The ship at the time was on Charter to the Admiralty, and the painting is at present in the hands of the Imperial War Museum.

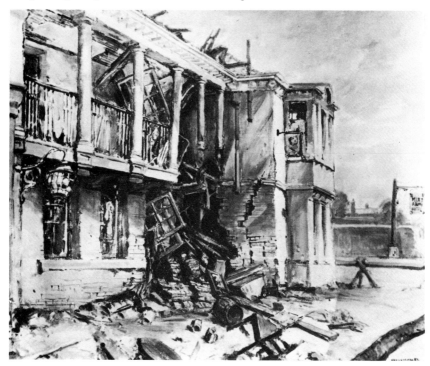

36   OIL PAINTING by Harry Morley, A.R.A. entitled *The Miles Arms Hotel, West Coast.* Commissioned by Ministry of Information, and shows the Hotel as it was on 2 September 1940.

ANTI-GOSSIP

Besides being put to a disadvantage by the strict war-time censorship, historians also suffer to some degree from the effects of the anti-gossip campaign. This was the censorship people imposed upon themselves by not talking about war-time events which they saw going on around them for fear of being overheard by enemy spies or traitors. The likelihood of such undesirables circulating in Avonmouth seems a rather improbable suggestion to us now, but after the fall of France in 1940 it was fully expected that the Germans would next invade this country, and the 'fifth columnist' scare was very real indeed. Even after 40 years and more have elapsed, some folk are still hesitant to speak about the important activities which happened in Avonmouth during the war years.

The Ministry of Information began the anti-gossip campaign early in 1940 by issuing posters to remind people how important it was not to disclose information which could be of use to the enemy. The posters appeared in Post Offices and on public transport, etc. One such declared:

> 'Lives are lost through conversation,
> Here's a tip for the duration,
> When you've private information,
> KEEP IT DARK!'

The every-day wartime slogan 'Be Like Dad, Keep Mum' was taken from the poster by Reeves, but the best remembered posters are the 'Careless talk costs lives' series by the clever Fougasse – alias Cyril Kenneth Bird. His funny Hitler faces and large Göring torsoes listening-in to conversations became quite famous. His, too, was the phrase 'Walls have ears' which became another wartime slogan. Thus it was that ordinary men and women went about their business living and working in Avonmouth, and for the most part not realising what vital and sometimes very dangerous activities connected with the war were going on right under their very noses.

This ignorance was not only bliss, but it was sometimes a blessing in disguise, judging from the following story which I was told after the war. It concerns a Railway incident on the line from Avonmouth to Bristol Temple Meads via Clifton Down. There were only steam locomotives to pull the trains during the war, and it was very difficult to black-out the glow of the fire-box and its steam reflections. Furthermore the engine cabs being open to the elements had to be blacked out by means of anti-glare tarpaulins, which made the cabs very hot and stifling for the men on the foot-plate. Due to the difficulty in preventing the fire-box glow being visible to raiders it was the Railway Rule that when an air-raid 'alert' was sounded, trains had to brought to a stand-still at the next signal, and remain there until the 'all clear' was given. On the night in question an 'alert' had been sounded, and already there was an up-train standing at Sea Mills Station. Another up-train was standing in Shirehampton Station, when an up-goods train arrived at Avonmouth Dock Junction signal-box at West Town Avonmouth, and was duly brought to a halt there by the signalman. Immediately the goods guard came up to the signal-box and questioned the signalman as to why his train had been brought to a stop. The signalman rightly pointed out that he was working to

37 ANTI-GOSSIP POSTER. One of many
Second World War posters from the clever
hand of *Fougasse* alias Cyril Kenneth Bird.

38 ANTI-GOSSIP POSTER. Another of the
famous posters by *Fougasse*.

Rule, and added, 'What's more, Jerry 'planes are in the vicinity at this very moment!' At this, the guard became very agitated and nervous, the colour drained from his face. He blurted out, 'This is a munition train mate, and we have tons of high explosives on board!' The signalman needed no further persuasion to get the goods train moving. After a few hurried words with Railway Control over the 'phone the goods train was given the go-ahead, and allowed to proceed with all haste and speed to the safety of Clifton Down tunnel, where it remained until the 'all clear'.

This incident shows that the anti-gossip campaign in one respect actually helped the Parishioners who had to live and work in Avonmouth during the war. If ordinary folks had been fully aware of the dangers of living in war-time Avonmouth, perhaps no one would have had the courage to have remained here, and who could have blamed them?

Footnote:

The phrase 'fifth column' was first coined during the Spanish Civil War in 1936, when one of General Franco's Commanders announced that he had five columns attacking Madrid, i.e. four advancing upon the City in battle order, and the fifth composed of sympathisers operating in the Capital itself.

V. PREPARING FOR WAR

The possibility of war was first considered by the Bristol City Council as early as May 1935, which resulted in the setting up of an Air-Raid Precautions Committee. During the next three years the problems of A.R.P. were considered by the Council from time to time, but in peaceful Bristol there seemed no great urgency about implementing plans. As always the costs involved aroused controversy. However, by the end of 1938 the A.R.P. Committee was working smoothly, and its activities had become so extensive that it became necessary to create four sub-Committees, and to each was delegated particular tasks.

ADMINISTRATION

In the Spring of 1939 the City Engineer, Mr. H. M. Webb, was appointed the A.R.P. Controller. He became the most important Official in the Administrative machine, and was in supreme command of the City when the emergency came. In addition to his responsibilities to Regional Headquarters, the A.R.P. Committee and the Emergency Committee, he was also required to maintain contact with the Ministry of Home Security. Quietly spoken and unflappable, Mr. Webb managed to do the work of several men, never lost his 'cool' and remained in the post until peace returned.

Emergency Committee

At the request of the Lord Privy Seal, the Bristol City Council appointed an Emergency Committee to take over the civil defence of Bristol in April 1939. The A.R.P. Committee had charge of equipment, and watched over the efficiency of the service and its general well-being, whereas the Emergency Committee confined its attention to the determination of policy and control of operations in emergencies. This Committee consisted of four extremely able men. Alderman Arthur W. Cox (Leader of the Labour Party on the City Council), Alderman F. A. Parish (Deputy Labour Leader), Alderman Sir John Inskip (Tory Leader) and Alderman A. Havergal Downes Shaw. Throughout the war these four men met daily to deal with the thousand and one problems concerned with the defence of Bristol, and although all were keen Party men, political differences were sunk in favour of the common task of winning the war. In all that time they never had a single cross word, and Bristol was fortunate in its Emergency Committee.

39 BRISTOL'S EMERGENCY COMMITTEE in session 1942, in War Room down in cellars of 19/21 Woodland Road, Bristol 8. *Corner position:* General Sir Hugh Elles (S.W. Regional Controller); *on his left:* Military Adviser and Ald. F. A. Parish (Committee Chairman). *Also included in picture:* Mr. H. M. Webb (City Engineer & Bristol's A.R.P. Controller) and Mr. George Gibbs (Deputy A.R.P. Controller & Lord Mayor's Secretary).

Alderman F. A. Parish, the Chairman, who died in April 1985, aged 86, was the last surviving member of the Emergency Committee. At 40, Mr. Parish was the youngest Chairman of any of the wartime Emergency Committees of the large Cities, and King George VI invested him with the C.B.E. for his services at the height of the bombing. As far as Avonmouth is concerned Alderman Parish is best remembered for having served on the Docks Committee for 40 years, and in particular for having been Chairman of that Committee for some considerable time.

It was made known in November 1938 that for defence purposes the Government proposed to divide the Country into various regions, with a Commissioner to each. Avonmouth, Shirehampton and Bristol came within the No. 7 South Western Region, which also included Gloucestershire, Somerset, Wiltshire, Devon and Cornwall. Within the first few months of the war, Sir Hugh Elles (a Tank Commander in the Great War) was appointed the South West Regional Commissioner, and he remained in the post until February 1945, when peace was in sight. Sir Hugh would have become virtual dictator of the South West Counties had Germany actually invaded this Country, and particularly if Bristol and the South West had found themselves cut off from London by enemy forces. Mercifully nothing of the kind took place. It was the opinion of those who worked with Sir Hugh that if the worst had come he was the sort of 'leader' they would have liked, and Bristol had complete confidence in him.

War Room

In 1971 when some of the West Country's store of wartime secrets were published for the first time, it came to light that two comfortable and spacious Victorian town houses in Cotham were chosen as the nerve centre of the civil defence operations in Bristol and the South West. In the roomy cellars of No's 19 & 21 Woodland Road, Bristol 8, beneath bomb-proof concrete and reinforced steel girders was set up Bristol's top secret War Room. It was here that Sir Hugh Elles and his staff, with the leaders of Bristol's Civil Defence Forces worked at their vital posts throughout the war years. The secret of 19 & 21 was well kept, and few people who passed along Woodland Road realised the true wartime role being played there.

40   19/21 WOODLAND ROAD, BRISTOL 8. Bristol's War Room was in the cellars of this house. *N.B.* Pill-box position in corner of garden, intended as last line of defence in event of invasion.   Photo: April 1980.

It was from this War Room that Bristol's air raid warning system was controlled, and where Sir Hugh kept in touch with all the five Counties in the South West. The first indication that Nazi bombers were approaching Bristol was flashed to this basement, with its heavy metal doors, gas-filter plant, escape hatches, wall maps and top priority telephone cables. Today, the only remaining evidence above ground of Bristol's once War Room is the brick pill-box at the corner of the garden. This would have been the last line of defence had Bristol ever been over-run by the enemy.

It is certainly ironic that 40 years on, at the time of writing, 21 Woodland Road should house the German Department of the University of Bristol!

Precautionary Measures

As from the Autumn of 1938, the newspapers almost daily carried articles giving hints and sensible advice as to the best way to protect either one's person or one's property in the event of enemy air attacks. Furthermore, in July 1939 the Government issued pamphlets giving instructions as to what to do in the event of an air raid.

For instance, householders were urged to clear their lofts and attics of papers and other inflammable materials which could be a fire hazard. People were also advised to keep their bath filled with water, so that there would be a supply on hand should a fire break out. This applied to those people who were fortunate enough in those days to have a bathroom with a suitable bath. Useful as it was, the Government's pamphlet did not seemingly cover every kind of eventuality, as the following Cook Street incident illustrates.

During one of the heavy Avonmouth raids, the water-mains were damaged, and Parishioners found themselves without any water supply. Mrs. Edith Room consoled her family that as far as they were concerned they were very fortunate in having plenty of water in the empty house next door. The neighbours had filled their bath before having evacuated themselves to the country for the duration, and kindly entrusted Mrs. Room with their key. So it was the morning after the blitz that the Room family armed with kettles and saucepans went into next door to get some water for their morning cup of tea, and to wash, etc., and were quite aghast to be confronted with a completely empty bath! During the raid a bomb dropped in the garden, and blast had come up through the waste-pipe and blown out the bath plug. All the precious water had drained away. However, all was not lost. Resourceful as ever, Edith provided the family's morning 'cuppa' by using the water in their hot-water bottles. The kettle that morning had to be boiled over the fire in the open grate, because Avonmouth was also without supplies of either gas or electricity.

70

41   BRISTOL CIVIL DEFENCE CORPS. (Shirehampton Division). Pictured at Shirehampton Junior School for stand-down 2 May 1945. *Divisional Warden:* W. M. Surtees, *Deputy:* C. V. Duggan.

AIR RAID SIRENS

After the Munich Crisis in 1938, changes began to take place in Avonmouth and Shirehampton in preparation for the possibility of war. The first indication that Air Raid Precautions were in earnest was the arrival of the air raid sirens, which were erected on the chimney-stacks of the Police Stations. In March that year Bristol Council had heard it would cost £37,000 to install an air raid warning system in the City, but that £24,000 would be provided by the Government.

At that time Avonmouth's Police Station was in Avonmouth Road at the junction of Green Lane, on the site at present occupied by A.T.S. car-park. Shirehampton's Police Station was at the bottom of Park Hill on the corner of Park Road, which has since been converted to a private house and business premises. The Port of Bristol Authority at Avonmouth had their own air raid siren. This was on the roof of 'V' Shed, at the West Wharf of the Royal Edward Dock. Having three sirens in the neighbourhood ensured that everyone in Avonmouth and Shirehampton heard the warnings of approaching enemy planes no matter which way the wind was blowing.

The sirens were first heard by the Parishioners of Avonmouth and Shirehampton during the night of Wednesday, 5 July 1939, when A.R.P. rehearsals took place in this area. The street lights were switched off for this practice, and the rising and falling sounds of the sirens in the darkness were a chilling foretaste of more frightening things to come.

Because of their wailing tones the sirens were dubbed 'moaning minnies'. There was also some variations in the pronounciation of the word 'siren'. Some Bristolians talked about the 'Syreens' just as they talked about the 'I-talians', whilst one man, oddly enough, insisted on calling them the 'Syrians'!

PRACTICAL AIDS

Public Air Raid Shelters

Whilst Prime Minister Neville Chamberlain was negotiating his second bid for peace at Munich, Mrs. Maund noted in her diary on 28 September 1938, 'Digging trenches on College Green'.

The speed in which Corporation Parks and open spaces in and around Bristol were dug up to make underground air raid shelters in September 1938 surprised one and all. The College Green shelter was a very large one built to accommodate 1,380 persons, and a similar underground shelter for the same number of people was installed in Queen Square.

Parks in the suburbs of Bristol were also dug up to make underground air raid shelters, and among them was Ashton Park and Avonmouth Park.

42   AVONMOUTH POLICE STATION, Avonmouth Road. Centre of A.R.P. Operations during the War. *Inset:* Avonmouth's air raid siren on the chimney-stack.   Photo: 15 June 1969.

43   PORT OF BRISTOL AUTHORITY'S AIR RAID SIREN. On roof of 'V' Shed, Royal Edward Dock, Avonmouth. *Left:* Fire-watchers' steel shelter.   Photo: March 1944.

Writing in the Avonmouth Parish magazine in 1938, the Vicar (the Revd. R. W. Philipson) reported:

'Our little park rapidly being transformed into a beautiful garden, has been turned into an unsightly mess, and a net-work of trenches where those caught in an air raid may shelter. . . .'

In such a low-lying Parish like Avonmouth, which is either at sea-level or below it, it is sheer folly, and a waste of money to dig trenches here at any time or for any reason, because of water-logging difficulties. This has always been one of Avonmouth's problems, and unfortunately will always remain one. It is not surprising, therefore, to learn that the trenches dug for air raid shelters in Avonmouth Park very soon became flooded, and had to be quickly filled in again!

As an alternative to the underground shelters, Avonmouth was provided with brick surface shelters erected in Richmond Terrace and Clayton Street to give cover for shoppers and workers who were caught away from home during air raids.

Perhaps the delay in erecting shelters at Avonmouth School, which were not begun until January 1940, was due to Avonmouth's drainage problems. Again these shelters had to be the brick-surface kind, and were built in the front and back yards of the School. They were first used by the pupils for the mid-day alert on 3 July 1940.

Domestic Air Raid Shelters

As adequate protection from bomb blast and flying shrapnel, the Government supplied three types of domestic air raid shelters. Andersons were partly buried in the ground, Morrisons were for indoors and there were the surface shelters made from reinforced bricks and concrete.

Domestic shelters were not obligatory, and only supplied on application. They were free to people whose income was below £250 a year, and with a charge of only £7 to those with incomes above this figure. This meant that the majority of homes in Shirehampton and Avonmouth could receive a free shelter if they so wished. Some foolish folks did not apply for a shelter in the first instance, and even ridiculed the people who did apply, jeering that the war would never reach these parts. How wrong they were! Needless to say, these same ill-advised people soon changed their minds about applying for a shelter, and were glad to do when the air raids got on the way.

The Anderson Shelter project was launched in November 1938, and within twelve months Andersons became a feature in most back gardens throughout the country. They were named after Sir John Anderson (Lord Privy Seal and Minister for Civilian Defence) and were the Government's answer to the

44   DOMESTIC ANDERSON AIR RAID SHELTER in situ 392 Portway, Shirehampton.
Photo: May 1980.

45   DOMESTIC BRICK SURFACE SHELTER in situ 6 Davis Street, Avonmouth. Photo:
May 1979.

46   DOMESTIC CONCRETE SURFACE SHELTER in garden of 104/102 Avonmouth Road, Avonmouth.   Photo: May 1979.

problem of providing shelter from glass splinters and falls of debris for houses without basements or cellars, and not much garden suitable for digging trenches. The Anderson Shelters were igloo-shaped and made of corrugated steel by the British Steel Industry. They measured 6 feet high, 4½ feet wide, 6½ feet long, and were buried in the ground up to a depth of 4 feet, with their roofs covered with at least 15 inches of soil and or/sand bags. They cost between £6 and £7 each, and on average 30/– (£1.50p) to erect. Altogether 2¼ million Andersons were erected throughout the country, of which Bristol had 41,450.

Anderson Shelters are seldom, if ever, seen these days due to the fact that most were dug out and returned to the Authorities soon after the war ended. What a joy it was to get rid of the Andersons, now that shelters were no longer needed, and in so doing it was helping post-war steel shortage. My Father despatched our Anderson in August 1945, only eleven days after V.J. Day, in his haste to relay the lawn which had been sacrificed in 1939 to make room for the shelter. A whole new generation has since been born and grown up without either having seen or known about Andersons. The one that remains in situ (at the time of writing) at 392 Portway must hold the record as being the very last in Shirehampton. Having been used as a garden shed since the war it has unwittingly become a rarity.

Shirehampton Parish managed extremely well with the Anderson shelters, some keen gardeners even landscaped the exteriors of theirs as rockeries, and made them gay with flowers. Because of the old drainage problem the Anderson shelters were of no use to Avonmouth, and none were ever erected in the Parish. As an alternative, the homes in Avonmouth were given individual surface shelters. These were either built of bricks and reinforced concrete with walls 14 inches thick, or were wholly built of reinforced concrete. As certain proof of the strength and stability of these surface shelters, my own in 1968 took three men using a pneumatic machine three days to remove, during which time they broke two drills!

Morrison Shelters were designed to be erected inside the house, for homes such as flats, not having cellars or gardens, and resembled a massive table made of steel with mesh sides. Because of the amount of space they took up in an average sized room, they were usually used as a table, with a bed inside them. Morrisons were to protect the occupants from falling rubble, and could survive almost anything save a direct hit. Even if the house actually collapsed, the Morrison Shelter usually survived, and by the end of the war more than a million were in use.

Although hospitals were kept very busy during the air raids, there were not so many casualties as had been anticipated. The casualty lists for Avonmouth and Shirehampton must be considered very slight when compared with the vast tonnage of high explosives that were dropped here. Certainly this was thanks to the various types of air raid shelters which were provided and put to good use.

47 MINISTRY OF HOME SECURITY POSTER. Gas attacks were regarded as one of the certainties of War in 1939.

Gas-Masks
(Officially called 'Respirators')

Gas attacks were regarded as one of the certainties of war in 1939. Fear of it was widespread, and dominated every other fear of war.

Poisonous gases were first used in the trenches on the Western Front during the Great War, and many remembered its terrifying use there, having either watched their comrades die, be blinded or maimed by it. Others suffered from the after-effects of gas for the rest of their lives, and remarks like, 'Poor man, he was gassed in the war' were heard all too often in the years that followed.

One such victim was the late Mr. Harper Brayley of 6 Green Lane, Avonmouth, who served in France from 1915 with the First 6th Gloucestershire Regiment. When recalling his experiences in the trenches, Mr. Brayley wrote in 1975:

'. . . the enemy were sending over shells filled with Mustard Gas, and I had a dose of it. The Germans also sent over gas shells that contained a new gas which we called "Lewisite", and it penetrated our respirators, and affected our lungs, and we were withdrawn from the trenches to have the respirators adjusted. The gas still affects my body after all these years. . . .'

Mr. Brayley died in 1976 aged 82.

Fore-warning that the next war would involve the entire population, men, women and children besides the Armed Forces, and predicting what this would be like, was brought home to people by the film 'Things to Come' made in 1935. H. G. Wells, the author, wrote this futuristic play specially for the screen; starring Raymond Massey and Ralph Richardson, it became the British Film of the Year. It first told the story of a town in peace-time, and again after it had been bombed, gassed and laid in ruins by the ravages of a modern war. As it turned out 'Things to Come' was an incredible forecast, especially as the story was supposedly to take place in the year 1940!

Little wonder then that at the Munich Crisis, when war seemed so imminent, there was a rush to obtain gas-masks when these were first made available on 30 September 1938, at various depots in and around Bristol. Shirehampton Police Station (then at the bottom of Park Hill) and Avonmouth National School were two of these depots. Supplies quickly ran out, but this was only a preliminary distribution. The general distribution of gas-masks took place in Bristol a few months afterwards, during February and March 1939.

Air-raid Wardens called at every house to distribute the gas-masks, to obtain sizes and fit them. They also demonstrated the correct manner in which they should be put on and taken off. Unlike the air raid shelters which were only supplied on application, and free only to house-holders whose annual income was below £250, gas-masks involved everyone, and were issued free irrespective to every man, women and child in Great Britain and Northern Ireland.

The gas-masks were a defence against three categories of war gases, i.e. Tear Gas, Choking Gas and Blister Gas (which included Mustard Gas and Lewisite Gas). There were always rumours that the Germans had new gases against which the respirators would be useless, and on 21 May 1940 it was announced that special filters would soon be distributed as a guard against a 'smoke' type of gas called 'Arsine'. The box containing the additional filter was known as the 'contex container extension', and this was fixed to the end of the gas-masks by adhesive tape.

There were four types of gas-masks issued. The large civilian 'duty' respirators had a flexible tube, and were intended for A.R.P. personnel and other workers with occupations in essential Services. The vast majority of the civilian population were given the black rubber kind which had a wind-screen eyepiece, and perforated green tin base. These were held in place with webbing straps at the back of the head, and came in three sizes, large, medium and small. (Men with beards had to shave them off before they could wear their masks!) Young children and toddlers were issued with 'Mickey Mouse' masks, so called because they had individual eye-pieces, and a nose flap, and the children were encouraged to treat the wearing of them as a game. Babies were given what was termed a 'gas helmet', but this was in fact a miniature air-tight chamber into which the baby was placed bodily, and filtered air was pumped into it by means of hand-bellows.

When the war broke out it was stressed that everyone should carry their gas-mask with them at all times. Some folk did, and some not. Before the end of the month the Lost Property office had a goodly stock of gas-masks which had been left behind by forgetful passengers on Public Transport! To aid in carrying them, some Manufacturers with an eye to business, soon put on the market specially designed gas-mask carriers with shoulder straps. A very high quality carrier in watertight cloth was advertised as costing only 3/6d (17½p).

In order to detect the presence of poison gas, large yellow circles were painted on walls in strategic places around the Parish, which we were told would turn red colour when gas was present. If and when this should happen, it was the task of the Air-raid Wardens to raise the alarm by touring round shaking rattles (similar to those used by fans at football matches). When the gas had disappeared, and it was considered safe to remove one's gas-mask, the Wardens would come round a second time ringing hand-bells as the 'gas all clear' signal.

No one actually enjoyed wearing their gas-mask, not even for practice purposes, but they did offer a little comfort inasmuchas the Government had

48 GAS MASKS *(Officially called Respirators)* on display at Devizes Library in September 1979. *L to R:* Handbell for Gas 'All Clear' signal, Duty Respirator for A.R.P. Workers, Protective box and General Issue respirator.

49 GAS MASKS on display at Devizes Library in September 1979. *L to R:* 'Mickey Mouse' respirator for children and Gas Helmet for babies. *N.B.* Book showing horse wearing gas mask!

50 STIRRUP PUMP. Issued for fighting small fires. This one rescued from old garden shed in Shire-hampton when destined for waste skip. Photo: October 1979.

51 HOW *NOT* TO USE A STIRRUP PUMP! To use effectively, stirrup pumps required at least three pairs of hands. Photo: October 1979.

done something by way of preparation. Britain resolved NOT to use poison gas warfare unless Germany should resort to it first. Mr. Churchill warned Hitler many times that if he should dare to use gas, then Britain would not hesitate to immediately retaliate, and with vastly greater force! According to Mr. Churchill, Britain had sufficient stocks of gas to 'wipe out half Germany!'

One now wonders if some of these stocks of poison gases to which Mr. Churchill so confidently referred might have been here in Avonmouth. During the war there was a strong local belief that the Imperial Smelting Corporation was engaged in the manufacture of poison war-gases. Furthermore it was always said that there were sufficient stocks down at the Smelting Corporation to wipe out half of Germany. Avonmouth was certainly involved in the manufacture of Mustard Gas during the Great War, so perhaps there could have been some truth in the rumours of its being made here during the Second World War. So far this has not been confirmed or denied.

By some miraculous stroke of good fortune, which still remains unexplained, the war took its course and concluded without either side having resorted to the use of poison gas, despite the fact that both Britain and Germany had stock-piled large numbers of chemical weapons. Could it be, I wonder, that Hitler himself hated the wearing of his gas-mask as much as the rest of us did?

Stirrup-pumps

Stirrup-pumps (which cost about £1.00 to produce) were intended as a practical aid to put out small fires. They were distributed free, one to every few houses for neighbours to share. Not surprisingly there was no time lost in trying them out when they were first issued, when fire-drill became a novel pastime. The disadvantage with stirrup-pumps was that to operate them properly required as least three pairs of hands, i.e., one person to direct the nozzle, another to use the pump, whilst a third and better still a fourth person was needed to keep the bucket filled with water. In the event, fires which got out of hand became beacons for following waves of enemy 'planes bringing their high explosive bombs. Often, therefore, stirrup-pumps were not used to extinguish incendiaries when these were falling thick and fast in the general panic and haste to put them out as quickly as possible. One such instance was vividly described by Mr. W. A. Hares who was on fire-watching duty with his crew during a short raid on Eastville night of 26 February 1941. At the time he noted in his diary:

'Fire-watchers are discussing the whereabouts of the fires, when all at once the familiar hiss of a shower of incendiaries sends us all scuttling for cover. I am standing in the doorway with F.K. Top floor is ablaze. My pals tear up over the stairs with me. What a sight meets our gaze! It's a fire-fighter's bad dream – you don't know which to start on first. My mates are on the top floor giving another the works. So I tackle the one in the office. No time for "finessing" with stirrup-pump or other fancy tackle. Two buckets of water straight on the damn thing, and up she goes. Then some sand on top. I rush down to the box-room on the next floor. Another couple of buckets of water dampens down the blazing cartons, and J. throws some more water over the now burning woodwork. Up into the form-room where another incendiary is lodged in the rafters. We throw water, but cannot reach it. We throw sand over the burning papers, drench the bench with water. Leave that and dash back to the office where the first one is getting a hold on the tables and stock. C. goes up to the bomb, thinking it is a blazing gaspipe, as it is lodged on the wall horizontally. Approaches the bomb with a bucket of water, and attempts to pour the water on to the fire. The bomb blazes more furiously – C. jumps – and throws the bucket as well! It makes me laugh. . . .'

Unlike gas-masks which had to be handed back to the Authorities when the war was over, stirrup-pumps were not re-called. Most of them were given a more pleasant role in peace-time, i.e., that of watering the gardens. Stirrup-pumps are not often seen now-a-days, but they continued to be used by Avonmouth Fire Brigade to put out domestic chimney fires in the days before 'smokeless zones'.

Precautions Against Flying Glass

At the outbreak of the war Manufacturers were quick to put on the market various kinds of materials to help prevent injuries from splintering and flying glass caused by bomb blast. The public took every advantage of these. There were the 'cellophane' types of transparent materials to stick on window-panes, and these proved quite successful when put to the test. There were also splinter-proof 'lacquers' available to be painted directly on to glass, but these did not prove so effective, especially against nearby blast. Shop-keepers stuck strips of brown paper across their plate-glass windows in the hope of keeping them intact when faced with blast, but again this practice proved of little use.

Public Mortuaries

Provision of Public Mortuaries was the most gruesome side of practical aids. The Government had envisaged astronomic losses of civilian lives in the war, and recommended adequate provision of Public Mortuaries to cope with large numbers of deaths.

Avonmouth's Mortuary was a red brick building at the far end of Richmond Terrace. That for Shirehampton was the Old National Schools in Station Road, requisitioned by Bristol Corporation at the outbreak of the war, and converted and used as an Emergency Public Mortuary until March

52 STATION ROAD, SHIREHAMPTON August 1982. *Centre:* The Old National Schools requisitioned as Emergency Public Mortuary from 1939 to 1945.

1945. An unfortunate incident occurred during the air raid on 29 March 1941, when a high explosive bomb fell just outside the national Schools. Two men happened to be passing at the time and both were killed at the Mortuary! Extensive damage was caused to the building.

Although both Mortuaries were put into use during the period of the air raids, on reflection, the loss of lives in Avonmouth and Shirehampton due to enemy action was not so great as had been feared, and to warrant the provision of two Public Mortuaries in this area. *(God be praised!)*

VI. THE DEFENCE OF AVONMOUTH

On the declaration of war in 1939, as in the Great War, Avonmouth became of great national importance. Once again the Parish played an essential role in the war effort as an artery in the life-line of men, war machinery, raw materials and – not the least – of food.

After the fall of France in 1940, Avonmouth's role became even more important, when increasing enemy pressure was brought to bear on ships using Britain's ports on her south and south-east coasts. With London and Southampton virtually paralysed, of necessity Britain's ports on the west coast became her main ocean gateways.

When the United States entered the war, Avonmouth was selected as their chief depot in the west for the importing of war supplies. Between 1942 and 1945 many thousands of American servicemen passed through the port, besides hundreds of thousands of tons of stores of all kinds.

The Government did all in their power to defend Avonmouth, even with the limited resources at their disposal during the early part of the war. The Parish was designated a 'target' area, and was given every facility of Britain's Defence System, namely: barrage balloons, anti-aircraft guns, searchlights, and observer posts. Additionally, during the height of the air raids a smoke screen was diffused in an attempt to hide Avonmouth completely from enemy raiders, together with decoy fires being lit – code name 'Starfish' sites.

All these were necessary precautions. The Germans too recognised the importance of Avonmouth, and it is not surprising that Hitler did his utmost to obliterate the Parish by his bombing air raids. Not one street in Avonmouth came through the war unscathed by German bombs.

Some Parishioners (the author included) consoled themselves in the belief that Hitler didn't really know where Avonmouth was! But when the aerial photograph taken by the Luftwaffe on 27 September 1940 came to light after the war, it showed the enemy's knowledge of Avonmouth and its activities to be remarkably accurate. The main German target area seemingly was the Imperial Smelting Works with their zinc spelter foundry, etc. Other targets highlighted were railway sidings, grain mills and warehouses at Avonmouth (Old) Dock, with special mention of the C.W.S. Flour Mills, which is where the author happened to be at the time the photograph was taken. The Germans were even aware of the Army barracks on Penpole Point!

Manning Britain's ground defences was no piece of cake. Many sites were in isolated and desolate places. The Regiments on duty had an unenviable job, in all winds and weathers, at times lonely and monotonous, tiring and often unrewarding. All sites had to be operational 24 hours a day, seven days a week for the entire length of the war, and in the face of enemy attacks. On 3/4 April 1941 a high-explosive bomb killed one soldier and injured seven more at the anti-aircraft gun site at Markham Farm, near Pill. The last and only fatal casualty in the final air raid on Bristol, 15 May 1944, was a serviceman killed at the searchlight site in King's Weston Lane; but the success of Avonmouth's defences can be judged from the fact that the Docks were prevented from working normally, due to enemy action, on only one single day.

ROYAL OBSERVER CORPS.

No matter how effective ground defences might be, they are of little use without their having knowledge of impending enemy air attacks. Providing this information was an important part in Britain's Defence System, filled by the Royal Observer Corps. Observer Centres covered the entire country, each controlling a number of posts, where day and night watch was kept for sight and sound of enemy aircraft.

Comparatively few people in Avonmouth were aware of the presence of the Royal Observer Corps using their eyes and ears in the defence of Avonmouth in the open fields behind St. Andrew's Road, amid Farmer Briffett's quietly grazing cows. The Avonmouth Post, one of 36 local posts, was near a barrage balloon site, reached through a five-barred gate, which in those days crossed St. Brendan's Way beside Park House. Here the skies were scanned day and night throughout the war, from the first week until the last, 24 hours a day.

The enrolling and training of members for the Observer Corps was begun as early as 1937, being under the general direction of the Chief Constable. Shortly before the outbreak of the war, however, the force was placed directly under the control of the Air Ministry. The Observer Corps was a civilian organisation, consisting of more than 30,000 volunteers, most of whom carried out the duties as 'watchers', 'plotters', or 'tellers' in their spare time.

In the passing on of up-to-date information about the whereabouts of enemy 'planes to Home Security, people engaged on important war work were saved wasting time unnecessarily in air raid shelters, when there was no imminent danger. The flight-paths of all 'planes, whether enemy or friendly, were plotted and tracked and the information passed both to Fighter Command, and neighbouring Observation Stations and/or Posts. Thanks to the vigilance of the Observer Corps many a friendly aircraft, during inclement weather, was guided to a safe landing.

In April 1941 King George VI recognised the valuable service being rendered to the war effort by the Observer Corps, and to rectify the lack of official recognition he granted them a 'Royal' title. Henceforth the Corps was known as 'The Royal Observer Corps', and the following December a new blue battle-dress type of uniform was approved for members.

BARRAGE BALLOONS

Both Avonmouth and Shirehampton saw the arrival of the barrage balloons at the very outset of the war, floating in the sky like huge silver piggy-banks. The balloon sites were manned by the Royal Air Force, and were so arranged that the balloons formed a defensive 'roof' over the Parish. Avonmouth and district had about a dozen.

The Germans had a healthy respect for the balloons – they not only shot them down whenever possible, but also located them on their aerial reconnaisance photographs as 'Sperrballone' (see plate 1). On 27 September 1940 there were eight balloons in Avonmouth, with another sea-going balloon flown from a barge anchored in the mouth of the River Avon, off Avonmouth. In addition there were at least two more balloons sited in Shirehampton.

The Barrage Balloons were only one of the factors in Britain's Defence System. Their primary object was to force attacking 'planes to heights at

53   BARRAGE BALLOONS. Hundreds went up in 1939 over important centres, including Avonmouth, to harass enemy aircraft attempting low level attacks. Photo: At an Oxfordshire airfield, May 1963.

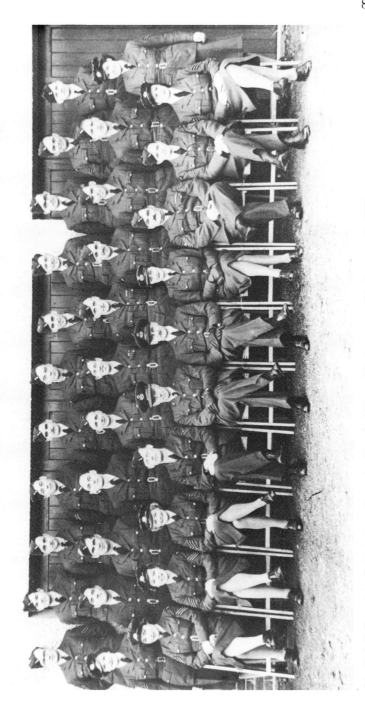

54 R.A.F. BALLOON PERSONNEL pictured at Twyford House Headquarters, Shirehampton in 1943.

55 BALLOON CREW at site 23, Cowley Farm, Avonmouth in 1943. (*N.B.* Picture includes two ducks and one dog!).

56 PAINTING by Dame Laura Knight, entitled *A Balloon Site, Coventry* depicting W.A.A.F. defending Industry, as they did in Avonmouth.

which accurate bombing and the machine-gunning of civilians was virtually impossible. The idea of using balloons as a weapon of Air Defence was first mooted by the Germans themselves, when during the winter of 1914/15 they tried a form of balloon or kite barrage to build up a stockade of nets in the sky to protect their industries. In January 1918 a British 'plane was caught in one such net and the two crew taken prisoner. After the war the pilot reported the dreadful mess which the balloon cable had made to his machine and British balloons were therefore developed between the wars. It was British policy to concentrate on developing balloons to operate at medium heights, and to leave the upper air free for fighter 'plane interception.

The balloons were made of specially treated rubber-proofed cotton fabric, many of them at Liverpool by the girls of Littlewoods, the firm of football pool promoters. They were painted silver to deflect the rays of the sun, and measured about 63 feet in length, just over 31 feet in height, weighed approx. 550 lbs, and were flown on flexible steel cables. The balloons were filled with hydrogen gas which is many times lighter than air. They had three stabilizers inflated with air at the back which looked like two huge 'fins' and a 'rudder' to keep them always riding head on to the wind, and to stay on an even keel.

Sea-going balloons were much smaller in size, and easier to handle than land balloons. These were painted in black and white squares for camouflage purposes, and with their pointed fin-like stabilizers they had the distinct appearance of chequered flying sharks. Besides being used to defend estuaries and docks as in the case of Avonmouth, sea-going balloons were successfully used to protect convoys, and were a serious obstacle to dive-bombers.

Considerable skill, strength and team-work was called for to fly the balloons. To keep a constant 24 hours a day guard on each, and manoeuvred according to the force and change of the wind required a complement of ten men to each site. In January 1941 it was suggested that the flying of balloons could be carried out by the members of the W.A.A.F. to relieve the men for other duties. At first this suggestion was received with some dismay, but any doubt of the capability of women for such a strenuous a task was soon dispelled. After training the girls proved equally as efficient as the men as balloon operators, although it was one of the hardest jobs undertaken by women in the war. The sites in Avonmouth and Shirehampton were thence taken over by the W.A.A.F., and forty and more years on, the women balloon operators stationed here, hold their reunion meetings to talk over times spent in defending Avonmouth.

For the most part, the balloons were either seen flying at low altitudes 500 feet, not much higher than the tree tops it seemed, or anchored down by dozens of sand bags. It soon became apparent to the general public that when the balloons were seen to be soaring to greater heights (they could reach 7,500 feet), then 'Jerry' was about, and we could expect an air raid warning any

57 W.A.A.F. BALLOON OPERATORS. Reunion of Site 23 Avonmouth Crew held at Rushyford, Co. Durham in May 1985. *L to R:* Mesdames Peggy Kenny, Betty Dixon, Vera Tandy, Peggy Jones, Marion Whitmore, Barbara Davis, Vera Bullet and Nellie Calvert.

minute. Folks therefore kept a watchful eye on the heights of the balloons.

Sometimes the balloons were a source of trouble, especially during bad weather. In high winds they proved very difficult to keep anchored, and sometimes were blown away during gales. For instance, a storm which occurred at the end of September 1939 tore loose many balloons in England, and it was claimed that 60 got as far as Sweden. One came down near Stockholm. Another (nick-named 'Jemima') at Cadbury's Recreation Ground at Bournville, broke loose and entangled itself in the electricity cables, cutting the supply and plunging Birmingham into darkness, at the same time bringing the City's electric tramcars to a halt. Balloons were particularly susceptible to lightning. They seemed to attract it during thunderstorms, and were instantly set on fire. One such regrettable incident occurred during an air raid over Bristol, and the unfortunate burning balloon lit up the entire surrounding area for all the world like one of Jerry's own flares. It has been claimed that during a thunder storm on 27 July 1940 Bristol lost 28 balloons through lightning.

These days the value of the barrage balloons is often dismissed as being only merely morale boosters, whereas in truth it is impossible to judge their real value in warding off enemy raiders. Sufficient to quote the attitude of the Nazi pilots themselves, recorded in William Shirer's 'Berlin Diary' viz: when speaking of the pilots '. . . they did not dare to go below 7,000 feet on account of the barrage balloons. . . .' (Compare with height of Clifton Suspension Bridge only 245 feet above high water!)

We can be profoundly thankful that by the presence of the balloons this area did not suffer the terrifying attacks by German Stuka dive-bombers which had enjoyed tremendous successes during Hitler's blitzkriegs in other European Countries, neither did German fighter 'planes fly in low machine-gunning our streets as they did in other theatres of war.

The only occasion known when a German raider came below the balloons locally, was on 22 February 1941, when a lone Heinkel Hell came over the entrance to the Royal Edward Dock after being shot down by the Portbury A.A. gun. In so doing the 'plane struck a balloon cable before crashing into the mud of the River Severn in Kingroad, off Avonmouth. The balloon cable helped in the 'plane's final destruction, which must have given the balloon crews guarding Avonmouth a great deal of satisfaction.

After the war, Avonmouth Rugby Club resumed playing on their pitch at Avonmouth Recreation Ground in West Town Road only after members had spent an entire summer in removing more than fifty heavy concrete blocks remaining from one of Avonmouth's wartime barrage balloon sites which had been stationed there, having been used for anchoring purposes.

ANTI-AIRCRAFT GUNS

At the beginning of the war there were only eight anti-aircraft gun sites employed in the defence of Bristol, three of which were located in or near Avonmouth. At first the sites were only temporary ones with sand-bag pits, which, as the war progressed were replaced with concrete. Each site was equipped with four heavy 3.7″ large calibre anti-aircraft guns.

Of the three local sites, only one was actually within the Avonmouth Parish boundary. This was to the north in a field between Rockingham Road Bridge and Holesmouth Railway signal-box, known locally as the Holesmouth gun, but its official name was Rockingham gun site. The other two were on the perimeter of Avonmouth across the River Avon, to the south at Markham Farm on the Failand hillside, and west at Portbury. The Markham site commanded an excellent sweep of the skies above Avonmouth, Shirehampton and Clifton. The Portbury gun was established in 1939, and of the three local guns was the most successful, having bagged two enemy aircraft to its credit.

With so many targets listed by Nazi Germany's Luftwaffe, Bristol was eventually defended by twenty battery sites supporting ninety-six heavy guns. These formed a close-knit circle 'round Bristol and Avonmouth, and sites ranged from urban districts like Eastfield Road, Westbury-on-Trym, to rural sites such as Pagan's Hill, Chew Magna. One of the first guns to arrive in Bristol was on Purdown, which Bristolians affectionately referred to as 'Purdown Percy'.

The units were 76th Heavy Anti-Aircraft Regiments (HAA) and were manned by the Royal Artillery, often in conjunction with the Territorial Army and sometimes the Home Guard. The 3.7″ guns required a crew of 9 or 11 men. The shells weighed 28 lbs, and had a maximum effective altitude of 32,000 feet. As a complete cartridge weighed half a hundredweight, loading the 3.7″ was no speedy operation, yet an efficient team could fire at least eight rounds per minute. The permanent sites were transformed into miniature villages, having their own mess, canteen, cookhouse, sickbay, maintenance shops and sleeping quarters, etc. It has been estimated each site required 140 men.

In the early days of the war Avonmouth had anti-aircraft guns sited on the top of Messrs. Silcocks and Paul's Silos in Avonmouth (Old) Dock. At the height of the air raids the Army brought in reinforcements in the form of mobile guns, which toured round Avonmouth firing from various strategic points. One of their favourite firing places was the railway level crossing at West Town Road. Perhaps the mobile guns made the enemy think that Avonmouth was more heavily defended than it actually was! These were manned by 98th Light Anti Aircraft Regiment, who were also responsible for searchlights and light machine guns.

As far as the General Public was concerned the A.A. guns did not fire half so much as we expected them to. Hearing the guns was the only source of comfort afforded to frightened and helpless civilians expecting death or injury at any minute. They gave everyone a sense of hitting back, and this was the generally held view everywhere.

One case in point. When the morale in London was at a very low ebb in September 1940 the powers-that-be gave orders for the heaviest possible barrage to be put up in front of the next Nazi raiders. The result was remarkable. Punctually to time the German bombers arrived over London, and were met by a roar of guns, which astonished them as much as it heartened the Londoners. The enemy had been flying at 1,200 feet, but as soon as the barrage opened up they climbed to 22,000 feet, and many actually turned back. At least nine raiders were brought down. Everywhere in London the following day people were saying, 'Thank God we are fighting back'.

The direct destruction of enemy 'planes was the most obvious purpose of A.A. guns, but this task was much easier for the fighter aircraft to accomplish, which was not generally realised. The value of the A.A. guns

58 PORTBURY A.A. SITE showing 3.7 mobile guns late 1939. *N.B.* Portishead and Electricity Generating Station in background.

59 SEARCHLIGHT AT PORTBURY. 210,000,000 candle-power beam probing the night sky. Photo: 1939.

60 ROCKINGHAM BRIDGE A.A. SITE, AVONMOUTH. Pictured in August 1973 when gun site remains were occupied by band of travelling people.

61 PORTBURY A.A. GUN SITE in September 1987 over-grown and derelict. (Similar view as plate 58).

was in the prevention of accurate bombing and in deterring enemy aircraft reaching their objectives, particularly at night. In the nature of things the guns were bound to play second fiddle to Fighter Command. They had the relatively humdrum job of breaking up large formations of enemy bombers, so that the fighters could get in amongst them, and suffered the frustration of not being allowed to fire because our own fighters were overhead.

When the war was over, the A.A. guns were taken away and the sites abandoned. Some ruins of the Rockingham A.A. site remained until 1973 when it was occupied by the 'travelling people', and now all traces have completely disappeared. The Markham site now forms part of a market garden, although the blast mounds are still easily recognised from the roadway. The Portbury site is very much overgrown with brambles which cover the tons of bricks and concrete remaining, and has become a blackberry pickers paradise. It is nevertheless claimed that the anti-aircraft gun sites in Avon County include some of the best preserved in the country, even though neglected.

Hitler undoubtedly had the knowledge and the wherewithal to wipe Avonmouth off the map, but thanks to Avonmouth's defences we have lived to tell the tale.

Firing at night

When a heavy anti-aircraft gun is fired, it produces a flash of flame some 25 feet high. This is not so noticeable in daylight, but at night it is a dazzling sight. There had never been a photograph published of this spectacular instant before, when in July 1940 the powers-that-be arranged for a Press photographer to take one.

The cameraman came to the A.A. site at Portbury for this purpose, where four heavy guns were guarding Avonmouth and Bristol. There was ample scope for the Pressman to get his picture, as Avonmouth and Bristol were at that time receiving plenty of attention from the German Luftwaffe. He therefore fixed his tripod and camera in position in daylight, focused all four guns in his view-finder, then settled down to wait, having first arranged to open the camera's shutter when the gun-position Officer gave the command 'Fuse!'

The gun site was not luxuriously appointed, and almost out in the wilds. There was only one Officer, who both slept and ate in his office. Everyone there slept in their clothes, except the cameraman, who ran out in his pyjamas and tin-hat whenever there was an alert, which was very often.

The enemy 'planes trying for Avonmouth were always too high for the A.A. guns to get a chance to fire. For eight days the poor man waited in vain for his picture, and almost ran out of patience. However, on the eighth night at 3.0 a.m., and in drizzling rain, the alarm was sounded yet again, and he rushed out to his camera. The searchlights caught and held the target, which was like a silver cigar pendant in the darkness. The gunners went into action, and as their Officer shouted 'Fuse!' the photographer opened his camera shutter – and waited!

There followed one almighty explosion. All four guns went off together, jerking the camera several feet into the air, and smashing the barrack-hut windows, but at the same time the salvo shot the tail off an enemy 'plane, and brought it down. Upon being congratulated by the Officer of having had a wonderful opportunity for a picture, the cameraman moaned in reply that he hadn't got a picture at all. It was a very depressed man who later 'phoned his office only to be instructed to return home.

Fortunately, the story had a happy ending. When in a determined mood to pursue this fiasco to its disappointing end, the photographer developed his film, to his great surprise and delight the triumphant picture showing Portbury A.A. guns firing at night emerged. Many similar photographs of guns firing at night were subsequently taken, but the Portbury night picture shown here can claim to be the very first.

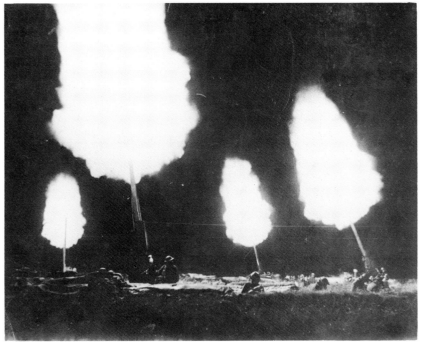

62   PORTBURY A.A. GUNS. First ever photograph to record A.A. guns in action at night.

SMOKE SCREEN

The use of smoke screens in Naval battles was well known. The most modern diesel-engined German pocket-battleship *Admiral Graf Spee* used a smoke screen several times when running from the Battle of the River Plate in December 1939, in her retreat into Montevideo.

But in the case of Avonmouth, when the Army stationed smoke generators with chimneys like sentinels at intervals along the Portway, Portview Road and St. Andrew's Road, it took the General Public by surprise. 'Fancy having a smoke screen', we declared! The generators were fired with thick black smelly oil, and were ignited during the air raids.

These small stationary generators were soon replaced by large mobile smoke generators, with huge chimneys, which were towed by Army lorries. They toured the parish to belch out black smoke in times of danger, according to the way of the wind.

A secret report which came to light after the war of a new type of smoke screen now makes very interesting reading. Avonmouth was chosen as the target for this exercise, which was carried out during daylight hours on 24 February 1944. The weather was slight mist, visibility four miles, no cloud, and wind N.N.E. at 10 m.p.h.

Twenty-four Esso generators of U.S. Army 79th Chemical Smoke Generating Coy. were deployed, spaced at 100 yards. They were ignited at 1515 hours, and allowed to burn for one hour. At the same time an Anson aircraft took off from Whitchurch airfield and flew over Avonmouth to observe the effects of the smoke screen.

It transpired that the smoke screen was plainly discernible from about 3 to 4 miles away, and the target fairly well covered, except that the larger buildings, the cranes at the Royal Edward Dock and balloon barrage could be seen, besides the oil tanks and piers. After the 'plane had climbed to 5,000 feet nothing could be seen, and Avonmouth was hidden. The smoke screen was reported as being by no means as unpleasant as the alternative Hasler screen from the point of view of the people who had to work in it, and traffic was not interrupted to any great extent.

It is also interesting to recall that when this exercise took place, Avonmouth Docks were crammed to capacity, and even overflowing with U.S. war machines of all kinds in the build up to the D-Day landings, only four months hence. Also to note that the very last Nazi 'plane over Bristol was on 15 May 1944, only three weeks before D-Day. It is good to know that every precaution had been taken in the event of the enemy inflicting a blitz on Avonmouth whilst housing so much military equipment.

STARFISH SITES

'Starfish' was the code name given to decoy fires, which were lit when Nazi 'planes were expected to inflict heavy air raids on cities or towns. The intensive air raids were termed 'blitzes', which was short for the German word 'blitz-krieg', meaning violent campaign, or lightning war.

The blitzes usually took the same set procedure. First came the marker 'planes, dropping parachute flares over the target area, which lit up the night sky, and floated down very slowly like chandeliers. On 4/5 April 1941 the whole of Bristol was illuminated by a large number of chandelier flares, fifteen of which were counted in the air at one time. The flares burnt for several minutes illuminating the ground, and also enabling night reconnaissance 'planes to photograph the results achieved by bombs already dropped. It was the duty of the A.A. gunners to shoot the flares out before they could be useful to the raiders. The first marker 'planes were soon followed by a second wave dropping incendiary bombs (fire bombs) to set the target alight. After giving the incendiaries a chance to take a hold, and begin their task of fire destruction, then a third wave arrived bringing their deadly high explosive bombs.

A case in point occurred on 16/17 March 1941, when incendiaries started a fire at a cottage in Moorhouse Lane, about three-quarters of a mile from the Imperial Smelting Corporation. As the cottage blazed furiously, it offered an easy target for the enemy bombers, and the fact they seized upon it could be judged by no fewer than 78 bomb craters being afterwards found in the neighbourhood.

The idea of decoy fires was therefore conceived, which would be lit when the first tell-tale flares were seen over cities or towns, in the hope that Jerry 'planes would drop their high explosive bombs in the countryside, or on unoccupied open moorland where they could do little damage.

The sites to detract from Avonmouth were in the region of Kingston Seymour, near Weston-super-Mare. Rivers were a certain guide to 'planes in the black-out, and the position of Avonmouth could not be disguised, being at the mouth of the River Avon where it joins the River Severn. Kingston Seymour was chosen as being geographically similar to Avonmouth, where the River Yeo joins the River Severn. This plan proved highly successful. Although starfish sites were tried in other places, none enjoyed the same success as in the case of Kingston Seymour defending Avonmouth.

VII. THE 'PHONEY' WAR

The first nine months of the war were called the 'phoney' war, a phrase first coined by the American newspapers, and soon adopted on both sides of the Atlantic. This described the period of uncertainty and waiting, from September 1939 to April 1940, with no great battles being fought on the Western Front, as had been expected. No one knew quite what would happen, although Hitler made many threats. No one could foresee what course the war would take, and Britain waited for Hitler to make the first move.

In the main, British hopes were pinned on the invincibility of the Maginot Line, the strong fortified defences on the Franco-German border built between 1918 and 1938, to prevent the Germans from invading France, and turning that country into a battlefield, as in the 1914–1918 Great War. It was for the defence of the Maginot Line that the British Expeditionary Force was rushed to France at the outbreak of the war in 1939. As in 1914, some contingents sailed from Avonmouth, when motor vehicles of all kinds requisitioned by the army, were rushed to the Docks. Some obviously having first received a thin coat of khaki paint, whilst others were still in their peacetime owners livery, e.g., Sunlight Soap, Lever Brothers, etc., with only 'War Dept' stencilled across their sides.

All quiet it may have been on the Western Front during the 'phoney' war, but this was certainly not the case on the high seas. As an Island, Britain depended on the control of her sea lanes linking her with the Commonwealth Countries and America. From the very first day of the war, when the Germans sank the defenceless *Athenia* with 1,400 Anglo-American civilian passengers and crew on board, they made it apparent they meant to attack Britain's sea lanes even more ruthlessly than they had tried to do in the Great War, in an attempt to starve Britain into submission. The Battle of the Atlantic, waged from 1939 to 1943, cost many thousands of brave seafarers lives.

The first battle of the war was that of the River Plate, 14/20 December 1939. The 10,000 ton German pocket-battleship *Admiral Graf Spee* acted as a commerce raider on the open seas from the outbreak of war, sinking nine British merchant ships. When she came face to face with the Royal Navy she ran from the battle, and was scuttled by her Commander in the Estuary of the River Plate on 20 December 1939.

EVACUATION

During the late 1930's it was fully expected that in the event of war breaking out, London and other large cities would be subjected immediately to large-scale German aerial bombardment. It was for fear of this happening that following the 1938 Munich Crisis the Government distributed Anderson air raid shelters and gas-masks, and hundreds of beds were held vacant in the hospitals. Plans for taking children and expectant mothers away from the cities to places of greater safety in the countryside had been first drawn up in the Autumn of 1938, so that the evacuation scheme could be quickly set in motion.

In point of fact less than 24 hours sufficed. The decision was taken on 31 August 1939, and next morning tens of thousands of children, and some teachers too, were shepherded from their school assembly points to the main-line Railway stations. By the evening of the fourth day the total number of passengers dealt with by the Railways was estimated at 1,200,000. The ages of the children ranged from 3 to 13 years. Each child carried their gas-mask, a change of clothing, and wore an identity label tied on their lapel.

It was a very trying time for families. Evacuation was not compulsory, and with many men already being called up, mothers were faced with a choice between keeping their children at home in possible danger, or sending them away to safety. As it happened the expected immediate mass bombing of London and other cities did not materialise, and by Christmas 1939 many evacuees had returned again to their homes. When the air raids actually started in earnest in the Autumn of 1940 a second full scale evacuation had to take place.

In a broadcast on 11 November 1939, Queen Elizabeth (now the Queen Mother) said, 'The King and I know what it means to be parted from our children, and we can sympathise with those of you who have bravely consented to this separation for the sake of your little ones'. When it was suggested to the Queen that Princess Elizabeth (aged 13) and Princess Margaret (aged 9) should be sent to Canada to safety, she replied, 'The children could not go without me, I would never leave the King, and the King will never leave'. The Princesses spent the war years living at Windsor Castle, where, deep underground, the ancient dungeons with their thick stone walls were strengthened with sturdy roofs, and converted into a series of air raid shelters.

Indeed, the King did not leave. He stayed at his post and shared with his subjects the dangers of wartime London, remaining in residence with the Queen at Buckingham Palace, which was bombed nine times. The Queen took instruction and practised the art of shooting with a revolver . . . 'Just in case it may come in useful!' . . . she said.

Queen Mary

The most important evacuee was Queen Mary. It was decided that in the event of war, Queen Mary (mother of King George VI) should come to Gloucestershire to live at Badminton House, the home of the Duke and Duchess of Beaufort, the Duchess being a niece of Queen Mary.

On the day war was declared, Queen Mary was staying at Sandringham, and the very next day, 4 September 1939, together with an entourage totalling fifty-three, she made the long journey from Norfolk to Badminton to take up her wartime residence. Queen Mary considered herself, quite rightly, a London evacuee, even though a reluctant one! A squadron of the Gloucestershire Hussars were detailed Her majesty's bodyguard during her stay at Badminton.

At this time Queen Mary was a very active 72 year-old, and very quickly became a familiar figure in the area, often seen either travelling through the County, or when making her many un-announced 'surprise' visits to local factories engaged on war work, to workers' canteens and the like, or when making her most welcome visits to wounded soldiers in hospitals at Tidworth, Bath or Bristol. On the day she visited Clevedon it was to witness the detonation of an unexploded mine which had been washed ashore nearby.

Queen Mary made it a habit always to offer lifts in her Daimler to servicemen and women whenever and wherever possible, and for this she became quite renowned. After some recipients found it hard to believe that they had been helped on their way by none other than Queen Mary, she had small metal medallions made bearing her crown and cypher, which she handed out at the journey's end, as proof of the experience.

Many of Queen Mary's important friends and relations came to Badminton to visit Her Majesty, and also members of other Royal families taking refuge in Britain during the war. One such visitor was Mrs. Eleanor Roosevelt (wife of the then United States President) who came to Badminton on 4 November 1942 to pay her respects to Queen Mary.

After spending the six war years living at Badminton, the time came in the Spring of 1945 for Queen Mary to say goodbye to Gloucestershire. Her parting words were, 'Oh, I *have* been happy. Here I've been anybody to everybody, and back in London I shall have to start being Queen Mary all over again!'

Bristol Status

For the purposes of the evacuation scheme, the country was divided into three distinct categories, namely 'evacuation', 'reception' and 'neutral'. At the outbreak of war Bristol was designated a 'neutral' area, but in practice the City immediately became a 'reception' area, when King's College London, the pre-clinical students of Middlesex Hospital, and some departments of the B.B.C. evacuated themselves to Bristol from London.

This sudden influx of people into the City, already full, naturally caused many problems. To find suitable lodgings for civil servants, professors, undergraduates, radio stars and a variety of office staff was not easy.

The University buildings had never before been so full, despite the fact that some staff and undergraduates of both University and College had already joined-up in the Forces, or been called away on war work. Whenever possible, the departments of King's College and the University were merged. The Great Hall of the University was transformed into a library for the visitors, only to be completely destroyed when the Great Hall was set on fire by incendiary bombs during the first blitz on Bristol 24 November 1940.

It soon became an open secret that the B.B.C. had descended on Bristol, when such famous radio stars as Tommy Handley, Ted Kavanagh, Jack Warner, Henry Hall, Sir Adrian Boult, Stuart Hibberd, Felix Felton and others were seen going about their everyday business, especially in the area of the B.B.C. Headquarters in Whiteladies Road, Clifton. This was much to the joy and delight of school-girl autograph hunters! Bristolians found themselves rubbing shoulders with well-known radio personalities in the local pubs, and shops like Lloyds the fishmongers can now proudly boast in having had Sir Adrian Boult and the announcer Stuart Hibberd amongst their regular customers during the war years. The Director of Variety, John Watt, and the B.B.C. Repertory Company (about fourteen variety Artistes and actors with the B.B.C. Chorus and some Orchestras) besides the B.B.C. Symphony Orchestra and the Director of Religious Broadcasting also came to Bristol.

To accommodate the B.B.C. evacuees various parish halls in the Clifton district were hastily converted into broadcasting studios, the one used principally being Clifton Parish Hall. It was from here that Tommy Handley broadcast live his radio series 'It's That Man Again', which became universally popular as 'ITMA'. Other wartime radio series broadcast from Bristol were Band Wagon, with Arthur Askey and 'Stinker' Murdoch, Mrs. Bagwash, Nausea, and the rest, also Garrison Theatre. At the kind invitation of the Dean of Bristol, the Very Revd. Harry W. Blackburne, the Daily Morning Service was broadcast from the Eastern Lady Chapel of Bristol Cathedral, and the set was inspected by Queen Mary during her visit to the Cathedral. However, after the windows of the Eastern Lady Chapel were grievously injured in the first blitz on Bristol, the Daily Morning Service was transferred to the B.B.C. studios in Whiteladies Road, Clifton.

After surviving the devastating blitzes and numerous air raids over Bristol during the winter of 1940/1941, the B.B.C. evacuated themselves for a second time in April 1941 to Bangor in North Wales.

Footnote:

The Parish Church of St. Andrew, Clifton stood at the end of Birdcage Walk, was first established in 1154, but rebuilt three times. On Sunday, 24 November 1940 during the first great blitz on Bristol it was struck by an oil bomb at 7.30 p.m., was totally destroyed, and has not been replaced. A plaque now marks the site occupied by the once lovely Church. The Clifton Parish Hall used by the B.B.C. was in Merchants Road, Clifton, and continued until the 1970's, when it was demolished in favour of the present Millar House block of modern flats in 1977.

Overseas Evacuation

When war broke out, many British parents sent their children overseas to be the guests of warm-hearted American families, who opened their homes for evacuees. Many Bristolians had relations living in Canada to whom they could send their offspring, stemming, no doubt, from the years prior to the Great War when the s.s. *Royal Edward* and the s.s. *Royal George* operated a fortnightly emigration/passenger service from Avonmouth to Canada. In 1939 the names of many local children were entered on shipping passenger lists, to await sailings to the New World, only to have their names hastily removed by their parents following the disastrous sinking of the s.s. *Athenia*. I personally know of two such instances.

The *Athenia* (13,581 g.r.t.) was of the Donaldson Atlantic Line, who, with her sister ship s.s. *Letitia* (see also under 'Hospital Ships') operated a regular service from Glasgow to Quebec/Montreal. Within a few hours of the outbreak of war a German U-boat, without warning, attacked defenceless *Athenia*, on her way to Canada, only 200 miles off the north-west coast of Ireland. Furthermore, the submarine surfaced and then shelled the liner, which sank with the loss of 112 lives. The Daily Telegraph of 6 September 1939 reported that a British destroyer in convoy to the liner located the submarine and sank her with depth charges, 150 miles from where the *Athenia* went down.

There had been 1,100 civilian passengers aboard *Athenia*, many women and children evacuees, and American civilians scurrying back to the U.S.A. away from war-torn Europe, together with 320 crew members. The survivors, who were picked up by a number of rescue ships, were returned to Glasgow to await the next available ship to North America.

This barbarous sinking shocked the civilised world, and it was said at the time to be directly contrary to Hitler's orders (though this may be open to doubt). The submarine Commander was ultimately held responsible for the loss of *Athenia* which caused much dispute.

The dangers of the Atlantic-crossing increased as did the U-boat menace, which led to a ban being put on children being sent overseas, although American families continued to offer hospitality for evacuee children.

63   DONALDSON ATLANTIC LINE *Athenia* (13,581 g.r.t.) Turbine twin-screw steamship, built 1923 and sunk the day War broke out, 3 September 1939.

64   EVACUEES Bristol school children leaving Temple Meads for Devon and safety 19 February 1941. 'Thumbs up' by Lord Mayor, Ald. T. H. J. Underdown.

Local Evacuation

It is quite extraordinary that whilst suffering some of the country's worst blitzes, as well as a long succession of air raids of varying severity during November and December 1940 and January 1941, Bristol officially remained a 'neutral' zone under the Evacuation Scheme. Many parents, realising the dangers, made private arrangements for the evacuation of their children, sending them to the comparative safety of the countryside at their own expense. Under the Government Scheme general evacuation could not take place until the status of Bristol was re-classified an 'evacuation' area.

The situation had become so serious in February 1941 that the Ministry of Health sanctioned a partial evacuation of Bristol's children, when 6,370 from elementary schools in badly bombed areas of the City left for the peace and security of Devon. Following further severe air raids the Ministry finally agreed in April 1941 that the whole of Bristol should be declared an 'evacuation' area. This resulted in a further 3,132 children being despatched to Somerset and Cornwall.

The children of Avonmouth and Shirehampton Schools took part in the first large scale evacuation. On 19 February 1941 53 children of Avonmouth School, accompanied by teacher Mrs. G. Giblett, who remained with them, boarded long trains at Temple Meads Station for 'unknown' destinations, which turned out to be Crediton in Devon for the pupils of Avonmouth School, and Holsworthy North Devon for the pupils of Shirehampton School.

The Lord Mayor and Lady Mayoress of Bristol, Alderman & Mrs. T. H. J. Underdown, were at Temple Meads to wave the children goodbye, and the Mayor of Torquay met most of the trains bringing evacuees to that town. Each child carried their gas-mask, kit bag and/or suitcase (and comics) with labels pinned to their coat lapels with their names. Surprisingly enough, there were no tears. Enthusiasm prevailed, with shouts of 'Goodbye' . . . 'Have a good time' . . . 'Mind you behave yourselves' . . ., etc. This was the first time in history British children had been evacuated within their own region. They were sent to Barnstaple, Bideford, Kingsbridge and Torquay amongst other places in Devon, besides Liskeard in Cornwall.

On 9 March 1941 a further eight children left Avonmouth for Truro, and in the following November five more went to Holsworthy. The actual number of Bristol children involved in all the various evacuations was 20,085.

Evacuation was not compulsory, so the local Schools had to remain open to cater for pupils who did not go away. This left the School buildings half empty, and the south-east wing of Avonmouth School premises whilst not being required for educational purposes was leased to the Board of Trade for the time being. In the meantime, the School was organised into two groups,

Juniors and Infants. In December 1941 the Avonmouth School attendance was reduced to 80, with only the Headmaster, Mr. Charles Northey, and Miss Wall to cope, as three other staff had either been called up or gone with the evacuees.

Most of the evacuees settled into their new surroundings quite happily. Those fortunate enough to be billeted on farms had a thoroughly enjoyable time with the animals, despite the long walks to and from School every day, along country lanes in all winds and weathers. Some evacuees, alas, became very homesick. For instance, one London schoolgirl evacuated to Devon took off in search of her mother, and was successful in locating her living in Oxford. There was also the case of two brothers, who, not understanding why this Hitler should separate them from their mother, set out one day to walk back to Bristol from Aveton Gifford. They got as far as Exeter before being caught by the long arm of the Law, and were returned to their new foster home. After a little while they set out to walk to Bristol a second time, and in the interest of the safety of the children, they were then allowed to return to their mother for keeps.

As the fortunes of war swung in favour of the Allied Forces, and the possibilities of air raids seemed less likely, some of the Bristol evacuees began to drift back home again. However, it was not until 26 October 1944 that the Official Order was given that all the Bristol evacuees (except those sitting for School Leaving examinations) should return home.

To the children of the 1940's, their evacuation is just a childhood memory. Many of the evacuees to Devon still vividly recall having seen the distant sky glowing red in the black-out when the Luftwaffe burned the City of Plymouth. The only tangible evidence now of Bristol schoolchildren having stayed in Devon is the regularity in which Bristol addresses appear in the visitors books of the country Parish Churches there during the years 1941–1944. The only evidence of Holsworthy having been host to so many children from Bristol is a single item in the Holsworthy Parish Council Minute book, recording a member having asked whether or not the evacuees would cause a rise in the Rates!

One aspect of the war effort which is overlooked, is the remarkably unselfish way in which families in the 'reception' areas invited into their homes the children of strangers, and cared for them, which was no light undertaking. This service of great value to the war effort was not overlooked by the Queen, who sent a personal message of appreciation and thanks to all the host families of evacuees for having given their hospitality so readily. The payments made for billeting evacuees was 10/6d (52½p) for the first child, and 8/6d (42½p) for each additional child per week. No doubt these payments were the forerunners of the present day Government Family Allowances, which is now taken so much for granted.

ST. MARY'S CANTEEN

The war was only seven days old when St. Mary's Canteen was born. Mrs. May Dixon opened the Vicarage garden gates, set up a trestle table and proceeded to provide cups of tea and sandwiches, etc., for drivers of the long queues of vehicles and other servicemen awaiting shipment to France from Avonmouth with the British Expeditionary Force. Mrs. Dixon was wife of the Revd. C. W. Dixon (Vicar of Shirehampton 1920–1949), and the Vicarage at that time was The Priory in High Street.

Very soon Mrs. Dixon's many influential and monied friends raised the necessary funds to provide a Canteen building, a large wooden hut which was erected on vacant land opposite the Vicarage, now occupied by The Lawn bungalows. An adjoining hut served as a games and recreation room. St. Mary's Canteen remained in business from the very first week of the war until the very last. It was most successful for the welfare and comfort of the troops stationed in or passing through Shirehampton.

Other Canteens were organised in Shirehampton during the war, one at the Methodist Church, and another run by Toc H, but St. Mary's was unique in staying open ALL day and EVERY day.

St. Mary's Canteen was staffed entirely by a dedicated band of volunteers, most being members of St. Mary's Mothers Union. Prices charged fitted the

ST. MARY'S CANTEEN, SHIREHAMPTON.

65 WATER-COLOUR by Mrs May Dixon, entitled *St. Mary's Canteen, Shirehampton.* *1939/45.*

pockets of servicemen, everything costing either one penny or three-half-pence (pre-decimal currency). Cheese on toast was a great favourite with the hungry troops, and oft-times the ladies were hard put to it to keep pace with orders. In January 1945 it was reported that the Canteen had served the colossal number of 1,183,221 snack meals to men and women of the Allied Forces, and men of the merchant Navy. All the profits, which ran into three figures, were donated to the Soldiers, Sailors & Airmen's Families Association. The only time St. Mary's Canteen closed its doors was for about a fortnight enforced through burst pipes in February 1945, when Victory was already in sight.

When Peace came, every Canteen helper was presented with a testimonial, designed by Mrs. Dixon, and decorated with her water-colour sketch of the Canteen, which read:

The Committee of St. Mary's Canteen
desire to place on record their
most grateful thanks to

....
for the devoted Voluntary Service
she gave so unstintingly, within its walls, for
the Comfort and Welfare of
His Majesty's and the Allied Forces
in the
Second Great War, 1939–1945.

(*Signed*) Clement W. Dixon (*Chairman*)
(*Signed*) May Dixon (*Honorary Secretary*)

Sequel:

The Canteen huts were sold in October 1947 for the princely sum of £500; the proceeds were spent on repairs to the Old Schools in Station Road, then returned to Parish use, after having been requisitioned by Bristol Corporation during the war years.

ROYAL VISIT

It was during the period of the so-called 'phoney' war, on Thursday 8 February 1940, that Avonmouth was honoured by the visit of the late King George VI and Queen Elizabeth (now the Queen Mother). The royal visit was to view the Docks, generally boost morale and the war effort. It was most unexpected, and came as a very pleasant surprise.

This was the fourth time a member of the Royal Family had visited Avonmouth, and the second time by the Sovereign Regnant and his Queen. The previous occasion Avonmouth was visited by the Monarch, was on 9

66   KING GEORGE VI & QUEEN ELIZABETH 8 February 1940. Inspecting members of
Civil Defence Services at Kellaway Avenue, Horfield, following their hush-hush visit to
Avonmouth.

July 1908, when King Edward VII and Queen Alexandra in a three day visit
opened and named the Royal Edward Dock. The welcome which Bristol
staged for them in 1908 with pomp and ceremony rivalled only that given to
Queen Elizabeth I in 1574.

In 1940, by stark contrast, the country was at war, so that every precaution
had to be exercised to ensure the safety of Their Majesties, and the greatest
secrecy observed until the very last minute. In consequence, there were
comparatively few people to see their arrival at Temple Meads Station, the
King in the uniform of a Marshal of the Royal Air Force, and the Queen
wearing a simple violet-coloured ensemble of dress and matching coat,
trimmed with grey lamb's-wool. But the news that the King and Queen were
in Bristol soon spread, and thousands of people, including children from the
various schools en route, cheered them as they drove by car along the
Portway to Avonmouth.

Their Majesties received a loud and rousing welcome from the children
lined up in front of Avonmouth School, and when they reached the Docks
they were cheered by hundreds of enthusiastic Dockers. After being taken to
the roof of a vast transit shed to get a birds-eye view of the Docks, they
inspected contingents of Navy, Army, Air Force and Merchant Navy
personnel, as well as members of the W.A.T.S. on the quayside.

The King and Queen left Avonmouth via St. Andrew's Road, and in so doing passed close by the Royal Lime Tree which had been planted two years earlier to commemorate their Majesties Coronation. Happily, Avonmouth's Coronation Tree survived the war, for much of the time in company with a huge static water tank. The lime tree continues to thrive to remind us of the valiant yet reluctant King who did not shirk duty when called upon to bear the unexpected burden of the Crown, who diligently shared the dangers and sufferings of his Peoples during the war and post-war years, and his Queen whose smile continues to captivate everyone, as it did on that memorable day in February 1940.

VIII. 'OUR FINEST HOUR'

The so-called 'phoney' war was merely the lull before the storm. It came to an abrupt end on 9 April 1940 when Hitler made the unexpected move by invading Denmark and Norway. The following month saw the opening of his Western Offensive on 10 May 1940, with the invasion of Luxembourg, Holland and Belgium, enabling the Nazis to invade France by the 'back door'.

German Panzer Divisions swept through the Low Countries in only a fortnight, achieving a complete victory. When the German attack came the Allies were entirely put off balance, and France soon began to crumble with the collapse of her army. The British Expeditionary Force was trapped, outnumbered, outgunned, encircled and in great danger of annihilation, but thankfully the British withdrawal to the French coast was achieved.

DUNKIRK EPIC – OPERATION 'DYNAMO'

From 24 May to 4 June 1940 an armada of hundreds of 'little' ships of all varying shapes and sizes, including eight of Bristol's familiar P.&A. Campbell's fleet of paddle-steamers, answered the call and crossed the English Channel to bring home the British Expeditionary Force stranded at Dunkirk. A miracle of fine calm weather descended on the Channel, enabling operations to be carried out which in rough weather would have been impossible.

The British troops drawn up in long winding lines on the beaches at Dunkirk showed perfect discipline in patiently waiting to be taken off. There was no panic, even though under constant attack, giving rise to the now well-known saying 'The Dunkirk Spirit'. With naval and air support, the 'little' ships carried out the amazing rescue of some 335,490 officers and men, which included some of the French and Belgium armies, over a period of nine days. Operation Dynamo was not without its losses, and some of the 'little' ships did not return, including three of Bristol's fleet of P.&A. Campbell paddle-steamers, i.e. *Devonia, Brighton Belle* and *Brighton Queen.*

The troops stood shoulder to shoulder on the rescue ships packed like sardines, there was no room for sitting, and no room for arms or equipment either, all had to be left behind. The ships disembarked at piers and docks along the south-east coast, where the men transferred to long trains for reception areas in all parts of the country. It was a tired and bedraggled army, but by no means a dispirited one, which returned home to the cheers and welcome of the British people.

Some of the Dunkirk trains arrived at Stapleton Road Station in Bristol, and the troops taken by double-decker buses to an emergency camp set up in Eastville Park, and were accommodated there for about two weeks under canvas beneath the trees. The local inhabitants warmly welcomed the troops into their homes for meals and baths. They were mostly soldiers from the North of England like Durham, Sunderland or South Shields, etc. Many lasting friendships were formed from that time with Bristolians, and at least two soldiers married local Eastville girls.

The tall iron railings which originally surrounded Eastville Park were taken as scrap metal to help the war effort, but not that fencing the section of the Park occupied by the Army, which is still there, as a reminder of the dark days of 1940.

The French Government soon capitulated, and asked Hitler for peace terms. Their Generals predicted that in three weeks England would have her neck wrung like that of a chicken! 'Some chicken', retorted Winston Churchill, 'Some neck!' *(To Canadian Government 20 Dec. 1941).*

INVASION THREAT

Britain stood alone in the face of tyranny, following the Dunkirk withdrawal, and became the last bastion of liberty in Europe, upon whose fortunes depended the future of all free peoples.

To the rest of the world the fall of France seemed to herald the final triumph of Germany, yet in Britain there was neither talk nor thought of surrender, only the resolve to stand firm. 'If the British Empire and its Commonwealth last for a thousand years,' predicted Winston Churchill, 'men will still say,

"This was their finest hour".' *(18 June 1940)*.

On the same day Hitler launched his great Western Offensive, 10 May 1940, Mr. Churchill (Chancellor of Bristol University) by the will of the country succeeded Neville Chamberlain as Prime Minister, and offered the people '. . . nothing, save blood, toil, tears and sweat' *(13 May 1940)*.

The first task of the new Prime Minister was to form a National Government, a coalition consisting of all three Political Parties, and also a small War Cabinet of eight members, which included Ernest Bevin as Minister of Labour & National Service. Mr. Bevin was well known to Bristolians from his being formerly a full-time official of the Dockers' Union, and Vice-President of Avonmouth & Shirehampton Labour Band. It was an astute Cabinet appointment, and one for which Bristol and Avonmouth later had good cause to be truly grateful *(see January 1941)*.

The National Government and War Cabinet stayed in office until the General Election of July 1945.

Beating the Invader

In the dark days of 1940, when Britain stood alone in 'Her finest hour', invasion by the Nazis seemed not only imminent, but was fully expected! When would Hitler invade us? was the question uppermost in the mind of everyone.

67   WARTIME PILL BOX POSITION on the foreshore of Royal Edward Dock, Avonmouth. Still there in September 1978.

Great preparations were made to prevent German troops from landing, as well as plans to resist them if they did so. The daily newspapers carried silhouette pictures issued by the War Office of German troop-carriers to enable the population to distinguish the enemy should they arrive. The warning of Germans invading was to be the ringing of the church bells.

As an invasion precaution pill box positions were introduced. Some 4,500 of them were built throughout the country between June and August 1940, which formed a triple line of defence, i.e., on the coast, 100 yards inland, and between 600/800 yards further inland. They were intended to house either a machine-gun post with three men, or four/five riflemen. Improvised road-blocks were hastily set up at strategic points, at cross-roads and the like, until such time as tank traps of a more substantial nature could be introduced.

To foil the enemy all place names and signposts were removed, and milestones either defaced or buried. (One such milestone marked '5 miles to Bristol' was buried and almost forgotten until 1985 when Avon County Council embarked on a pavement laying scheme. After 44 years the milestone came to the mind of Mr. Edgar Light, the roadman who had buried it mid-way between two old oak trees! It was then recovered, restored and returned to its original position.)

To deter the landing of troop-carriers, cairns, such as piles of stones were placed on the Downs and in open spaces near Bristol. Farmers were requested to erect their haystacks in the middle of fields, as against in the corners as was the custom. (The cairns on the Downs were not removed until the autumn of 1944.)

Owners of motor-cars and motor-bicycles were asked to be ready to put their vehicles out of action should the invaders arrive, and to destroy any maps they possessed.

The Government's general instructions, should the invasion be attempted, was to stand firm, and carry on. Voicing the sentiments of the silent millions of his countrymen Winston Churchill insisted, 'We shall go on to the end, we shall defend our island whatever the cost, we shall fight on the beaches, in the fields, in the streets, in the hills, we shall never surrender.' *(4 June 1940)*

Meanwhile, across the English Channel the German armies were consolidating their conquests. Hitler and his staff looked across the narrow expanse of water and considered the best way of subduing the small islands that rashly stood between Germany and the domination of Western Europe. Operation Sea Lion was Hitler's plan to invade Britain.

Troop-carrying barges began to mass menacingly in the harbours along the French coast in the summer of 1940, lying in wait ready for a swoop on the English coast. R.A.F. Bomber Command was instructed to go in and flatten them, and they did so with excellent effect.

Like Philip of Spain and Napoleon before him, Hitler failed to gain control

68   TANK TRAP. Remains of road block in Napier Miles Road, King's Weston.   Pictured in May 1988.

69   MILESTONE at Northwick Road, Pilning, with inscription removed to foil would-be invaders, and not yet replaced!   Photo: April 1988.

of the English Channel, and his Operation Sea Lion came to nothing. In the end he decided not to risk an invasion of Britain after all, a decision which was generally felt to be one of the unexplained miracles of the war. The only bit of British soil to be occupied by the Nazis was 'our dear' Channel Islands, as Mr. Churchill once described them.

Thankfully Britain's church bells remained silent throughout the war years, except on one occasion. Sunday 15 November 1942, when they rang our merrily to mark the great victory in the Battle of Egypt. It was also the day of Thanksgiving Services held nationally for Britain's wondrous deliverance from the enemy when she stood alone in 'Her finest hour' during the years 1940 and 1941. The church bells were then silenced again until V.E. Day 8 May 1945 when they gloriously proclaimed the final Victory.

HOME GUARD

A peculiar characteristic of the British sense of humour enables us to laugh at ourselves when in a tight corner! Nowadays the Home Guard is considerd a figure of fun, made so by the popular T.V. and Radio programme 'Dad's Army', whereas, when the Home Guard was originally formed in 1940 the situation was very serious indeed, and far from a laughing matter. Britain at that time had its back to the wall, and with an army only half equipped in the face of threatened invasion, things looked pretty grim.

Only four days after the change of Government and Prime Minister, the newly appointed Secretary of State for War, Mr. Anthony Eden, made the now considered historic broadcast speech to the nation on 14 May 1940 calling upon all able-bodied men between the ages of 17 and 65 (not already called-up) to assist in the defence of our country. 'You will not be paid', he said, 'but will receive a uniform, and will be armed.'

The response to Mr. Eden's broadcast was overwhelming as men all over the country flocked to the Police Stations in their hundreds to obtain their application forms to join the new citizens army, my father included. He returned home with an arm-band bearing the initial letters 'L.D.V.' (Local Defence Volunteers) a name which perfectly described the new force for home defence, to guard against enemy parachutists. Mr. Churchill's new name for the 'L.D.V.' was adopted on 24 August 1940, from then on it was known as the 'Home Guard'.

The vast majority of the volunteers were old soldiers having enlisted in the 1914–1918 Great War, and were anxious to serve their country again. Members were given rifle-drill practice, instructions in how to throw hand-grenades and the use of machine-guns, as well as flag signalling courses. In due time the Home Guard handled anti-aircraft guns.

The initial response for volunteers was so tremendous that many months

LOCAL DEFENCE VOLUNTEERS

CITY & COUNTY OF BRISTOL

This is to Certify that

L. BROWN ,

has been enrolled in the Local
Defence Volunteer Force for the
City and County of Bristol.

A. F. CHAPMAN
Lt. Col.
Zone Commander

OAVI. 234.14ot Ref to.

Signature of Volunteer

L Brown

70   L.D.V. CERTIFICATE OF
ENROLMENT issued to Leonard
Brown of Dursley Road, Shirehampton (Author's father) May
1940.

71   LOCAL DEFENCE VOLUNTEERS 18 June 1940. Old soldiers handle rifles again!
Detachment drilling on the Close at Clifton College preparing to defend the Country.
(Later renamed the Home Guard).

passed before this new enthusiastic army could all receive a uniform or be suitably armed. Eventually the Home Guard members were issued with a battle-dress type of uniform indistinguishable from regular Army uniforms, except for the shoulder flashes with the words 'Home Guard'. In 1940 the Government was sadly lacking the necessary equipment with which to arm the Home Guard, as so much Army equipment had been left behind in France, save for obsolete rifles, shotguns and a sprinkling of artillery, so that knives and home-made 'coshes' became a stand-by. The volunteers were determined to use anything should the occasion arise!

In October 1940 Mr. Churchill announced that 1,700,000 men had voluntarily joined the Home Guard. This was an eye-opener to Berlin, where Ribbentrop's 'Decadent British' theory still held in spite of Dunkirk. In the course of time the Home Guard became a well-clad, well equipped, efficient part-time army, which released thousands of servicemen for duties overseas.

14th Gloucestershire (City of Bristol) Battalion Home Guard

The local Battalion of Home Guard was formed by four sub-divisions having merged. Early in June 1940 a detachment of Local Defence Volunteers was recruited in Avonmouth and Shirehampton by Captain R. A. Pobjoy and Major Ivor Westlake, which formed a platoon of 'C' Company commanded by Major S. H. Piper, D.S.O. A week later a large detachment was raised by Major A. G. Ashford numbering over 100 employees of Industrial firms in Avonmouth Docks, including the Port of Bristol Authority, which formed part of 'S' Company. These two detachments became the nucleus of the 6th Battalion (Avonmouth) Home Guard formed in September 1940, and which later became the 14th Gloucestershire (City of Bristol) Battalion Home Guard.

Soon afterwards the National Smelting Company's detachment joined the 14th Battalion, and in September 1940 Major D. W. Ware was appointed Battalion Commander, with Major A. G. Ashford Second-in-Command. In February 1942 the Hallen and Pilning Platoons (Commanded by Lieut. W. E. Ford) also joined the 14th Battalion, and in October 1942 Lt. Col. D. W. Ware was succeeded by Lt. Col. A. G. Ashford, who held the Command until 'Stand-down' in 1944.

The Women's Home Guard Auxiliary was authorised in April 1942, and 30 volunteers enrolled. The ladies reached a remarkably high standard of efficiency in a very short time, and gave invaluable service as drivers, telephonists, clerks and in the Intelligence sections.

From 1943 until 'Stand-down', the 14th Battalion comprised: Battalion Headquarters (Lt. Col. A. G. Ashford), H.Q. Coy. (Capt. H. G. Hill), 'A' Coy. (Capt. A. G. Ford), 'B' Coy. (Capt. E. F. Derrick), 'C' Coy. (Mayor I.

72 14th GLOS. (CITY OF BRISTOL) BATTN. HOME GUARD. December 1944. *L to R: Front row* – Capt. E. B. Murrell (*Sub Unit Medical Officer*), Capt. A. G. Ford (*O/C 'A' Coy.*), Capt. H. G. Hill (*O/C 'H.Q.' Coy.*), Capt. R. F. Pearn, (*Adjutant*), Major R. A. Pobjoy (*Second in Command*), Lt. Col. A. G. Ashford (*Commanding Officer*), Major W. Woolley (*Senior Medical Officer*), Major Ivor R. Westlake (*O/C 'C' Coy.*), Capt. H. W. White (*O/C 'D' Coy.*), Capt. E. F. Derrick (*O/C 'B' Coy.*) and Major W. E. Ford (*O/C 'E' Coy.*). *Middle row* – Lt. J. R. Freeman, Lt. R. L. Maby, Lt. J. A. Stephen, Lt. R. H. B. Cogan, 2nd Lt. T. Morgan, Capt. C. R. Northey, Lt. H. C. Owen, 2nd Lt. F. Pullin and 2nd Lt. J. P. Shufflebottom. *Back row* – Lt. O. Clark, M.M., Lt. C. C. Boon, M.M., 2nd Lt. F. G. Cox, Capt. H. A. de F. Ford, Lt. H. D. Beavis, Lt. R. H. Bubbear, 2nd Lt. S. F. Mason, 2nd Lt. A. W. Attfield and Lt. R. H. England.

73 HOME GUARD 'C' Coy. 14th Glos. Battn. in 1944. *L to R: Top row:* Anon., T. Hunt, C. (?), Anon., R. Plumley, B. Britton, A. Chambers, H. Westlake, – Dudridge, Anon. and – Davis. *Third row:* J. Taylor, R. Peters, Anon., – Nicholls, A. North, Anon., J. Toye, R. Oliver, A. Maggs and Anon. *Second row:* W. Boyle, B. W. Salmon, J. Ellert, W. Wall, Anon., Captain C. R. Northey (2nd I/C), Major Ivor Westlake (O/C), R. Bubbear, E. Dart, J. Newman, – Parish and R. Higgin. *Front row:* Anon., R. Newman, J. Howes, T. Collier, Anon., G. Tanner, C. Trueman, A. Fry and Anon.

74 WOMEN'S HOME GUARD AUXILIARY (Attached to Glos. Reg.). Pictured at Tithe
Barn Headquarters, High Street, Shirehampton *c* 1942.

R. Westlake), 'D' Coy. (Capt. H. W. White) and 'E' Coy. (Major W. E.
Ford).

Captain Aubrey Ford was a member of staff at the C.W.S. Flour Mills at
Avonmouth, and Major Ivor Richard Westlake was better known locally as
the talented hairdresser, whose popular salon was in Avonmouth Road
opposite the Avonmouth Tramways Garage. Major Westlake had an
intimate knowledge of Avonmouth and district, and who better therefore to
have charge of the Home Guard Company for this area. In 1944 Major
Westlake was awarded a Certificate of Merit for his war-time services. His
Second-in-Command, Captain Charles R. Northey, was better known to
the children of Avonmouth, as being the Headmaster of Avonmouth
National School (1936–1955).

The 14th Battalion engaged in several exercises by night and by day, either
on its own or in conjunction with other Home Guard Battalions, and
sometimes with regular troops as the 'enemy'. Very successful week-end
camps were held near Severn Beach and, when transport restrictions
permitted, at Uphill near Weston-super-Mare. One of their busiest periods
was on 15, 16 and 17 March 1942 when a mock 'invasion' of Bristol, on a
grand scale, was carried out. For three days the City was realistically in a state
of siege. Verdict: 'Bristol was *not* captured'.

During the heavy air raids experienced by Avonmouth, invaluable service
was rendered by members of the 14th Battalion living in the vicinity. They

assisted Police and National Fire Service in directing traffic, in fighting fires, and in rescue work besides acting as guides to visiting Fire Brigades. In recognition of these services a commendation was received from General Sir Hugh Elles, the S.W. Regional Commissioner.

Altogether 246 members of the 14th Battalion went into the Regular Forces, besides 29 who joined the merchant navy. All these members could assure their Commanders that the training they received in the Home Guard was of great help to them.

The Allies Victory was already in sight when the Home Guard was disbanded in 1944. Bristol's 'Stand-down' parade took place on Sunday, 3 December 1944, when crowds of people turned out to cheer the Home Guard for the last time. The various local Companies formed five columns which marched down Park Street, Bristol, the salute being taken by Brig. M. Angel-James, V.C., on College Green, opposite the Lord Mayor's Chapel.

Earlier in the day the 14th Battalion had held their 'Stand-down' ceremony at Shirehampton, at which the Battalion Commander took the salute, before they took part in the Bristol march past.

I have received The King's command to express His Majesty's appreciation of the loyal service given voluntarily to her country in a time of grievous danger by

JOYCE SMITH

as a Woman Home Guard Auxiliary.

The War Office,
London.

Secretary of State
for War

75   WOMEN'S HOME GUARD AUXILIARY Service Certificate 1944 in respect of Joyce Smith, a Shirehampton volunteer.

76   BRISTOL HOME GUARD STAND-DOWN PARADE, Sunday, 3 December 1944.
Pictured marching down Park Street, Bristol. Salute taken by Brig. M. Angel-James, V.C.
on College Green.

IX. FIRST TASTE OF WARFARE

On hearing over B.B.C. Radio the grim news of the Dunkirk withdrawal, my Father declared, 'Hitler's next stop? . . . here! As it turned out his prediction was not very far wrong. After Dunkirk, Hitler lost no time in turning his attention towards Avonmouth and Bristol. In fact within sixteen days German 'planes appeared in the vicinity.

On 20 June 1940 at 2.0 a.m. searchlights at Portishead stabbed the night sky with their beams, probing for enemy aircraft droning overhead. They were engaged for 15 minutes, and in that time ten bombs were dropped; four fell near a house known as 'Rockleigh', and the remainder in the mud and shingle seventy yards from Battery Point at Portishead, but the air raid warning was not given on that occasion. That same evening the German radio announced, '. . . Bristol, one of the greatest trading cities, has been bombed', yet we who lived here were not aware of the fact!

We had heard the sirens wailing their blood-curdling 'alerts' on a couple of occasions during A.R.P. Exercises following the 1938 Munich Crisis, but when the warning siren awoke us, startled and frightened, at half-past midnight on the morning of Tuesday, 25 June 1940, it was no practice run. This time it was the real thing, the Germans were in the skies above us, and we were experiencing our first taste of warfare.

Grabbing a torch, gas-mask and eiderdown, and not stopping to dress, we hurried to the Anderson shelter in the garden in our night clothes. Already we could hear the distinctive drone of the Luftwaffe which, according to my father who was on night duty, had been in the area for some considerable time before the 'alert' had been sounded. We sat shivering in the shelter waiting for the worst to happen, and were profoundly thankful that it was mid-summer, and the hours of darkness were soon over. Not long after daybreak the siren sounded the 'all clear'.

As far as Avonmouth and Shirehampton knew this first air raid had been of a reconnaissance nature, as there had been no hostility in this area, but not as far as Bristol was concerned. Shortly after midnight the first H.E. bomb fell among a few old houses and shops near Champion & Davies factory in Lower Maudlin Street, Bristol. The factory itself, which was being used as a Red Cross Depot, was hit by another bomb. A further attack was made on Knowle at about 1.30 a.m., and bombs also fell in parts of St. George and Bedminster, and the districts mainly affected were St. Philip's, St. Paul's and Brislington. The objective of this first raid was thought possibly to have been Temple Meads Station, as nine H.E.'s fell on Railway property, two of which failed to explode. Other unexploded bombs were located at Temple

Gate and Victoria Street. Bristol's first air raid lasted from 12.30 a.m. until
2.45 a.m., during which time the City was hit 50 times, five people were
killed, 14 seriously injured and 19 slightly injured.

  This first raid taught us much about being prepared for air raids in future.
My parents immediately brought our beds downstairs, and made our air raid
shelter comfortable with bunk beds and hurricane lamps for light and
warmth. A year later on 22 June 1941 Germany attacked Russia, and the air
raids here became spasmodic. But it was not until 21 December 1941 that my
parents considered it sufficiently safe for the family to move back upstairs to
sleep once again.

ESCAPING THE BOMBS

  Britain first experienced air raids during the Great War, when the Germans
sent over aeroplanes and Zeppelins to bomb London and towns on the east
coast. On two occasions Zeppelins penetrated as far as the Midlands, and
with the furnaces there open to the heavens, it is little wonder the enemy
found their objectives without difficulty.

  Bristol in those days was out of range of the enemy. However, with the
rapid development of aircraft between the wars, both in range and speed, put
Bristol as far as air raids were concerned, in the front line during the Second
World War, especially after overrunning France and the Low Countries the
airfields of which the enemy were able to use to good advantage.

  Finding their objectives in the darkness was a great worry to bomber
pilots, who utilised rivers and canals as good signposts. Enemy 'planes,
taking off from occupied Countries crossed the English coastline around
Plymouth, then followed the course of the Bristol Channel and the River
Severn up to the Midlands, and ultimately to Merseyside, returning by the
same route, which came to be known as 'The Northerly Rat-run'. This put
Avonmouth and Bristol in the enemy flight-path, and the local sirens
sounded the 'alert' every night for week after week during the winter of 1940/
41.

  It was a practice with my family to try and estimate where the raids had
taken place each night, judging by the time it had taken the raiders to return.
A former Luftwaffe airman claimed that when on bombing missions, their
'planes were guided by a 'beam' or wireless signal, which, if on proper course
and over target, would automatically release their bomb load. However,
there was always the fear that damaged aircraft returning from raids on other
places might drop their bombs haphazardly in order to get home more easily,
which happened to Avonmouth on more than one occasion. Avonmouth
was certainly not the safest of places to stay the night during those very
dangerous times.

Older Parishoners who had no ties in Avonmouth, and others who did not actually work in the Parish, quite understandably, evacuated themselves to the country districts for the duration of the war, some folk even leaving their homes empty for kindly neighbours to look after. As the raids intensified it was a common sight in Avonmouth to see people at dusk on bus stops armed with blankets and rugs as they departed to sleep the night at the homes of friends living in Sea Mills or Westbury-on-Trym, where they considered it to be safer. After visiting Burrington Combe in December 1940, Mrs. Maund noted in her diary having seen a large colony of caravans parked in the space facing the Rock of Ages occupied by people who had fled from the City. Many others slept in their cars along the Combe at the side of the road – some had made tents with tarpaulin, hung washing on lines tied to the rocks, with cooking-pots and children in evidence. She learnt from a cafe proprietress there that cottagers and farmers were being besieged by people wanting night accommodation.

With the nightly exodus leaving so many houses in Avonmouth unoccupied over-night, it is a miracle that whole streets were not razed to the ground, considering the tens of thousands of incendiary bombs dropped on the Parish. As a target area troops were brought into Avonmouth during air raids to help deal with the incendiaries.

It was a commonly held belief, that if a bomb 'had your name on it', then you would not hear it coming. A cold comfort, and a fact which could neither be proved nor disproved. On the other hand no one heard land-mines coming, or parachute-mines as they were sometimes called. Land-mines were, in fact, ordinary sea-mines of gigantic size over 8 feet in length, dropped silently by parachute. Mines were not only larger than bombs, but because they exploded on the surface on impact, their lateral destructive force was greater. One fell in Priory Road, Shirehampton on Good Friday, 11 April 1941, destroying several houses and killing five people, whilst two which dropped near Victoria Park, Bedminster, damaged about 700 houses. One of the latter left a crater measuring 75 feet long and 25 feet wide.

What is said to have been the most destructive weapon used against Britain during the Second World War, was not the high explosive bombs, or even the flying-bombs and rockets sent over in 1944 (of which Bristol was out of range) but the incendiary bombs, which made a 'plopping' or 'rattling' noise as they landed. A grey coloured cylinder measured 13½″ long, 2″ in diameter and weighed 2 lbs, and they were dropped in their thousands. Each Incendiary Container was purported to hold 36 incendiary bombs.

The effects of the German raids on Britain showed that in built-up areas, incendiaries caused far more destruction than an equivalent weight of high explosive bombs, but the incendiary could not be used as a weapon of precision. Their purpose was to set alight the centre of towns to serve as a

78 INCENDIARY BOMB. One of the many thousands which the Germans dropped on Avonmouth and Shirehampton during air raids.

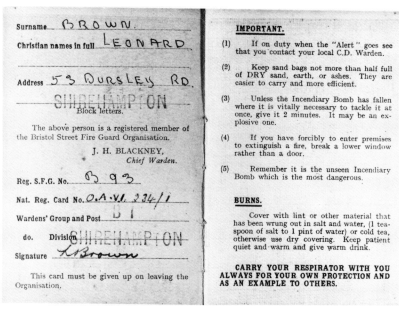

Surname BROWN.

Christian names in full LEONARD

Address 53 DURSLEY RD.

SHIREHAMPTON
Block letters.

The above person is a registered member of the Bristol Street Fire Guard Organisation.

J. H. BLACKNEY,
Chief Warden.

Reg. S.F.G. No. B 93

Nat. Reg. Card No. O.A·VI. 234/1

Wardens' Group and Post D 1

do. Division SHIREHAMPTON

Signature L Brown

This card must be given up on leaving the Organisation.

IMPORTANT.

(1) If on duty when the "Alert" goes see that you contact your local C.D. Warden.

(2) Keep sand bags not more than half full of DRY sand, earth, or ashes. They are easier to carry and more efficient.

(3) Unless the Incendiary Bomb has fallen where it is vitally necessary to tackle it at once, give it 2 minutes. It may be an explosive one.

(4) If you have forcibly to enter premises to extinguish a fire, break a lower window rather than a door.

(5) Remember it is the unseen Incendiary Bomb which is the most dangerous.

BURNS.

Cover with lint or other material that has been wrung out in salt and water, (1 teaspoon of salt to 1 pint of water) or cold tea, otherwise use dry covering. Keep patient quiet and warm and give warm drink.

CARRY YOUR RESPIRATOR WITH YOU ALWAYS FOR YOUR OWN PROTECTION AND AS AN EXAMPLE TO OTHERS.

79 BRISTOL STREET FIRE GUARD ORGANISATION. Membership card for Leonard Brown (Author's Father). Set up in January 1941, and operated until September 1944.

beacon and aiming point for subsequent waves of attackers with H.E. bombs. During the few seconds after the incendiary struck and ignited, it was a perfectly simple task to extinguish it – all that was required was a smothering agent, preferably sand. Some, however, were fixed with an explosive device designed to maim the person extinguishing the bomb.

Providing sufficient people to put the incendiaries out proved a problem when they were falling thick and fast. After the disastrous city fires of November and December 1940, the Government realised that much of the damage caused by incendiary bombs may have been avoided if they had been dealt with immediately on landing. The Government therefore made 'fire-watching' compulsory, and took powers to conscript all employers and employees to share if necessary in the protection of their places of work from fire bombs. The new organisation was called The Fire Guard, and it remained in force until 12 September 1944.

Hitting the enemy back in like measure was easier said than done. The day after taking office as Prime Minister, Mr. Churchill gave Bomber Command authority to attack Germany. But Britain was at a disadvantage having only medium range aircraft unable to take the war into the heart of Germany, and Berlin was 165 miles away. This predicament led to the Ministry in 1942 requesting a design for a bomber capable of reaching Berlin.

In the meantime the U.S.A. came into the war and their Flying Fortress bombers, capable of carrying 8,000 lbs of bombs, with a range of 1,850 miles became available. With their highly accurate Norden bomb-sights, a series of daylight attacks at great heights were made on Berlin. But even Flying Fortresses suffered heavy losses, due to the lack of long-range fighter escort. The British design long-range bomber was eventually adapted, and became the experimental Brabazon civil luxury 'plane intended to cross the Atlantic non-stop, which was made at Filton in 1946, the forerunner of present-day Concorde.

The story of the air raids over Britain has many aspects. If credit for the final Victory rightly goes to the Fighting Forces, then the endurance and courage of the people against the terror loosed upon them surely played its part. A radical social change took place during the war with a spirit of comradeship, fostered by a mutual danger.

X. UNDER FIRE

Diary of enemy air raids as they particularly affected the parishes of Avonmouth and Shirehampton –

20 June 1940

A prologue to the local air raids was enacted at 2.0 a.m. when enemy aircraft first appeared in the vicinity. They were engaged by the searchlights at Portishead for 15 minutes, but no 'alert' warning was given, and the sirens remained silent. (For details see *First Taste of Warfare*.)

25 June 1940

The first air raid warning was sounded at 12.30 a.m. (For details see *First Taste of Warfare*).

3 July 1940

Today the first bombs were dropped on the Parish of Avonmouth. They fell in a field adjoining Cowley Farm, near the National Smelting Company, and no damage was caused.

14 July 1940

There were two air attacks on this day. At 1.0 a.m. seven High Explosive bombs fell near St. Andrew's Road Railway Station at Avonmouth, which put the signal-box out of action, and slightly damaged the railway track, causing it to be temporarily closed to traffic. At 8.0 a.m. three 'planes attacked Avonmouth. Twenty-nine railway trucks and 20 private tank wagons were slightly damaged.

1/2 August 1940

A single enemy 'plane, flying at considerable height, shortly after midnight, scattered propaganda leaflets in their thousands over southern England, some of which fell in the Backwell district near Bristol. When picked up they proved to be the size of a small newspaper headed, 'A Last Appeal to Reason by Adolf Hitler', and gave an English translation of a speech delivered by the Fuehrer to the Reichstag on 19 July 1940.

Hitler still hoped for peace with Britain, being convinced that his great victories in Europe of spring and summer, together with the samples of German bombing England had already experienced, would persuade this country to capitulate. The Germans could not believe that Britain would go on fighting alone, what was to them, so clearly a hopeless war. The leaflets entreated the English to give up the useless struggle, and accept the generous terms which Hitler was prepared to offer. But this was no longer the same

80   GERMAN LEAFLET RAID. Reader
in a S.W. District studying one of the
propaganda leaflets dropped in thousands by German 'planes during night
of 1/2 August 1940.

Britain with whom Hitler had dealings at Munich in 1938. Britain was now fortified, and inspired by their new War Leader, Prime Minister Churchill.

It was much to Hitler's surprise, therefore, that his propaganda leaflets were gathered up to help the paper salvage drive. The appeal which they contained was treated as a huge joke, and became the cause of uproarious laughter. Hitler's tone changed, with the result that the German air offensive was launched 8 August 1940, and waged until 5 October 1940, known as the Battle of Britain.

11/12 August 1940

A crude-oil bomb was dropped at the West Town suburb of Avonmouth, besides unexploded bombs which fell in the mud of the rive bank on the opposite side of the Avon, near Sheephouse Farm, Easton-in-Gordano.

Shirehampton was bombed for the first time, when at midnight 14 H.E.'s fell in and around the Village. An Electricity sub-station was damaged, one house demolished and a few others damaged. The entrance of the air raid shelter in the playground of St. Bernard's R.C. School at the corner of Station Road and Pembroke Avenue received a direct hit. No harm was done to the

81 ST. BERNARD'S SCHOOL PLAYGROUND. Although receiving a direct hit at entrance
to underground shelter in Station Road, Shirehampton, no harm came to those in the
shelter beneath. 11/12 August 1940.

shelter beneath, and ten people inside, one of whom was Mrs. Mary Cox,
remained uninjured.

In recalling her experiences in July 1986, Mrs. Cox wrote:—

'Besides my late husband, Frank, and myself in the shelter, there were two Roman
Catholic priests, Mrs. Andrews and her young daughter aged about 7, Mrs. Grant
with her young son Stanley, and two others. Fortunately, the bomb was only a 50
pound one. Later on in the war when 2,000 pounders were being dropped, we should
have been no more, but apparently we were ear-marked for survival. The shelter
lights were still on and I could just see Frank's head above the rubble, where he was
digging out young Stanley, who, once he had climbed free through the hatch, ran
around the playground making a high pitched noise like a falling bomb . . . we soon
put a stop to that! One Catholic priest had a broken leg. I was blown the full length of
the shelter, with no injuries whatever, though for six weeks after the event I lost my
voice. Father O'Connell banged his head on the hatch door in his haste to get out, and
we were all reduced to mild hysteria laughing at him. When we reached our home on
the opposite side of Station Road, I suggested to Frank that he ride down to
Avonmouth on his bike, to let my family know all was well if they heard any reports
in the morning. My husband was covered in dirt, plaster, and everything else that
goes into the building of a shelter, and I insisted that he washed his hair before he
went, not to appear like someone from outer space!'

During the same raid a string of seven H.E.'s fell in Stoke Bishop, in a line
from the back of 26 Old Sneed Avenue to a field east of Eastmead Avenue.
The back corner of one house was blown out, and other damage was confined
to broken glass, gas and water mains. One bomb, reported to be of a
'whistling' type, fell in a back garden at Manor Park, Redland, and damaged
the windows of six houses.

15/16 August 1940

About a dozen bombs landed in the sea near the North Pier of the Royal Edward Dock, eight near Rockingham Farm and a further 17 around Hallen.

24/25 August 1940

Houses No's 57 and 58 Richmond Villas, Avonmouth, received a direct hit, whilst six more bombs landed in the sea.

27/28 August 1940

At 9.0 p.m. an attack was made on Avonmouth Docks with both incendiary and H.E. bombs, which fell at the Petroleum Board's Canning Factory at Holesmouth. Other incendiaries were dropped in Avonmouth itself, and in the countryside towards Lawrence Weston.

28/29 August 1940

At Lawrence Weston six small craters were found near Katherine's Farm.

September 1940

At the beginning of the month, enemy objectives appeared to be Avonmouth Docks, which were attacked on three occasions, without serious damage.

In attempting to sever the railway line linking Avonmouth with Bristol, the number of bombs which were near misses is unbelievable. One fell on the railway allotments between Shirehampton Station and Hung Road bridge, missing the 'down' line by about only six feet. Another bomb landed on the railway allotments near Woodwell Lane, missing the 'up' line by about 30 feet and luckily did not explode. The Army Bomb Disposal men, in recovering this bomb, to the amazement of everyone, left behind a crater quite as large as if the bomb had actually exploded. However, the 'down' line near Sea Mills station was temporarily blocked by a bomb at about this time, whilst another unexploded bomb estimated to weigh about 250 lbs. remained wedged in the mud at Sea Mills Creek, and was not discovered until April 1951.

1/2 September 1940

Bombs in the same salvo caused a direct hit in Avonmouth on the Miles Arms Hotel and a house in Davis Street (No. 34), where two occupants were killed. Slight damage was caused to the G.W.R. line on the Docks. In the same raid, six bombs caused damage to several houses in Stoke Bishop.

A photograph of the bomb-damaged Miles Arms Hotel was published in the Evening World on 3 September 1940 with the caption, 'The result of a direct hit from a bomb on an hotel during a night raid on a South West Town'. The same paper carried a photograph of the bombed house in Davis Street, Avonmouth, which bore the caption, 'A woman and her child were killed after a bomb had struck this private house during the night raid on a

82   DAVIS STREET, AVONMOUTH (No's 32, 30 & 28). *Evening World* caption read, 'A woman and her child were killed after a bomb had struck this private house during a night raid on a South West Town'. 1/2 September 1940.

83   MILES ARMS HOTEL, AVONMOUTH. After receiving a direct hit during a night raid of 1/2 September 1940. *N.B.* Passing Policeman carrying tin-helmet and gas mask.

South West Town'. The woman killed was Mrs. Ellen Mary Cook (aged 34) and her daughter Elizabeth (aged 5).

Miles Arms Hotel

The Miles Arms Hotel, which takes its name from the Miles family, formerly Squires of King's Weston Estate, and landowners of Avonmouth, was built in 1907. At the outbreak of war in 1939 the Hotel was requisitioned by the Army and used as their Embarkation Headquarters. Very strict security precautions prevailed at that time, requiring all the guests and residents at the Hotel to be turned out, and forced to find alternative accommodation. They were not allowed to return to live at the Miles Arms again until after D-Day in 1944.

When the Hotel was bombed in September 1940, the Germans had, in effect, hit a military target. The blast from bombs was sometimes known to do peculiar things, as here recalled by Mrs. B. A. Francis who in 1940 was a telephonist at the Avonmouth Exchange at the Post Office in Avonmouth Road.

'After an air raid on Avonmouth, in which the Miles Arms Hotel was badly damaged, quite a lot of glass was scattered. A wine-glass from the Hotel, however, survived the blast, and came to rest 250 yards down the road on a window-sill of the Post Office. The wine-glass stood, complete, upright and not even cracked. It was surrounded by fragments of glass. We took the glass into the office, and the Postmaster suggested we returned it to the Miles Arms, where we were told to keep the glass as a souvenir.'

The artist, Mr. Harry Morley, A.R.A., painted in oils the Hotel as it was on the morning of 2 September 1940 after being struck by the bomb (see 'From Peace to War – War Artists').

3/4 September 1940

Shirehampton raided. Bombs fell on the National Smelting Company's works damaging only a water main. Others dropped in the vicinity of Cowley Farm, Katherine Farm and Poplar Farm.

7 September 1940

Londoners experienced their first taste of the blitz on this night, when 250 German bombers struck hard at the capital. For the remainder of 1940 and into 1941 Londoners were subjected to a relentless pounding from the air.

10 September 1940

The services of the bomb disposal experts were stretched to the limit at this time. The No. 7 Bomb Disposal Company of the Royal Engineers was billeted in High Street, Shirehampton, opposite the George Inn, when an unexploded bomb landed nearby, and Second-Lieutenant Frederick John

84 BOMB DISPOSAL SQUAD VICTIM.
Last resting place at Canford Cemetery of 2nd Lieut. F. J. Ingram, Royal Engineers, killed attempting to defuse an unexploded bomb at Shirehampton, 10 September 1940.

Ingram (aged 36) went to deal with it. Unfortunately, the bomb had a delayed action fuse, and Lieut. Ingram was seriously injured. He died on the way to the Bristol Royal Infirmary, and two others were also badly injured. Demands on the Bomb Disposal Company were so great, that only two Sappers could be spared to attend the Officer's funeral, and had the distressing duty of driving the Army truck carrying his body from St. Bernard's Roman Catholic Church to the Cemetery at Canford.

15 September 1940

This date marks the climax of the Battle of Britain, in the course of which from August to October 1940, the Germans lost 1,733 aircraft (not the 2,698 claimed by the British) whilst the R.A.F. lost 915 fighter 'planes (not the 3,058 claimed by the enemy). This resounding British victory, considered one of the major turning points of World War II, will ever be immortalised by the words of Winston Churchill, 'Never in the field of human conflict was so much owed by so many to so few'.

15/16 September 1940

Sunday night. According to German sources, Avonmouth was their target on this occasion, and allocated 4 × 20 Flame bombs, 60 General purpose

H.E.'s and 16 Incendiary containers, but against this record was noted 'Target not hit'. Even so, three soldiers of the Gloucestershire Regiment at 'T' Camp, Shirehampton were killed through enemy action on this date, namely, Private Frederick William Bailey (aged 30), Private Job Langford (aged 43) and L.-Cpl. George Alfred Hall (aged 29) who died next day at Southmead Hospital.

Wednesday, 25 September 1940 – First daylight raid on Filton

It was a beautiful sunny morning, with lovely blue skies, and hardly a cloud to be seen, when a large force of about 100 aircraft approached Britain from the south. Following the course of the Bristol Channel, half made for the Welsh Coast, and the rest, estimated to be about 50, turned in over Avonmouth.

The time was 11.40 a.m., and the 'planes flying in strict 'V' formation, made an impressive sight. Having no interception, those who saw them quite naturally assumed they were 'ours', but in fact they were German Luftwaffe from Villacoublay near Paris, Heinkel bombers with Messerschmitt long range fighters as escort, weaving in and out, above and beneath the formation of bombers. Their objective was Bristol Aeroplane Works at Filton, which they found without difficulty, and which was completely at their mercy without any British 'planes to oppose them. In 25 terror-filled minutes (the 'alert' was sounded at 11.40 a.m. and the 'all clear' at 12.05 p.m.) they let loose 168 bombs, causing a high death-roll and much havoc.

The B.A.C. works was a legitimate military target. Blenheim, Beaufort and Beaufighter aircraft were being constructed there at the time. The German News Agency put out the claim, 'This factory will not produce any more aircraft', but in actual fact only eight 'planes were so seriously damaged as to be irreparable.

In June 1945, Mr. W. R. Verdon Smith, C.B.E., Chairman of Bristol Aeroplane Company, in an address to shareholders, said, 'At mid-day on 25 September 1940 Filton was chosen by the enemy to be the subject of a heavy attack; in that raid 91 of the Company's employees were killed, nearly 200 suffered injury, and considerable damage was done to the premises'.

Several months were to elapse before the damage caused that morning was made good, but more serious than this was the loss of life. Six shelters full of people were struck, with appalling results. Some of the bombs did not explode for several hours after the raid, and a number of members of the Bristol Medical Service were injured whilst they were digging in the ruins for survivors.

From the German point of view the morning's work was highly satisfactory. The only consolation as far as Bristol was concerned was at 11.50 a.m. a Heinkel 111 from Chartes was shot down by the Portbury Gun

85   NINE HEINKEL 111 BOMBERS in formation. It is believed this photograph was taken
on the day of the first daylight raid on Filton, 25 September 1940.

site operated by 237 Batt. 76th H.A.A. Regiment. All five members of crew bailed out and were taken prisoner. The 'plane crashed at Racecourse Farm at Lower Failand.

Friday, 27 September 1940 – Second daylight raid on Filton

On this day history almost repeated itself of two days earlier, but not quite! It was a fine sunny morning once again when a large wave of Luftwaffe bombers with fighter escort turned in over Avonmouth making for Filton, and at about the same time 11.30 a.m. But here the similiarities of the two days ended. In an attempt to repeat his exploits of Wednesday 25th the enemy soon learnt his mistake. This time the R.A.F. was ready and waiting for him.

A squadron of Hurricanes posted to Filton on the day before, soon scattered the assailants like a flock of sheep, and with the aid of anti-aircraft fire, the Luftwaffe was driven off before they could inflict any damage. Some of the 'planes immediately headed for home, jettisoning their bombs wherever they could, doing little, if any damage. Crowds of Bristolians came out into the streets to watch the 'dog fights' taking place in the skies above the City, ignoring warnings and protestations from the Air-raid Wardens to take cover. Ten German aircraft were destroyed and two British.

A Messerschmitt fighter was shot down and crashed at Stapleton Institution (now Manor Park Hospital). Both crew members were killed. Another Messerschmitt was shot down and crashed at Radstock. The Pilot bailed out, and was taken prisoner, but the parachute of the Observer failed to open, and his body was later found near Kilmersdon Colliery Railway.

From the British point of view the daylight raid of the 25th was a complete disaster, but was made up for on the 27th which was a resounding success, and was certainly a great boost to local morale. It was later established from German records that the target on the 27th had been the Parnall Aircraft Ltd's factory at Yate where gun-turrets were being manufactured at the time. But whatever the target might have been, it was certainly not reached, and the enemy soon learnt that daylight raiding was not a profitable undertaking. The two daylight raids on Filton are now recognised as being part of the Battle of Britain. The raid on the 27th proved of particular significance to Avonmouth.

The German PK (Propaganda-Kompanie) men later named Kriegsberichter (war correspondents) were a unique military body during the Second World War. Made up of former journalists, photographers, wireless reporters, and cameramen they were civilians turned war correspondents. Their task was to accompany the troops into action and report on their experiences, and often operated as a pair, one reporting in writing, the other by photographs or movie film. At the start of the war the Luftwaffe pilots refused to take PK men with them on their operations, not

86 MESSERSCHMITT FIGHTER 109E, known to Luftwaffe pilots as *Emil*. As fast as the
British Spitfire, but less manoeuvrable. Also handicapped by its short range.

87 PART WRECKAGE OF HEINKEL 111, at Racecourse Farm, Failand. Brought down by
Portbury A.A. guns. Five crew parachuted out and were captured 25 September 1940.

wanting any spectators. To get over this problem, on Goebbel's orders, PK men were trained as gunners and bomb aimers, so becoming members of crew.

Sitting beside the Pilot of a Heinkel on that fine September morning, with his precision Leica camera with telephoto lens at the ready, a PK man took an excellent aerial photograph of the Parish of Avonmouth (see plate 1). After Intelligence analysis this photograph, no doubt, became a useful aid in the bombing which Avonmouth later received at the hands of the Luftwaffe.

12 October 1940

Avonmouth had another raid, which didn't last long, i.e., 10.15 p.m. until 11.55 p.m. One H.E. fell in the Royal Edward Dock, damaging the railway near the Transit Station and a few trucks were derailed, but otherwise no interference.

15/16 October 1940

Shirehampton raided. H.E.'s and incendiary bombs were scattered in Shirehampton Park. Druid Stoke, Henleaze and Westbury-on-Trym were all damaged by bombs, during this long raid, which began at 7.45 p.m. and continued until 6.20 a.m. carried out by Dornier 'planes from Nantes and Brest airfields in Brittany.

14/15 November 1940

A bright moonlit night saw the start of a new phase in Luftwaffe bombardment. Hitherto their mass aerial attacks had been reserved for London, but now started a series of heavy night attacks directed against industrial and military installations in smaller British towns and cities. Coventry was singled out for the first ruthless assault. It lasted nearly all night, during which time the beautiful 14th Century Cathedral was totally destroyed, causing an outburst of public outrage.

In recent years it has been claimed that the Prime Minister knew just hours before the raid that a blitz on Coventry was coming, but took the decision not to evacuate the City for fear of giving away the closely guarded secret that the German signalling code had been broken, and wireless signals were being intercepted and decoded. In any case, it is doubtful if a city the size of Coventry could have been effectively evacuated with only a few hours notice.

Sunday, 24 November 1940. Bristol's First Blitz

The Germans were well schooled in the Englishman's Sunday, when inner cities were largely depopulated, and hoped to use it to his advantage, expecting also that civil defence vigilance would be somewhat relaxed. On seven of the nine Sundays in November and December 1940 Britain's big cities were attacked by the Luftwaffe, and Bristol was no exception.

88 KING'S WESTON AVENUE, SHIREHAMPTON. Occupants rushed furniture from houses when adjoining dwellings were ablaze. *Left:* Mr. H. W. Yeoman.

89 ST. MARY'S CHURCH, SHIREHAMPTON. E. J. Thomas inspecting charred floorboards caused by incendiary bomb during the early blitzes. Photo: July 1976.

The worshippers attending Bristol's Churches for evening services on 24th November 1940 hardly had time to return home, before the sirens sounded the 'alert' at 6.21 p.m. with the arrival of 60 Heinkel's from Villacoublay, Dreux and Chartres airfields near Paris, led in by Pathfinders from Vannes dropping flares. By the time the enemy 'planes turned for home at 11.59 p.m. Bristol's Mediaeval City was a raging inferno.

The hostile 'planes attacked in waves of two or three at regular intervals, raining down thousands of incendiary bombs. The red sky of Bristol burning could be seen for miles around – as far as Stinchcombe Hill at Dursley. A thousand years heritage perished in this one night, as did Wine Street and Castle Street hitherto Bristol's renowned shopping centre. 'Bristol,' declared the German Official News Agency, 'has been wiped out', and certainly the 'City of Churches' had in one night become a city of ruins.

A high wind was blowing across the target area, and whilst it did not account for the vast destruction over so wide an expanse of Greater Bristol, this certainly was responsible for the obliteration of the most ancient parts of the city. The situation was further handicapped by damage done to mains, causing a failure of water supply with which to douse the fires. The reserve water from tanks and reservoirs was soon exhausted, and there only remained the supplies from the River Avon and harbour using fire-floats. For many days the six square miles of the city burned. Apparently, the enemy air-crews themselves could smell the results of their savagery, judging from the following conversation which took place during a German operational flight over London:–

' "Can't you smell anything, lads?", the Flying Officer cried out unexpectedly. He sniffed and sniffed. I controlled the fuel system, and looked to left and to right of the engines, sniffing the air as well. Dammit, he was right. The 'plane reeked badly with an evil smell of burning. "I can't find anything, our machine seems alright", I cried back. "I've had the smell in my nostrils for some time, but I didn't want to say anything" the Mechanic reported. But what can it be? It certainly isn't our bird. "Well then, it must be the smell of London burning", the Commander answered calmly. And we learned later he was right; other aircrews had made the same observation.'

There was a little consolation in that not *all* the enemy 'planes engaged in this first great blitz on Bristol returned afterwards safely to their base. A Dornier from Lanveoc Poulmic in France got lost on the way back from bombing the City, and crashed at Rame Head near Plymouth after hitting a barrage balloon cable. All four members of the crew baled out, and were taken prisoner. Three were captured by nearby villagers armed with broom handles! The fourth crew member was rescued in the darkness from the sea by two men in a rowing boat which was slowly sinking due to a hole in the bottom. Two of the German airmen were armed with pistols, but did not use them.

The official casualty list for this raid was 200 killed, 163 seriously injured and 526 slightly hurt.

25 November 1940

After the devastating blitz experienced by Bristol the night before, Avonmothians quite naturally thought to themselves 'Now it's our turn', when the 'alert' was given and bombs began to fall on the Parish just before seven o'clock. A shed at the Petroleum Board's Canning Factory was destroyed, and the National Smelting Company was hit and fires started. The remaining damage in the Docks was of a minor character.

90 BUSINESS AS USUAL. In Bristol's Districts where shops were destroyed, life went on cheerfully, with trucks and stalls trading in the open.

In Avonmouth itself a Bank, two Churches and several houses were damaged. Four bombs fell near the West Town Dock entrance gate, doing small damage to railway sidings. One unexploded bomb at the premises of Messrs. Bodey, Jerrim & Denning was dealt with by naval personnel. As a result of this raid there was a failure of electricity supplies, and altogether 14 H.E.'s and an estimated 100 incendiary bombs were dropped.

26 November 1940

In the evening between 6.35 p.m. and 7.30 p.m. a shower of incendiaries, preceded by flares, were dropped over Avonmouth and Shirehampton. Only a few incidents were reported, as the majority fell on Shirehampton Golf Links and Hallen Marshes. Mr. Ralph Pendergast (aged 53) received injuries through enemy action at the National Smelting Company, and died at Bristol General Hospital the same day.

2 December 1940. Bristol's Second Blitz

This large-scale raid, which lasted from 6.16 p.m. until 11.0 p.m., was, according to the Germans said 'to conclude the work of the destruction similar to Coventry and Southampton' begun during the first blitz on 24 November. The Official casualty figures were 156 killed, 149 seriously injured and 121 slightly injured, which included three local deaths, i.e. Alice Makin (aged 53) and Joan Weaver (aged 23) both killed at 103 Westbury Lane, Sea Mills, and Lieut. Ernest William Jones, R.E. (aged 52) at 56 Station Road, Shirehampton.

It has since come to light that Bristol, on this occasion, did not receive all the bombs intended by the enemy due to the following reasons, explained by a dorsal-gunner of one of the Dornier 'planes detailed on this raid, leaving Deurne (Antwerp) airfield, who remembered his experiences more than 30 years later:

'The briefing was short and to the point. The whole Gruppe was to attack Bristol. We were flying in formation, and so high that everybody was wearing their oxygen masks. When nearing the English coastline a clumsy movement by the navigator caused his maps to drop from his lap. He asked me to retrieve them, so I undid my straps and leant down to look for them. In so doing the pipe of my oxygen mask unnoticed became loose, and shortly afterwards I lost consciousness. Luckily, the pilot noticed that something was wrong, made a quick dive, jettisoned his bombs into the North Sea, and made for home. On the way back I recovered consciousness, but it had been as close a shave for me as it had been for the people of Bristol. II/KG3 (another aircraft in the same flight) neatly dropped its bombs into a swamp, mistaking the 'starfish' decoy fires for the target, and Bristol itself was spared. The following day, however, reconnaissance aircraft discovered the error, and a report was drawn up. As a result Göring was enraged, and ordered a new attack.'

This was probably the reason Bristol suffered three blitzes in the space of a fortnight.

6 December 1940. Bristol's Third Blitz

Bristol's third big air-raid in quick succession, began just after 6.30 p.m. and lasted until 11.28 p.m. Casualty figures for this raid were 100 killed, 80 seriously injured and 108 slightly injured. A H.E. struck the railway alongside the 7.10 train from Bristol to Salisbury which was derailed, and accounted for many of the casualties. But the attack was rent with the most terrific anti-aircraft barrage so far experienced by Bristol.

11/12 December 1940

In an isolated raid on Shirehampton, two H.E.'s damaged about 250 houses.

Monday, 16 December 1940

'Tis not the walls that make the City, but the people who live within them', quoted King George VI, when he came to Bristol on 16 December 1940 to see for himself the devastation and wanton destruction caused by the Nazi bombs, and to give his sympathy and encouragement.

His Majesty was welcomed at the City gate by the Lord Mayor (Alderman T. H. J. Underdown), the Regional Commissioner (General Sir Hugh Elles), the Sheriff (Mr. C. H. W. Davey) and the Emergency Committee of the City Council. It was the King's second visit to Bristol in 1940, and again for

91 KING GEORGE VI meets A.R.P. workers whilst on 'see for himself' tour of bomb-damaged Bristol, 16 December 1940. *Far right:* Lord Mayor, Ald. T. H. J. Underdown.

security reasons there were no advance announcements of his intended visit, which was without pomp or ceremony. Somehow, though, the news of his coming leaked out, and Bristol gave His Majesty a warm and enthusiastic welcome.

The King toured on foot the bomb-damaged areas, and the distress which he saw was real enough, but there was no sign of despondency. On the contrary, Union Jacks fluttered on bomb-craters to bear witness to the unconquerable spirit of Bristol which survived the air raids. His Majesty's words of sympathy greatly cheered the large crowds, particularly those in residential areas which had received the heaviest blows. Shouts of 'God Bless You' and 'We can take it' were proof enough of Bristol's determination to win through.

There was another Royal visitor to Bristol on that memorable day. Queen Mary also came to inspect the bomb-damaged areas, and at the same time took the opportunity of taking lunch with the King at the Council House. In subsequent months she paid visits to the Hostels, a British Restaurant and large factories to cheer the War-workers.

Bristolians happily spent a quiet Christmas with almost a month's respite from air raids.

January 1941

The bitter cold weather of January added to the horror of fires and bombs. For this month, Avonmouth came only second to London (with Bristol third) in the list of towns on which more than 50 tons of H.E.'s were dropped in raids.

After enduring four consecutive nights of bombing at this time, when raiders flew through a corridor in ack-ack defences, there were certain misgivings amongst Bristolians about the apparent ease with which enemy 'planes were getting through to the City. Due to an acute shortage of guns and ammunition, not a shot was being fired until after the bombs were dropped.

The hole in Bristol's defences was under discussion at one of the daily meetings of the Emergency Committee at this grim time, when Sir John Inskip asked the meeting whether anyone knew a Cabinet Minister? Alderman Parish replied, 'I know Ernest Bevin' (the then Minister of Labour). Next morning Alderman Parish was sitting in Ernest Bevin's office in Whitehall, telling him that the people of Bristol were seriously disturbed about the situation. He listened to what Alderman Parish had to say, and then told him, 'Leave it to me, and I will see what can be done'.

A few days later, Ernest Bevin wrote a letter to Alderman Parish, the contents of which remained secret until May 1971, when it was published for the first time, as follows:

'Dear Parish – I have looked into the matter about which you spoke to me when you came to see me some little time back, and you can take it that the position is being rapidly and substantially improved. This is, of course, for your private information, and I cannot go into details about the arrangements which are being made. But I think they should prove satisfactory.'

Within a week the gap in Bristol's ground defences had been filled by four of the most modern ack-ack guns available, and with them came skilled crews to man them. That same night the German aircraft arrived to bomb Avonmouth. Instead of finding a clear path through the corridor above Bristol, this time they were met with such determined flak that the leading 'planes detailed to drop marker incendiary bombs were scattered. Troops were able to extinguish the incendiaries, and when the raid proper started, the target was in darkness.

3/4 January 1941. Bristol's Fourth Blitz

This almost dusk-to-dawn raid was, to that date, Bristol's longest, lasting 12 hours. The weather was bitterly cold. While flames poured from blazing buildings, coats of ice from the jets of benumbed firemen formed on adjoining houses, and great sheets of ice on the roadways added to the plight of those bravely attempting to quench the fires. Mr. Frederick Hooper, who was serving as a Messenger with the Fire Service at the time, described the night of 3/4 January 1941 as follows:

'Water froze in the hose, due to drop in water pressure as often happened then, and escapes and ladders were frozen to buildings. A turn-table ladder was frozen to the roof of the General Hospital, with tons of ice hanging in great icicles from the ladders. It took over a week, using hot water from the Hospital to free it. Hose could not be drained of water and rolled up, but had to be folded (or flaked) and collected by lorries. At Coronation Road Fire Station in Bristol the hose was piled to the roof in a great heap, and coke braziers kept burning day and night, with men pulling at the hose, trying to disentangle each length, thaw it, and drain it.'

The clothing froze on the firemen's bodies, so that they were encased in ice, and movement of any kind became difficult.

Casualty figures for this raid were 149 dead, 133 seriously injured and 218 slightly wounded. But even this raid did not satisfy the enemy's lust for indiscriminate bombing of non-military targets. In less than 24 hours Bristol had to endure yet another all-night ordeal of fire and destruction.

It was during the 3/4 January raid that the Germans dropped their biggest bomb on the City, which fortunately did not explode. '*Satan*', a 4,000 lb monster, which fell at Beckington Road, Knowle, measured 8' 11" long (without the tail) and 2' 2" in diameter. When the Bomb Disposal Unit recovered it in April 1943 they had to dig down 29½ feet. '*Satan*' rode in the Victory Parade through London . . . the very last plan the Germans could have thought of for its disposal!

92   LIKE A PANTOMIME FAIRY COACH. Fire-escape ladder covered with icicles during the twelve hours air raid on Bristol, 3/4 January 1941.

4/5 January 1941

The severe weather conditions did not deter the enemy. This attack began just after 7.15 p.m., and was concentrated on Avonmouth, where showers of incendiaries fell on the Docks, and minor damage was done to buildings of National Importance. Fires were dealt with speedily, and by 10.0 p.m. they had all been extinguished.

German records confirm the target as having been Avonmouth on this occasion, with 103 aircraft over the target, who dropped 82 tons H.E.'s and 735 incendiary containers (i.e., 26,460 bombs). Fire appliances, pumps and men were rushed to Avonmouth from as far away as Kenilworth, Nuneaton and Bilston in Staffordshire to help deal with the ensuing fires. The

93   FIRE ENGINE. A 1932 Leyland Titan Pump Engine of type used to fight the blitz fires 1940/1941. This 'oldie' pictured at Patchway Service Station in September 1987 with Fireman Gordon Pratton. Photo: by Colin Momber.

94   AVONMOUTH FIRE STATION in Green Lane. Centre of fire fighting operations during the air raids. *Inset:* Original name set in wall. *Photo:* June 1969.

distinctive feature of this raid was it being the longest period to date between the air raid 'warning' and 'raiders past', i.e., 6.20 p.m. to 6.59 a.m. 12 hours 39 minutes.

Mr. Robert Arnold (aged 59) of 75 Barrow Hill Crescent, Shirehampton, died at Southmead Hospital from injuries received.

10 January 1941

This comparatively short raid lasted 2 hours 15 minutes (6.30 p.m. to 9.15 p.m.) when two H.E.'s were dropped on Shirehampton, and one outside the Shell-Mex south garage at the Royal Edward Dock, Avonmouth, damaging five petrol lorries.

Thursday/Friday, 16/17 January 1941. Avonmouth Blitz

Bristol had something of a respite from enemy attacks from mid-January to the end of February 1941, but not so Avonmouth. Avonmouth was singled out for a particularly heavy and concentrated attack on this night, when considerable damage was done to the Docks and property. Not a street in the parish came through this raid unscathed, which was thereafter referred to as 'The Blitz on Avonmouth', and those who lived through it found it an experience they would never forget.

German sources confirm Avonmouth was the target, with 126 aircraft dropping 124 tons of H.E. and 1,480 incendiary containers (53,280 bombs). The raid lasted nearly 11 hours, from 7.08 p.m. until 5.39 a.m. next morning, with only one lull at around midnight, when it was assumed the nightmare was over, but Jerry returned for a repeat performance, which proved more savage than the first. Not to help matters, the weather was bitterly cold, and water was turning to ice, freezing up the fire-fighting equipment. As was the usual procedure in the blitzes, the path-finder 'planes came first dropping flares to illuminate the target, followed by waves of 'planes dropping incendiaries, and last but not least came those bringing H. E. bombs.

Early in the evening showers of incendiaries were let loose over the Dock area, and many fires broke out. The Fire Services were given prompt assistance by the Military Forces, and their combined efforts succeeded in extinguishing the flames, saving many vital buildings from complete destruction. To help fight the blaze, sand was issued, and this proved a great help.

In the early hours of 17 January, however, more incendiaries were dropped, starting further fires, which quickly got out of control, and illuminated the target for the subsequent waves of bombers. The German airmen found their task easy, and the damage they did to Docks property and Industrial buildings was considerable.

The Port of Bristol Authority reported that their premises destroyed included the Workmen's Shelter and Library near Gloucester Road Dock

95   CROWN TERRACE, WEST TOWN, AVONMOUTH. *c* 1910. So severely bombed 16/17 January 1941, inhabitants were evacuated, and their homes were never rebuilt.

gate, the Haven Master's Office, the shed at the old Passenger Station, conveyor galleries between the granaries and various offices. The following list of damage done to private concerns gives an idea of the havoc caused, and included premises of Rowland Bros. and Mountstuart Ltd. completely destroyed. Buildings belonging to Silcocks Ltd. and R. & W. Paul Ltd. were seriously damaged, and the Shell-Mex garage was destroyed, besides an oil tank at the Anglo-American Installation caught fire. 'V' shed was burnt, 'R' and 'U' sheds were badly damaged, and to a lesser degree Hosegoods Mill, Beldam Packing Co., and Elders & Fyffes straw shed. At Robinsons Mill (now B.O.C.M.) three barges and a timber shed were set on fire, and two ships berthed on the quays were also damaged. On the *s.s. Coracero* (7,250 g.r.t.) the First Officer, Norman L. McLeod (aged 27) was killed, and some of the crew were injured. The other ship involved was the *s.s. Llanwern* (4,966 g.r.t.). (Both ships survived this raid only to be later sunk at sea, the *Coracero* by torpedo from a submarine on 17 March 1943, and the *Llanwern* on 26 February 1941 after being bombed by an enemy aircraft.)

In Avonmouth Village the Police and Fire Stations were set on fire, also many houses, and Avonmouth Parish Church was gutted. About 50 houses were demolished and ten times as many damaged. Such devastation was caused at West Town, where some 200 folk lived, that they were evacuated whilst the raid was still in progress, and so severely damaged were their homes that they were never rebuilt.

96   CATHERINE STREET, AVONMOUTH on the morning of Friday, 17 January 1941, after receiving a direct hit by a German bomb during the previous night. Miraculously there were no casualties, despite No's 3, 4 & 5 being demolished.

97   RICHMOND TERRACE, AVONMOUTH. 16/17 January 1941. Children discover Christmas decorations among the ruins. Happily the family were safe in their shelter.

To deal with the numerous fires, appliances, pumps and men were rushed to Avonmouth from all parts of Gloucestershire, Somerset, Wiltshire and Devon. Movements of pumps and personnel continued all the next day and following night, and relief crews were still arriving until the following Saturday, 25 January.

In comparison with the violence of this attack, the following fatality list must be considered light:

Gilbert Edward Llewellyn Bailey (aged 46) at Avonmouth Road.
Albert Edward Carter (aged 49) at Avonmouth Road.
John Henry Johnson (aged 37) at Avonmouth Road.
Frederick Chard (aged 73) at 55 Cook Street.
Niel Beck Jespersen (aged 25) at Davis Street.
Alfred Richard Dunn (aged 49) at 4 Crown Terrace, West Town.
Albert Edwin Hopper (aged 46) at 6 Crown Terrace, West Town.

Writing in 1943 of his experience of this night, Mr. A. Simmons of St. Andrew's Road, Avonmouth, said:

'Though I have travelled all over the world during my seafaring career, and weathered many a storm, being torpedoed twice, under shell-fire from enemy submarines, suffered frost-bite due to exposure in open boats, yet I maintain that the blitz on Avonmouth 16/17 January 1941, was easily my biggest nightmare. During that blitz, my wife, married daughter and grandchild – a mere babe – were with me under the stairs. Outside it was as if brimstone and fire were falling from heaven. What touched me most was that the baby knew as if by instinct that something was wrong, and clutched my fore-finger each time a bomb fell. And there we stayed, huddled together under the stairs, as did thousands of others, expecting death or injury every moment, until the "all clear". I have since done a voyage to sea, and back again in convoy, without incident!'

Telephone communications with Avonmouth were cut off, and gas supplies were interrupted for several days. Indeed, Friday, 17 January 1941 was the blackest day in Avonmouth's history. It was also the only day during the entire war, that, due to enemy action, the Docks were prevented from working normally.

During this raid a bomb fell on the Theological College in Stoke Hill, Stoke Bishop, as did four more on the Downs. Ham Green Hospital was also damaged by fire.

Footnote:

The difficulties faced by visiting fire-fighters cannot be over emphasised. Besides the rigours of the black-out driving with masked headlights, and falling bombs, roads were very icy, without signposts, being in the main narrow and winding, without today's motorways. On reporting at Avonmouth assembly point, the visiting firemen were given guides to show them the way to the fires needing their attention.

An incident, of which I have been told, but so far have been unable to find official confirmation, concerns a fire-engine on its way to Avonmouth which over-turned on the Portway, killing two fireman. After the vehicle was righted, it continued on its journey to help deal with the Avonmouth fire.

Poole Street Incident

In Poole Street, Mr. W. Walker was in the garden with a neighbour after putting out incendiary bombs, when they heard a solitary 'plane overhead, which they thought was a British night-fighter, until they were aware of a bomb falling, which was probably a land-mine. Mr. Walker dived very quickly into his air raid shelter *(centre picture)* where his wife and three children were already taking cover. By a miracle, no lives were lost. The bomb landed in the street in front of No's 18, 20, 22 and 24 Poole Street, which were all destroyed by blast, leaving the Walker's bed *(left foreground)* hanging half in and half out of the bedroom wall!

After the site was cleared, it housed a large static water tank, until the war was over, when the four houses were rebuilt to their original design, and Mr. Walker returned to live out the rest of his life at No. 22, his original home.

98   POOLE STREET, AVONMOUTH. 16/17 January 1941. The scene after the land-mine explosion.

99　ST. ANDREW'S PARISH CHURCH, AVONMOUTH. The nave during Dedication
Service of new extensions, 30 November 1935.

100   ST. ANDREW'S PARISH CHURCH, AVONMOUTH. The morning after the blitz on
Avonmouth, 16/17 January 1941. (Same view as plate 99).

St. Andrew's Parish Church

At 2.40 a.m. it was reported that the Parish Church was on fire, which quickly reduced the building to a burnt-out shell. Avonmouth Church had stood only half built for some 40 years, not being completed until 1935, and only then mainly due to a very generous gift from Dame Violet Wills of £4,000 towards the £7,000 completion cost. Heart-breaking indeed for Parishioners to see their Church razed to the ground due to enemy action after only five years completion.

Some of the incendiary bombs that 'rained' on Avonmouth that night fell on the Church roof, too high to be extinguished, and in consequence set fire to the pitch-pine ceiling, and soon the entire building was ablaze. Amongst the possessions lost was the War Memorial to the Parish Dead of the Great War, a very fine organ, a valuable 'Breeches' Bible dated 1615 in a case of old oak wood taken from Bristol Cathedral which had been the gift of Mr. B. S. Lightfoot, and the prized Lectern Bible presented to St. Andrew's by King Edward VII to commemorate his visit to Avonmouth in July 1908 to open and name the Royal Edward Dock.

An eye-witness to the disaster was Mr. Fred Day, who says:

'I asked the fireman to let me into the Church to retrieve the "Breeches" Bible. "Give me three minutes", I begged. The organ was ablaze, the roof timbers falling, and the north wall with the Ten Commandments engraved on it was crumbling, and they would not let me in. I asked why water was not being used? to which the Fireman-in-Charge replied, "Look here, this place is only used one day out of seven – the Docks, warehouses, and factories take priority". It was a freezing cold night, and water was turning to ice.'

Only the Church Vestries and Tower escaped the flames, and fortunately for posterity the Church Records and most of the silver was rescued. Through all this St. Andrew's well-known Church clock never stopped!

During the same night, four homes were blitzed in Richmond Terrace, which caused a woman to come out into the street, shaking her fist at the German bombers, and shouting out, 'Yes, Hitler, you can bomb our people and our homes, but you can't bomb God!' How very true.

Because of censorship the loss of the Parish Church was not reported in the newspapers until some days later, and then referred to as 'Church in the Bristol area destroyed in a recent raid', unlike Christ Church at Pill which was destroyed by incendiaries during the same raid, and which was mentioned by name in the newspapers.

To many, 17 January 1941 must have seemed like the end of the world, especially to the Vicar of Avonmouth, Revd. R. W. Philipson, and Mr. Enos Lee, for so long the devoted Secretary of St. Andrew's Parochial Church Council. Together they had strived to complete the Church building, and now their work was tragically reduced to a heap of rubble and ashes. Mr. Lee died a matter of weeks afterwards on 5 May 1941, from what could only be imagined of a broken heart. Volunteers cleared the Church of debris, and his funeral service was held in the Church ruins. Mr. Philipson left Avonmouth the following year to become Vicar of Drayton in Somerset. (For restoration of St. Andrew's Church, see *Total Sum – Aftermath*.)

Footnote:

'Breeches' Bible is actually the Geneva Bible, which is a revision of great importance in the history of the English Bible. It was undertaken by English exiles at Geneva during the Marian persecution, and first published in 1560. In Genesis Chapter 3 verse 7 it reads 'breeches' instead of 'aprons'.

5 February 1941

A welcome Royal visitor to Avonmouth was the late Duke of Kent, in R.A.F. uniform, who arrived by car. After touring the Docks in company with the Lord Mayor of Bristol (Alderman T. H. J. Underdown), Chairman of the Docks Committee (Alderman A. W. S. Burgess) and the General Manager of the Docks (Mr. R. H. Jones), the Duke went on to tour the blitzed areas of the City.

101 H.R.H. DUKE OF KENT on 5 February 1941. After visiting Avonmouth Docks seen touring bomb-damaged areas of Bristol. *Left:* General Sir Hugh Elles, the S.W. Regional Controller.

On 25 August 1942 the Duke was killed on War Service, when a 'Sunderland' flying boat in which he was travelling to Iceland crashed on a lonely mountainside in Scotland. All occupants, except the rear-gunner, were killed.

22 February 1941

Today's air raid was the shortest, lasting a mere 13 minutes, and was the one which gave the folk of Avonmouth the most gratification.

Saturday afternoon was wet, blustery and overcast, when the 'alert' was given at 1.59 p.m. as a German Heinkel 111 from Dinard in Brittany approached Avonmouth from the sea. Almost immediately the A.A. guns at Portbury opened fire, and shot the aircraft down. The 'plane banked over Avonmouth spraying the Docks with machine-gun fire as it did so. There was a loud twanging noise as it struck one of the barrage balloon cables before it crashed into the mud in Kingroad at 2.12 p.m. The bomb-load was jettisoned into the Rivern Severn before the raider crashed.

An eye-witness to the drama said that when the A.A. guns opened up, the 'plane's engines appeared to falter. It began to circle with black smoke pouring from its engines and wings, and then nose-dived, hitting the mud with a tremendous crash, followed by an explosion. There was only one survivor from the crew of five, and he was the Pilot, who made a successful parachute descent, and was taken prisoner. The bodies of the Observer and the Flight Engineer were later recovered from the wreckage, and buried at Greenbank Cemetery in Bristol. The remains of the Wireless Operator and Air Gunner were never found.

The news that a German bomber had been shot down gave a significant boost to the morale of blitz-weary Bristolians, who applauded the extremely good shooting of the local A.A. gunners. The Unit to which this He.111 belonged was constantly in action over the Bristol area, from shortly after the fall of France until it was withdrawn from Brittany to participate in the attack on Russia in June 1941. It eventually transpired that the target for this lone bomber had been the aircraft works at Yate, and was the second time that a daylight raid on Yate had been attempted and failed.

Sequel:

About 20 years after the war was over, the farmer at the former Portbury gun site received a surprise visit by a German and his wife. It was Leutnant Berndt Rusche, the Pilot of the Heinkel He111, who brought his wife to show her where the guns had been that shot him down, and where he was brought when taken prisoner on that Saturday afternoon in 1941. He spoke perfect English, but his wife could only speak German.

102 WRECKAGE OF NAZI BOMBER. Remains of Heinkel 111 from Dinard, seen in mud at Kingroad, shot down at 14.12 hours on Saturday, 22 February 1941, by No. 2 A.A. Gun at Portbury.

103 LAST RESTING PLACE OF TWO GERMAN AIRMEN, Greenbank Cemetery, Bristol, killed when their Heinkel was shot down 22 February 1941. Four of crew of five lost their lives, one survived and was taken prisoner. Photo: April 1980.

27 February and 7 March 1941

In only five days, the enemy attempted yet a third daylight raid on Yate, and this time he was successful, with disastrous results. Parnall Aircraft Ltd's factory was high on the German target list, because of its important contribution to the British war effort. Captured documents clearly revealed this when the war was over, which subsequently came into the possession of Parnall's, including an Ordnance Survey map covering Yate, and an aerial photograph taken by a German reconnaissance aircraft on 29 August 1939, five days before war was declared!

At 2.30 p.m. on 27 February 1941 a single enemy aircraft, in broad daylight and unchallenged, passed over Charfield railway station, flying at such low altitude that the Swastika was plainly visible. The 'plane followed the railway line to Yate, with the undercarriage lowered to foil the defences, and to create the impression that it was a British aircraft about to land on Yate airfield. It shed its bomb-load of six H.E.'s and one oil bomb before anyone in the factory could take cover, and then it escaped into low lying cloud. The bombs were falling as the sirens sounded the 'alert'. The casualties might well have been higher had it not been for three H.E.'s not exploding, as there were around 4,000 workers in the factory at the time.

On 7 March another daylight raid on Parnall's by a single raider was pulled off, again causing extensive damage to the works and this time stopped all production. The Ministry of Aircraft Production then ordered total dispersal of the factory to Boulton Mills at Dursley, which was achieved in a week in a mammoth round-the-clock operation.

Altogether 52 workers lost their lives through these daylight raids on Yate.

13 March 1941

There was very little enemy air activity at night over Britain during the month of February and early March 1941, which it was generally concluded was due to the weather. However, night raids started once again in mid-March, and continued through April, some of which proved to be Bristol's heaviest raids of the war.

During this raid, shortly before 10.0 p.m., a shower of incendiaries fell on Avonmouth Docks and village. A few minor fires were started, but they were quickly brought under control. In Shirehampton about 50 houses were damaged.

14 March 1941

This week some notable successes were gained against German night raiders. Radar had played an important part in the Battle of Britain in plotting incoming bomber formations, and alerting A.A. defences and R.A.F. Headquarters. It was now also playing a vital part in helping British fighter pilots to 'see' in the dark. At the same time the British public were given to understand that pilots' better night vision was due to their eating large amounts of carrots!

Local people cheered when an enemy raider was brought down at Whitfield near Falfield during the night. The Heinkel 111 heading for Glasgow with a full bomb load, was intercepted by a Beaufighter somewhere in the neighbourhood of Codrington. A rattle of machine-gun fire was heard, followed by the engines of the bomber cutting out. Shortly afterwards a vivid flash was seen in the sky as the 'plane crashed to earth on fire.

All members of the crew were killed – the bombs scattered over the neighbouring fields. Following German raiders, seeing the fire, also dropped bombs, so that it was a tricky business for those who attempted to get near the crashed 'plane. There were no casualties to civilians, but of the Heinkel crew, one was thrown out of the 'plane and killed and the others were burnt in the wreckage. All four are buried at Greenbank Cemetery at Bristol.

16/17 March 1941. Bristol's Fifth Blitz

This mass attack was considered to be Bristol's heaviest raid of the war so far. Casualty figures were higher on this night than at any time during the war – 257 killed and 391 injured. German records state that 162 aircraft were over the target, Bristol/Avonmouth, dropping 166 tons of H.E.'s and 940 incendiary containers (33,840) bombs).

For eight hours showers of bombs were 'rained' on Bristol, with serious loss of life, and the firing and collapse of many houses. The high casualty list inflicted, was partly caused through a major incident at a shelter near St. Gabriel's Road, Easton, and a direct hit on the crypt of St. Barnabas Church, Ashley Road, Montpelier. Here scores of men, women and children were sheltering during this heavy raid, when a bomb crashed through the Church roof into the crypt killing 18 people outright, with 6 more dying in hospital. Although the Church was heavily damaged by blast, it was repaired and reopened on 12 June 1943.

Avonmouth's main incident was the burning of a cottage in Moorhouse Lane, about ¾ mile from the National Smelting Company. As the cottage blazed furiously, it offered an easy target for the enemy bombers. That they seized upon it could be judged by the fact that no fewer than 78 craters were afterwards found in the neighbourhood.

29/30 March 1941

An estimated fifty-five long-range bombers carried out a sharp but not long raid on Avonmouth. It lasted nearly 1¾ hours, during which time a number of fires were started in the Dock area, and three oil tanks belonging to the Anglo-American Oil Co. burnt furiously. Seeing that one tank contained 3,800 tons of Vaporising Oil, another 4,900 tons of Spirit and a third some 2,000 tons of Kerosene, it is not surprising that they were still burning the following day. Some of the pipe-lines were damaged, though not seriously, and efforts to save other tanks were successful. At the Shell-Mex & B.P. North Installation, the can filling shed was destroyed.

The only other fire of consequence was at the 'A' Wheat shed, which was being used as a locomotive repair shop. Most of the building, its machinery and contents were destroyed. Slight damage was done to the permanent way and trucks in the Dock Railway area, whilst at St. Andrew's Road Station one H.E. hit the platform. Vital installations however escaped serious damage.

The Germans officially claimed they had bombed Avonmouth with good effect, and issued the following communique:

'Berlin, Sunday
'Last night, strong German bomber formations attacked the industrial and harbour installations of Avonmouth on the Bristol Channel. This operation was carried out with great success. A number of small and large fires were caused.'

In Shirehampton bombs damaged the Emergency Mortuary at the National Schools in Station Road, where two men passing at the time were killed. The Temperance Hall (meeting place of the Salvation Army) and Mr. Arthur Neale's Ironmongery shop in Park Hill, besides the Greyhound Inn in Park Road were completely destroyed. The Police Station buildings and a number of houses were severely damaged. Of the six people killed in this raid, four (including one woman) belonged to H.M. Forces. Six others were badly injured and eleven less severely injured. Those killed were –

George Henry Upham (aged 42) and his wife, Evelyn Mary (aged 40), of Chelwood Road, Shirehampton, killed at Park Road.
Richard Charles Harris (aged 21), Ordinary Seaman, *H.M.S. Ariguani*.
W. T. Sparks (aged 34), Coder, *H.M.S. Caballa*.
R. W. Webster (aged 37), Sub-Lieut. *H.M.S. Ariguani*.
Edna Constance Webster (aged 30), of Normanton, Derbyshire.

The Greyhound Inn

The Greyhound Inn was a Shirehampton Public House of uncertain age, which stood in Park Road, quite near The Green. According to some folk with long memories, Park Road itself was at one time known locally as 'Scott's Lane' after Mr. Thomas Scott who was once the proprietor of the Greyhound. Mr. Scott left there in 1905, and was succeeded by Mr. Edward Grigg who stayed until 1909. Mr. Samuel Hill took over the Greyhound in 1909, and his wife Alice was the last in a long line of proprietors from 1931 until 1941.

Mrs. Hill and her daughter (now Mrs. Walter) had already closed the pub for the night, and taken shelter elsewhere when the bombs fell. In returning

104 THE GREYHOUND INN, Park Road, Shirehampton *c* 1935 where Mrs. Alice Hill was proprietor from 1931 to 1941.

105 THE GREYHOUND INN, Park Road, Shirehampton. All that remained after receiving a direct hit by a German bomb during the night raid of 29 March 1941.

106   SITE IN PARK ROAD, SHIREHAMPTON which formerly housed the Greyhound Inn, now replaced with lock-up garages. Same view as plate 104.   Photo: July 1988.

for a coat, Mrs. Walter heard the screeching of the bombs falling, and threw herself into the gutter, which miraculously saved her life. All that was left of the Greyhound was its smartly painted inn-sign swinging at the front gate, and a picture-frame hanging on the remains of a bedroom wall.

It was afterwards concluded that four of the people killed in this incident must have been sheltering in the inn porch. Neither the Temperance Hall, the Ironmongers shop nor the Greyhound Inn were ever rebuilt, and now one can only ask why not?

The derelict site once occupied by the Greyhound Inn, now houses seven lock-up garages.

April 1941

During this month three heavy raids were made in rapid succession – 3 April (four hours), 4 April (five hours) and on 11 April (Good Friday) when there was a dreadfully severe two phase attack, lasting many hours.

3/4 April 1941

German records confirm that the target for the raid, on this bright moonlight night, which lasted from 9.0 p.m. until 1.0 a.m., had been Bristol/Avonmouth. Seventy-six aircraft were reported over the target area dropping 80 tons of H.E. and 546 incendiary containers (19,656 bombs).

When the attack developed, it was on a line between the Horseshoe Bend and Filton. Avonmouth had a few scattered incidents, but at no time was the raid heavy. Avonmouth and Shirehampton were both hit by H.E.'s, and several vehicles of a Military Convoy on the Portway were damaged. Slight damage was done in the Docks area, and roughly 1,000 houses were damaged, but Utility Services were only moderately affected.

Total casualties for this raid numbered 22 killed, 56 injured and 34 slightly injured. Those killed included:

George William Pomphrey (aged 40) at Shirehampton Road.
Lilian Elizabeth Mountford (aged 40) at 514 Portway.
Rose Small (aged 71) at 514 Portway.

At Markham A.A. Battery a H.E. killed one soldier (Gunner Henry Edgar Hendy, aged 23) and injured seven others. Also killed, Private Henry James Chapman (aged 21) Royal Corps Signals of Shirehampton Transit Camp.

4/5 April 1941

It was soon apparent that Avonmouth was once again the target, when thousands of incendiaries were dropped over a wide area. Many hundreds burnt out harmlessly on high ground on the south side of the River Avon, whilst those that fell over Avonmouth and Shirehampton were dealt with quickly and effectively.

The whole of Bristol was illuminated by a large number of 'chandelier' flares, fifteen of which were counted in the sky at one time. Eight were seen over Avonmouth. Anti-Aircraft fire drove the raiders off their targets, with the result that damage to Docks, Railway property and Military objectives was kept to a minimum. The A.A. barrage, in fact, was considered the heaviest yet put up in Bristol.

The most serious effects at Avonmouth were felt by the National Smelting Works, where several departments suffered heavily enough to badly disrupt production, particularly the Fertiliser and Acid plants. At Shirehampton, a H.E. bomb which fell on the Portway near the Railway Station, broke the water mains, and water gushed forth and flowed down to the Lamplighters like a river.

Considering the scope of this raid and the number of H.E.'s dropped, casualties were small, i.e., 3 dead, 12 seriously hurt and 9 slightly injured.

It was officially reported that during this raid four enemy aircraft were destroyed – two accounted for by night-fighters, and two by A.A. guns. One of these, a Heinkel 111 from Le Bourget in France, whose target was Avonmouth Docks, was identified in the moonlight by a Beaufighter, who shot it down in flames. After jettisoning the bomb-load over the countryside, the Heinkel crashed at Reddings Farm, Hewish, near Weston-super-Mare, and of the five crew, two were killed, and three taken into custody after making parachute descents.

Footnote:

Shirehampton's water supply having been cut off by a bomb, the Parish's age-old springs and wells came into their own again. Householders were directed during this emergency to collect water from Bucklewell in Woodwell Road, and folk came from as far away as Dursley Road with their buckets. The pump at No. 2 Pembroke Road was also used as a water supply during the same emergency.

7/8 April 1941

Single raiders dropped H.E.'s and incendiaries in Shirehampton. Shirehampton Road and King's Weston Road were temporarily blocked.

9/10 April 1941 (Maundy Thursday)

Bombs were dropped on Avonmouth where the Cinema received a direct hit and was destroyed. Superficial damage was done to Messrs. R. Silcock's Mills, as well as to railway sidings on the Docks.

Avonmouth Picture House

Avonmouth Picture House stood at the corner of Collin's Street and Portview Road. In April 1912 a licence was granted to Mr. Gilbert Davies in the name of the 'Portview Picture Theatre', using premises formerly occupied by the Shire Avon Steam Laundry Company. The name became 'Avonmouth Picture House' in the early 1920's when Mr. W. J. Rolph took over as Manager, ably assisted by his wife.

The 'Bug-House', as the cinema was more readily called, is still affectionately remembered for the immense pleasure it afforded both young and old alike. Twice-weekly programmes were offered, besides a children's matinee on Saturday afternoons, otherwise known as the 'tuppenny rush'.

The joy of seeing such silent film stars as Elmo Lincoln and Pearl White in the early days, with the pianist playing her heart out, made twice-weekly visits to the Picture House a *must* for most families in the Parish. Standards in showing improved as the years went by, and 'talkies' were introduced. After the show there was always the fish-and-chip shop to visit, situated conveniently on the opposite corner of Collin's Street.

When Shirehampton's super-de-luxe cinema, The Savoy, opened in October 1933 it surprisingly had little effect on attendances at the Avonmouth Picture House, which continued happily under the Rolph's management until it disappeared entirely on receiving a direct hit by a bomb on Maunday Thursday, 10 April 1941. Hitler's bomb did what The Savoy

107 AVONMOUTH PICTURE HOUSE c 1920 with the projectionist, Mr. Harrison. The only photograph so far found to be in existence of Avonmouth's once so-popular cinema. Bombed 9/10 April 1941.

108 COLLIN'S STREET/PORTVIEW ROAD JUNCTION. Site of Avonmouth's former Picture House, which received a direct hit on 9/10 April 1941, and not replaced. Photo: August 1981.

failed to do in bringing down the final curtain at Avonmouth Picture House.

The site was subsequently cleared, and the adjacent buildings re-erected, but only the office block was replaced, and not the former Picture House.

11/12 April 1941 (Good Friday). Bristol's Sixth Blitz

This heavy two-scale raid, frequently talked about as 'The Good Friday Raid', was the sixth and final large scale attack on Bristol. The savagery of that night appeared to be all the more wanton because of the day upon which it was committed. The enemy claimed to have had 153 aircraft over the target, Bristol/Avonmouth, dropping 193 tons of H.E.'s and 969 incendiary containers (34,884 bombs), with the result that 180 people died, 146 were seriously wounded and 236 received slight injuries.

Incendiaries and H.E.'s were dropped by waves of 'planes after they had broken through a particularly heavy A.A. barrage shortly after 10 o'clock. Bombing continued for about 1¾ hours, then at seven minutes to midnight the sirens sounded the 'all clear'. Thirteen minutes later the enemy were overhead once more, and did not finally depart until 3.52 a.m. The second raid was by far the more serious, creating great havoc.

Bombs fell in and around Avonmouth Docks. A large bomb completely destroyed numbers 6 to 16 Richmond Terrace, Avonmouth, when Rosina May White (aged 33) and Patricia Orman (aged 9) both lost their lives. At Shirehampton a landmine fell in Priory Road, at the back of the houses and blew them into the street. Blast from this bomb blew a piano from a front room through a wall into a back room on the opposite side of the road, at the same time five persons were killed, i.e.,

> Frederick William Bishop (aged 70) at 43 Priory Road.
> Emily Fermandell (aged 30) at 43 Priory Road.
> William Arthur Fermandell (aged 4) at 43 Priory Road.
> Alice Rowles (aged 22) at 45 Priory Road.
> Private Albert Edward Fletcher (aged 24), R.A.M.C., at 47 Priory Road.

A Fireman was also killed during this raid, Archibald Charles Hancock (aged 30), A.F.S., at High Street, Shirehampton.

The Prime Minister, Winston Churchill, witnessed this raid, and gave his own account of it in his book 'The Second World War', as follows:–

> 'On 12 April 1941, as Chancellor of Bristol University, I conferred a number of Honorary Degrees. My wife came with me. Our train lay for the night in a siding in the open country, but we could see and hear the heavy air raid on the City of Bristol. We pulled into the station early in the morning, and went straight to our Hotel. There I met a number of dignitaries, and almost immediately started on a tour of the most stricken parts of the City. I spent an hour driving round the worst-hit places, and then repaired to the University. The bright academic robes of some of the principal actors did not conceal the soaked and grimy uniforms of their night's toil.'

Not a man to wear his heart on his sleeve, Mr. Churchill was seen more than once to have tears rolling down his cheeks, when some of the people who had lost everything ran to greet him. He grimly promised the enemy, 'We will give it them back', and gave a one sentence message to the people of Bristol, 'Carry on – all will be well'.

In his annual report on the Fabric and Furniture of St. Mary's Parish Church, Shirehampton, the Vicar, the Revd. C. W. Dixon, wrote of an extraordinary feat of bomb blast, as follows:–

'Mercifully this year there is no damage by enemy action to report. That this is so is nothing less than a miracle, for the parachute-mine which fell in Priory Road on the night of Good Friday, with such tragic results, might quite easily have shattered every pane of glass in the Church. We must count ourselves highly fortunate when we consider that the blast broke shop windows on both sides of the High Street, that our total damage was one small pane of glass cracked!'

As it well known, St. Mary's Church consists mainly of windows, and standing as it did between the explosion in Priory Road and the shops in High Street, it is quite remarkable to have survived with so slight damage as a cracked pane. St. Mary's escaped a similar fate to that of St. Andrew's Avonmouth and Christ Church Pill in being burnt down, when an incendiary bomb which penetrated the roof in the very early days of the blitzes, was seen by a passing soldier who broke into the Church and extinguished it. The scar made by the incendiary on the Church floor remained for many years as a thank-offering for the Church not having been burned down (see Plate 89).

7 May 1941

R.A.F. night fighters were now taking a toll on German bombers. On 4 May 1941, thirteen of the enemy 'planes fell to fighter aircraft, and three nights later a further 24 were destroyed, including a Heinkel He111 from Tours in France, whose target was Liverpool. The raider was shot down near Wrington by a Beaufighter, all five members of crew being taken prisoner. Four nights later, all records were broken when night fighters shot down a grand total of 33 bombers.

The increase in our night fighter 'kills' was largely due to 'Radiolocation', Britain's 'secret weapon', which had now reached such a state of perfection that raiding by night became a very risky business for enemy bombers.

The Last Blitz

Although generally reported as being the last blitz, the night of the full moon, 10 May 1941, was certainly a devastating and concentrated attack on London. Westminster Abbey, the British Museum, five hospitals, churches, business premises and other public buildings being either bombed or burnt out, and the Houses of Parliament were severely damaged. The Commons debating chamber was wrecked, which meant the Commons met the following morning in a building which had been held in readiness for such an emergency.

Definitely the last of the large-scale bombing on British towns ended with an attack on Birmingham on 16 May 1941. The blitzes had lasted only six months, but to we who had been on the receiving end, it had seemed like an *Eternity*.

31 May 1941

The Auxiliary Fire Service suffered casualties during this Whit-Saturday raid, which lasted from 0.15 a.m. until 3.30 a.m., when a bomb destroyed the A.F.S. Station in Westbury Lane, Sea Mills, near the Park Gates, and damaged about 40 houses. Two people were killed and 12 injured. One A.F.S. man lost his life and five were wounded. The fatal casualties were – William Ashley Rowe (aged 52) of Stoke Bishop (Chief Superintendent Engineer at Elders & Fyffes Avonmouth and a part-time Fireman) and Eleanor Mary Ray (aged 55) at 30 Elberton Road, Westbury Lane.

109   A.F.S. STATION at top of Westbury Lane, Sea Mills. One A.F.S. man was killed and five wounded when this Station near the Park Gates was hit during the air raid 31 May 1941.

22 June 1941

Hitler's pact with Russia had always been an uneasy one, when quite without warning the whole military might of Germany was hurled against Russia at dawn on 22 June 1941. Mr. Churchill immediately announced that Britain would give all possible aid to Russia, because he said, 'Any man or State who fights against Nazism will have our aid – any man or State who marches with Hitler is our foe'.

For the second time in their history the Russian peoples found themselves having to fight for their very existence. History had repeated itself, but whereas Napoleon went in search of gold, Hitler was in search of oil. Both Dictators found, to their cost, that the Russian winters, and the Russian scorched earth policies, were more than they had bargained for.

From June 1941, enemy air raids over this part of Britain, thankfully, became sporadic.

27 July 1941

When the new R.A.F. airfield at Broadfield Down was built during the Second World War (which is now Bristol's Lulsgate Airport), no-one in their wildest dreams could have envisaged that the first aircraft to use the new hard runways would be a German bomber!

It was a misty morning on 27 July 1941 when an unfamiliar-looking aeroplane circled over Lulsgate Bottom airfield, still under construction, and made a perfect landing. The time was 6.20 a.m. The 'plane then sped along the runway to the end where the men were at work, and had to pull up sharply before coming to grief on rough ground beyond the runway. It was, in fact, a Junkers 88 from Brest in France, returning from a bombing mission on Birkenhead Docks.

Keeping over the sea, the Junkers mistook the mouth of the Bristol Channel for that of the English Channel due to mist and bad navigation. Furthermore the 'plane had become a victim of a British 'secret' weapon, in that the Germans' 'beacon' had been put off 'beam' through interference by a transmitter at Lympsham near Weston-super-Mare.

The pilot of the Junkers got out, followed by his crew, and walked across to the workmen. 'What part of France is this?' he asked in French. The man laughed, 'This isn't France', he replied, 'You're in England'. The pilot whipped out a revolver to cover the retreat of his crew and himself back to the 'plane, and the story goes that an astute workman with great presence of mind, drove his mechanical digger into the path of the Junkers to prevent it from taking off. In the meantime, the Military attached to the airfield arrived with tommy-guns, and the four German aircrew were taken into custody.

The aircraft was a prized capture, and the face of the British Intelligence Officer was wreathed in smiles. It was a brand new Junkers 88, then an advanced type containing various latest ideas, which had fallen into our hands intact. The captured aircraft became EE205 with 1426 (E.A.C.) Flight at Duckford, and was scrapped in 1947.

April/May/June 1942 'Baedeker' Raids

On being given a taste of his own medicine, the enemy did not like it one little bit. Following raids by the R.A.F. on the Baltic ports of Lübeck and Rostock, an official spokesman in Berlin announced that as reprisal the Luftwaffe would bomb every English cathedral city marked with three stars in the German Baedeker guide-book. In attacking 'open' and undefended cities it was obvious the enemy intended to cause the greatest possible damage with the least cost to himself. It was no idle threat.

The first of the so-called 'Baedeker' raids took place on 24 April 1942, when the Luftwaffe attacked the historic City of Exeter, where considerable damage was inflicted on many ancient buildings, including the famous 12th century Cathedral. There quickly followed attacks on Bath *(25 and 26 April)*, Norwich *(27 and 29 April)*, York *(28 April)* and Canterbury *(31 May)*, besides Weston-super-Mare heavily blitzed *(28 and 29 June 1942)*. Numerous buildings and monuments of great historic value were blasted and/or demolished in all these raids.

Casualties at Bath were very heavy – the city was dive-bombed and machine-gunned, and with no previous experience of air-raids, the devastation caused was considerable, and the confusion very great. Between the night of the first blitz on Bath and 4 May, Bristol assisted her stricken neighbours by sending 34 rescue parties, besides numerous canteens and personnel to help with food and salvage, whilst the Bristol Corporation Housing Manager took over the work of housing repairs, etc.

Two months previously Bristol assisted with sending aid when Exeter was the victim of enemy attack, the same also applied when Weston-super-Mare was raided.

17 April 1942

Raiders dropped four bombs on Avonmouth. Two fell in the mud and a third demolished a building near the old Passenger Station at the Royal Edward Dock. The fourth bomb fell on the new oil-jetty under construction in the River Severn, near the North Pier of the Royal Edward Dock, causing some slight damage (see *Docks-ology–Petroleum*). There were two casualties, but only one was sent to hospital.

28 August 1942

On a sunny morning, flying at 20,000 feet above unsuspecting Bristol, a single Nazi fighter-bomber aimed a 500 lb. bomb at the heart of the City. It dropped in Broad Weir, near the junction of Philadelphia Street – the time

110 PASSENGER STATION, South Pier, Royal Edward Dock, Avonmouth. Opened 29 April 1910 by Lord Mayor, Mr. C. A. Hayes, to coincide with maiden voyage of passenger liners *Royal Edward* and *Royal George*. Bombed 17 April 1942 and not rebuilt.

was 9.20 a.m. at the rush hour. At such a great height, the 'plane was thought to be on reconnaissance, and the siren did not give the 'alert' until after the bomb had struck.

Three double-decker buses full of passengers were waiting at bus stops, with men, women and children going to work or school. The buses were set on fire instantaneously, and the casualties totalled 45 killed, 26 seriously injured and 30 slightly injured. This was the highest death-roll of any single Bristol incident. It was also the last bomb to fall on Bristol in 1942.

1943

There were no air-raids during 1943, although the enemy occasionally issued fantastic statements of the damage the Luftwaffe had done to Bristol.

On 29 August 1943 Fireman Frederick Alan Peters (aged 34), N.F.S. of Horfield, was drowned in the Royal Edward Dock at Avonmouth whilst dragging for a box lost overboard from a fire-boat earlier in the day.

15 May 1944

This is the last entry in the Official Record of the Battle of Bristol – the last scene in the last act which had lasted almost four years.

At this time Avonmouth Docks was crammed to capacity with war materials of all kinds in readiness for the D-Day landings planned for only

111 AVONMOUTH VILLAGE viewed from C.W.S. Flour Mills in July 1948, shows the Village after the Nazis had done their worst. *Left:* Bombed houses in St. Andrew's Road. *Centre:* Burnt out shell of St. Andrew's Church. *Right:* Bomb sites in Richmond Terrace and Richmond Villas. *Foreground:* Allotments.

three weeks hence. When the sirens sounded the 'alert' at 2 o'clock that morning, everyone was on tenterhooks. Perhaps Jerry himself had an inkling that 'something was up'. But thanks to the heavy barrage put up by the A.A. gunners (manned at that time by the Home Guard), the raiders were mainly beaten off.

Slight damage to property was caused when ten H.E. bombs fell in the Bristol operational area – three in Bedminster Division, five at Abbots Leigh and two in King's Weston Lane, where a serviceman was killed at a searchlight site. He was the only casualty in this the final raid on Bristol.

At seven minutes past 3.0 a.m. the 'all clear' was sounded. The German bombers had turned tail for home, and they never came back. Bristol's and Avonmouth's ordeal was over. *God be praised!*

XI. TOTAL SUM

The official details of Bristol's air raids were published for the first time in November 1944, when it was disclosed that the total number of 'warnings' had been 548, and that bombs were dropped on 76 occasions. Altogether 1,299 people had been killed in the City, and 3,305 were injured.

Over 3,000 houses were totally destroyed, and nearly 90,000 properties were damaged. Apart from London, only Liverpool published higher figures for casualties and property damaged. One effect of this not generally appreciated, is that Bristol lost between 10% and 11% of its rateable value. Repairing the City's public services proved a costly business – putting sewers in order again, repairing water mains, electricity and gas supplies, etc.

Bristol, known for centuries as the 'City of Churches', suffered grievously in the destruction of many of her historic places of worship. Sixteen Anglican Churches were completely destroyed, seven (including Bristol Cathedral) were severely damaged, and twenty-eight suffered from blast and/or fire. Additionally, fifteen Bristol Churches of other Denominations had been destroyed, and fourteen damaged.

After each raid the Army moved in to clear the streets and demolish dangerous buildings. On the humorous side, Bristol almost lost its leaning tower of Temple Church in Victoria Street, which Sappers thought was due to Nazi bombs, and they almost pulled it down. Just in time someone persuaded them it had leaned that way, five feet out of perpendicular, since the year 1460! The rubble from bomb sites was cleared away very quickly, in the public interest, and also to prevent the enemy in subsequent raids detecting the extent of havoc wrought by previous bombings.

Some of the rubble from demolished bombed Bristol buildings was taken by ship to New York as ballast, and formed the foundations of the East River Drive. A bronze plaque was unveiled there on 9 June 1942 with a glowing tribute to the people of Bristol – see plate 112. After research undertaken by Temple Local History Group, a replica plaque donated by B.B.C. Radio Bristol was unveiled at Broad Quay by the Lord Mayor of Bristol, Councillor Mrs. Joan Jones, on 16 July 1986.

It is quite amazing that after all these years unexploded German bombs are still found in the neighbourhood, as in the case of one in the playground of Shirehampton Infants' School in October 1966 dealt with by the Royal Engineers, and another recently discovered about a mile from the Severn Bridge in January 1988, which the Royal Navy blew up.

One wonders, fifty years on, exactly what Hitler had achieved by his indiscriminate bombing of homes, hospitals, schools and Churches, and by making thousands of civilians homeless, injured or bereaved? The answer is precisely . . . *NOTHING!* Long before embarking on the blitzes Hitler had decided not to invade Britain, so all that destruction had been wrought out of sheer spite. This only made the British people all the more determined to fight on regardless, until Hitler and his band of gangsters had been brought to Justice.

AFTERMATH

It was quite amazing how quickly the blackened bomb-sites became covered with wild flowers and herbs, bringing a message of hope in a world gone mad. The deciduous shrub, Buddleia davidii, not usually considered a 'wild' plant, with its long spikes of mauve flowers so beloved and attractive to butterflies and bees, positively thrived on the derelict sites. Reporting on this phenomenon, Frederick C. Jones (1892–1964), the well-known Bristol local historian wrote –

'In 1941 I tended a pigeon which had nested in St. Katherine's Chapel in St. Peter's Church, and fed a white dove which had built her home in the chimneypiece of the Abbots Lodgings. In 1942 the writer noticed at the south-east corner of High Street, pink antirrhinums in bloom. On the site of St. Clement's Chapel yellow flags grew out of the paving stones. St. Peter's churchyard was made gay by masses of rose-bay willow herb – four to five feet high – and six months later by a blaze of golden daffodils. A large altar-stone in St. Mary-le-Port churchyard was enveloped in pink balsam, whilst the ruined steps of the pulpit were covered in yellow snapdragon and foxgloves, above which hovered a bevy of butterflies. Elsewhere grew bracken, sallow willow, sowthistle, coltsfoot and ivy-leaved toadflax.

112 BRONZE PLAQUE. America Salutes Bristol. This plaque at East River Drive, City of New York, was unveiled in June 1942.

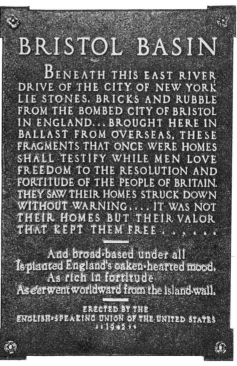

BRISTOL BASIN

BENEATH THIS EAST RIVER DRIVE OF THE CITY OF NEW YORK LIE STONES, BRICKS AND RUBBLE FROM THE BOMBED CITY OF BRISTOL IN ENGLAND... BROUGHT HERE IN BALLAST FROM OVERSEAS, THESE FRAGMENTS THAT ONCE WERE HOMES SHALL TESTIFY WHILE MEN LOVE FREEDOM TO THE RESOLUTION AND FORTITUDE OF THE PEOPLE OF BRITAIN. THEY SAW THEIR HOMES STRUCK DOWN WITHOUT WARNING.... IT WAS NOT THEIR HOMES BUT THEIR VALOR THAT KEPT THEM FREE......

And broad-based under all
Is planted England's oaken-hearted mood,
As rich in fortitude
As e'er went worldward from the island-wall.

ERECTED BY THE
ENGLISH-SPEAKING UNION OF THE UNITED STATES
·· 1942 ··

113 RICHMOND TERRACE BOMB-SITE, AVONMOUTH. Late 1940. Local children put the bomb-site to good use for their games of cricket. *Far right:* Kay Butcher.

Vegetable marrow flourished in Bridge Street in 1942, tomato plants in Victoria Street, barley and oats in the Centre, and broad beans on Bristol Bridge. In 1943, in turning the corner from Bath Street, the writer passed suddenly into what seemed to be a thick white mist, but which proved to be thistledown. In 1946 the west entrance of St. Peter's Church was completely obscured by bushes, while the site of the altar and chancel was covered by trees.'

Strange as it seems, that Buddleia having thrived so well during the war, is now considered by some itself a destroyer and a pest, through causing damage to old buildings.

Top priority was given after the war to rebuilding homes destroyed, which were constructed to their original design, so that Avonmouth no longer carries any scars of war. It is now impossible to detect which houses were rebuilt. The main exception to this are the sites in Richmond Terrace and Richmond Villas, on which Bristol Corporation have substituted flats for elderly people in place of the houses lost.

Some homes in Avonmouth, however, were never rebuilt. This applies to those lost at West Town, where the land was taken over by the Port of Bristol Authority, and that district now finds itself beneath the M.5 Motorway Avonmouth Bridge. The West Town Mission Chapel, opened in 1885, is not remembered after the great blitz of 16/17 January 1941, and it is presumed it was lost then also. Two other Avonmouth prominent pre-war buildings not replaced were, Avonmouth's Picture House, which stood at the corner of Collin's Street and Portview Road, and Avonmouth's Library near Gloucester Road Dock Gate, opened originally in 1896. The Library was not replaced until a classroom in Avonmouth National School was fitted out as a Lending Library, and opened in October 1973. Two buildings on the Docks which were bombed and not replaced, were the old Passenger Station at the entrance locks to the Royal Edward Dock, and the Workmen's Shelter at the Gloucester Road Dock Gates. In Shirehampton the Greyhound Inn and the Temperance Hall were not rebuilt.

It was some years before materials were available for the rebuilding of Churches, but St. Andrew's Avonmouth was fortunate in being allowed to be partially repaired, and was reconsecrated for worship in 1942.

Resurrection of St. Andrew's, Avonmouth

After the loss of the Parish Church, gutted in January 1941, services continued to be held at the Missions to Seamen Chapel in Portview Road, until that too was blitzed a few months later during the Good Friday raid. Services were then held in the Social Centre, adjacent to the Church.

In 1942 St. Andrew's was destined to become the first war-damaged church in Bristol to be partially repaired and restored, and Mr. P. Hartland-Thomas (who had been the architect for the completion of the church in 1935)

114 ST. ANDREW'S CHURCH, AVONMOUTH. Members making the restored Church 'Ship-Shape and Bristol Fashion' for the re-Dedication Service and Induction of the Revd. G. C. Lake as fifth Vicar of Avonmouth, 19 June 1942.

115 ST. ANDREW'S PARISH CHURCH, AVONMOUTH as it was from June 1942 until rebuilt under the War Damage Commission, and re-Consecrated 29 November 1957.

had the unusual distinction of designing and building the same church twice in seven years.

The arches separating the south-aisle from the nave were bricked in, and the south aisle (being the least damaged portion) was roofed over to provide a chancel and sanctuary on the site of the former Lady Chapel. The war-time girders used for the roofing still remain to this day, having been retained in the permanent church. All the fittings and furniture for the repaired St. Andrew's were collected from other bombed Bristol Churches, principally that of the blitzed and closed church of St. Raphael's in Cumberland Road.

The restoration work took six months to complete, and the temporary St. Andrew's was re-Dedicated by the Bishop of Bristol, the Rt. Revd. C. S. Woodward, on 19 June 1942. At the same service the Revd. G. C. Lake was inducted fifth Vicar of Avonmouth. Happily, therefore, Avonmouth Parish Church was the scene of the memorable services held later during the war, on the occasions of the National Days of Prayer, and services of Thanksgiving for Peace in 1945. The temporary building sufficed for the next sixteen years until materials for building Churches were again made available.

St. Andrew's was re-designed and re-built in 1957 under the War Damage Commission at a cost of £32,000. The Architect this time was Mr. F. L. Hannam, who kept the main aisle on the site of the former Lady Chapel. This accounts for Avonmouth Church having 'turned about' in its history, making a smaller church seating only 200 instead of 600 formerly, but providing a church more convenient for present-day requirements. Some of the fittings taken from St. Raphael's Church, which had originally been intended as a Sailors Church, were incorporated in the permanent St. Andrew's, so that appropriately the pulpit, font and clergy stalls from that church with their seafarers motifs should now find a permanent home in Avonmouth.

The 'modern' St. Andrew's was re-Consecrated (for the fourth time in its history) on St. Andrew's Eve 29 November 1957 by the Bishop of Malmesbury, the Rt. Revd. E. J. K. Roberts.

Footnote:

The Church of St. Raphael the Archangel, Cumberland Road, Bristol, was erected in 1859, at the expense of the Revd. Robert H. Miles (Rector of Bingham, Nottingham, fourth son of Mr. P. J. Miles of Leigh Court) and together with almshouses adjoining, was endowed for 'decayed' sailors belonging to the sea-port of Bristol. It was known as the Seamen's College, and the total cost was £10,000.

The church had a chequered existence. In consequence of the 'high church' ritual of the Revd. A. H. Ward, the Bishop of Bristol, Rt. Revd. C. J. Ellicott, withdrew his licence in 1878 for divine services, and the church, which was unconsecrated, was closed for several years. In 1893 the founder abandoned his design of connecting the church with the almshouses and it was then converted into the Parish Church of a new District, whereupon it was Consecrated by the Bishop on 30 May 1893, and Mr. Ward became the first Vicar.

After one of the blitz's St. Raphael's was closed, and the Vicar transferred to St. Simon. In 1946 it was declared redundant, demolished and entirely removed. At the time of writing, the site is being developed with luxury apartments, and only the east wall of the former church now remains as witness to the once Seamen's College.

XII. DOCKS-OLOGY

As one of the main terminals of the Atlantic Life-line, Avonmouth was destined to become one of the busiest ports in Britain during the Second World War, handling what has been estimated as some 42 million tons of goods. Thousands of ships bringing vital supplies of food and raw materials for Britain, poured into Avonmouth Docks. When the convoys put into port it was not uncommon to see ships berthed *three* deep around the wharves. At the same time, troops and supplies sailed from Avonmouth to the B.E.F. in France, around Africa to the Western Desert Forces and to the Mediterranean.

Proposals to extend the Eastern Arm of the Royal Edward Dock by 1,100 feet, together with additional constructions, had been sanctioned in September 1938, at a cost of £642,700. Work had already begun on this project when war was declared, and in consequence the work was hurried forward. By 1941 four additional deep water berths, a new wharf at the Oil Basin, and other improvements were operational.

After the fall of France, when Britain's ports on her south and east coasts became virtually paralysed, the diversion of shipping to the West Coast ports brought heavy responsibilities to Avonmouth. Railway trucks, barges and other equipment was sent to Avonmouth from that area, and large numbers of London Dockers also arrived.

'The Dockers job is just as important to the War Effort as if they were in the trenches firing machine-guns', declared Ernest Bevin, the Minister of Labour & National Service. Mr. Bevin took office in May 1940 when the war was going very badly for Britain. He lost no time in bringing in new emergency measures to meet the National crisis situation. By placing Dockers under a new control this ensured that ships would be discharged with the utmost rapidity, that goods were cleared through the ports with greatest possible expedition, and that men could be transferred from one port to another as and when required. Both ships and labour became *pooled* under the direction of the Ministry of War Transport.

116 SELF-PROPELLED U.S. 105 mm GUN being unloaded by floating crane at Avonmouth (Old) Dock ex *Amelia Earhart (7,176 g.r.t.)* 7 January 1944.

117 W.V.S. MOBILE CANTEEN serving hot drinks and snacks etc. to Dockers at 'O' Shed, Royal Edward Dock, Avonmouth in August 1944.

The co-operation which existed between the various Port Authorities and organised labour in those critical years could not have been better. The Avonmouth Dockers worked 12½-hour shifts (8.0 a.m. – 8.30 p.m.) Mondays to Fridays inclusive, and handled more tonnage in one shift than most other ports working two 8-hour sessions. In theory work stopped at 12 noon on Saturdays and 5.0 p.m. on Sundays, but it often continued without respite. Weekends were frequently the busiest times for stevedores, when ships were required to be discharged or loaded to fit in with convoy schedules on Monday mornings. The Dockers work did not go unnoticed. In 1942 Lord Leathers, the then Minister of War Transport, telegraphed 'Heartiest congratulations to all concerned in discharge of *Port Melbourne*'. The Blue Star Line quoted the unloading of *Canadian Star* as an example to all other ports, and later, Major R. Hannevig of the U.S. Transportation Corps wrote to express his appreciation of the work done on *Midnight* in 1944. These are only three typical examples of many other messages received.

Several Dockers continued working long past the time when men are considered able to perform such heavy work. Two such were Mr. J. Pring, who continued working until aged 89, and Mr. E. Hartney aged 86.

The work of the W.V.S. mobile canteens were what Dockers best remembered of the war years, serving them throughout winter and summer months alike with refreshments alongside the ships working to ensure the minimum loss of working time. At the close of the war the W.V.S. Dock Canteen service had made a handsome profit of £3,750 – half of which went to the Dockers Benevolent Fund, and the remainder shared amongst charities nominated by the W.V.S. So large a profit, despite the low charges, gives some idea of the tens of thousands of snacks served.

The large influx of dock workers from London and other ports created problems when it came to transport. Very long queues, sometimes four deep formed beside Avonmouth Park at 5.0 p.m. waiting for buses. Special bus services, and also extra trains became necessary, most having *standing room* only. For the first time in history a new innovation was practised with bus conductors collecting fares on the roadside at peak hours.

Mr. Arthur E. Waters, Chief Superintendent at the stevedoring firm of C. J. King & Sons Ltd. Avonmouth, was awarded the British Empire Medal for his services at Avonmouth Docks during the Second World War. Familiarly known as 'Johnny-All-Night' indicates the kind of working hours he imposed on himself and the dockers in getting ships turned round as quickly as possible during those critical war years. The British Empire Medal was also awarded in King George VI's Birthday Honours list in 1944 to Reginald Leslie Fenton, Chief Mechanical Foreman at Avonmouth Docks. These are only two of a number of awards received by members of Avonmouth Docks workforce in recognition of wartime services.

BUILD-UP TO D-DAY

Since the evacuation from Dunkirk, Britain's ultimate aim was to get back across the Channel and drive the enemy out of France and the Low Countries. The building-up of the necessary troops and equipment for such a great onslaught took four years.

In 1942 the American Forces arrived, and considered the enormous tonnage required to equip the Forces for an invasion of Europe, which seemed a hopeless task. But when the Americans put the problem to the Bristol work-force, they replied, 'Let's have a try – we think it can be done'. The U.S. made Avonmouth their main depot in the west for importing war supplies, and subsequently many thousands of G.I.'s passed through the port.

Three tank-engines, each weighing just over 46-tons, were sent on loan to the Port of Bristol Authority from the United States, to assist with shunting operations on the Docks. Coloured and white G.I.'s (although segregated in their own army) worked side by side with Avonmouth Dockers whose other task was to instruct their Allies in the specialised business of stevedoring. Later it was reported that Avonmouth-trained Americans had acquitted themselves well on the African Coast and elsewhere.

Many peculiar looking vessels began to appear. For example, parent-ships for landing-craft, cross Channel steamers adapted to land infantry, train-ferry boats which had brought U.S. tanks across the Atlantic, besides landing-craft and novel ships from the Great Lakes. Strange American Army vehicles came too, such as Duck amphibious transports (DUKW), White half-tracks and ubiquitous Jeeps, never before seen in this Country.

Every possible space on ships was utilised. Besides aircraft packed in crates and stowed in ship's holds, many more came across the Atlantic loaded on the decks of oil-tankers. These were landed on the wharves on their wheels, and towed away on Sundays, when necessary sections of the roads were closed to traffic. (St. Andrew's Dock Gate and the railway level-crossings had to be specially widened for this purpose.) After being towed to Filton they were cleaned up, fitted with engines, then taken into the countryside in the area around Westonbirt, and parked under the trees until they were required for service. The section of Filton Airfield where these U.S. aeroplanes were dealt with is still known today as the 'American' section.

Avonmouth and surrounding district was chock-a-block with war machinery of all kinds during the build-up to D-Day, which had over-flowed from the Docks. It was a common sight to find aeroplanes, tanks, Jeeps. lorries, etc., parked on *both* sides of the Portway. Other road-users on these occasions had no alternative but to ride in the middle of the road. Messrs. T. J. Wise & Co. Ltd. Shipping Butchers (one of the two Bristol slaughterers

118 U.S. LOCOMOTIVES at Avonmouth 24 March 1944. Off-loaded to barges prior to being unloaded elsewhere in the Dock, making for quicker turn-round time.

119 U.S. 0–6–0 TANK ENGINE 30 August 1944. One of the three tank-engines each weighing over 46 tons sent on loan from America to the Port of Bristol Authority, during shunting operations.

120   OIL TANKER at Royal Edward Dock, Avonmouth 15 February 1944 having arrived with Republic P.47 ('D' version) Thunderbolt Fighter 'planes stowed on her decks.

121   U.S. ARMY TANKS stowed in ship's hold newly arrived at Avonmouth Docks ready for discharge. 16 November 1943.

given Ministry meat contracts during the war) had their Avonmouth cold stores housing a strange cargo in 1944 when hiding landing-craft due to take part in the D-Day landings.

For security reasons, all movements of troops and Military equipment took place under cover of darkness. Even so, before the Normandy Invasion the Germans themselves told us of large concentrations of landing-craft assembled in Bristol's port, and on D-Day they named Avonmouth a springboard of the invasion. How right they were.

On 21 June 1946, Lieutenant-General John C. H. Lee, who had been the brains behind the movement and supplies of the U.S. Invasion Forces, returned to Bristol to receive an Honorary Degree at the hands of the Chancellor of Bristol University, Mr. Winston Churchill. That same evening Lt-Gen. Lee came to Avonmouth especially to convey a personal message of thanks to Dockers and other members of the Avonmouth workforce from General Eisenhower. He assured everyone of General Eisenhower's lasting gratitude for the great contribution Avonmouth had made to Victory.

122 LT-GENERAL JOHN C. H. LEE at P.B.A. Canteen, Avonmouth. 21 June 1946. Conveying to dock workers General Eisenhower's personal thanks for their magnificent service and contribution to Victory. *Right:* Mr. J. Pring, aged 89 and still working. *Left:* Mr. E. Hartney, aged 86.

PETROLEUM

'An army marches on its stomach', said Napoleon, which was undoubtedly true in the 19th century, but in the 20th century, armies primarily marched on their jerricans of petrol. Avonmouth played a major part in the War Effort in supplying vast quantities of petrol consumed by our mechanised Forces.

In August and September 1943, when the R.A.F. bombing offensive had reached new heights (and before the oil pipelines came into use), no less than 200 special trains, conveying well over 20,000,000 gallons of fuel were run weekly over the L.M.S. Railway system. This was largely a haulage from ports in the west to aerodromes in the east – from the Mersey (Liverpool) and the Severn (Avonmouth) to bomber bases in Lincoln and East Anglia. Each time the R.A.F. raided the enemy on the Continent, several trainloads of petrol were sent off to air bases to replenish depleted stocks.

The Petroleum Industry first established itself in Avonmouth in 1889, when a bulk oil installation belonging to the Anglo-American Oil Company was opened at Broad Pill, in what is now Avonmouth (Old) Dock, with an oil-jetty out into the River Avon (the scene of several shipping collisions in the river). In 1921 the Western Arm Extension to the Royal Edward Dock was completed, and this became the present Oil Basin. Further berths were added during the 1930's.

The war was only three weeks old when on 29 September 1939 all the Oil Companies, i.e. Anglo-American Oil Co., National Benzole Co., Shell Mex & B.P., Trinidad Leaseholds Ltd. with their associated companies voluntarily amalgamated to form the Petroleum Board, and for the duration of the war they pooled their resources of men and equipment. The various brand names of petrol gave way to one grade only called 'Pool'.

A large Canning Factory was opened at Holesmouth, to the north of Avonmouth, where thousands of tons of petrol were filled into five-gallon cans. This not only made for easier storage, but also enabled the Forces to carry their supplies of petrol with them. The majority of the work-force employed at the Canning Factory during the war was made up of women.

Special pipelines were laid down, so that petrol could be quickly distributed from Avonmouth to London and other places, and this great undertaking was carried out so quietly that few people realised what was happening. Three extra berths in the Royal Edward Dock were adapted for the use of oil-tankers, and when importation was at its greatest, an average of no less than 91,000 barrels a day was handled. Subsequently Avonmouth became linked directly with Berlin through P.L.U.T.O. (Pipeline Under the Ocean).

In 1944 four and three quarter million tons of oil was handled by

123 UNITED STATES *Stephen W. Kearney* (7,176 g.r.t.) at 'T' Shed, Royal Edward Dock, Avonmouth 4 January 1945. Five-gallon cans of petrol stowed in ship's hold for shipment to the Armed Forces.

124 JERRICANS. Somewhere in England, L.M.S. women porters transferring petrol cans from lorry to rail trucks – perhaps being returned to Avonmouth Canning Factory for refilling.

Avonmouth. Never before had any port in the United Kingdom handled so much oil in a period of twelve months. This record achievement was recognised when a telegram of congratulations and thanks from Downing Street was received by the Oil Companies at Avonmouth. A writer in the Petroleum Times of 11 October 1947, spoke of this work as 'a stupendous effort, reflecting the highest credit on all concerned'.

Insomuch as every gallon of petrol for Britain and her Fighting Forces in those days had to be shipped from America across the U-boat infested Atlantic, it is not surprising that petrol rationing was introduced almost at once, and commenced 16 September 1939. At first private motorists were allowed five gallons per month to drive about 150 miles.

To lessen the demand for travelling, 'Holidays at Home' became the order of the day, and bicycles came into their own. Hitch-hiking, not previously practised in pre-war days, now became common, especially by members of the Forces. The petrol ration was gradually reduced in stages, until June 1942, when, not before time, it was abolished altogether to private users.

Commercial petrol, which was dyed red, was issued to farmers and others for essential work, which soon became available on the black market. The Police became very vigilant about the misuse of Commercial petrol, and if traces of red were found in the engine of a non-commercial vehicle, the owner was fined heavily, or even given a jail sentence, as in the case of the famous actor, Ivor Novello.

By the end of 1942 the vast majority of private cars had been laid up for the duration. A wartime story, which is still related with humour and affection, concerns Mr. R. E. Hadlow, the Manager of one of Avonmouth's Oil Installations, who took to riding a horse to work. Strange as it seems, Mr. Hadlow was surrounded all day and every day by thousands of tons of petrol, yet could not use one single drop himself. Interestingly enough, on 23 May 1940 the price of petrol was raised to 1/11½d per gallon retail (predecimal coinage) representing about 9p per gallon today's prices.

Petrol rationing was ended on 26 May 1950, but was re-introduced for six months in 1956, due to the Suez Crisis. Branded petrol became available again from 1 February 1953.

The Tidal Oil-Jetty

In the event of the entrance to the Royal Edward Dock at Avonmouth being so damaged by enemy action as to prevent oil-tankers from bringing their precious cargoes into the Oil Basin, a precautionary measure was taken by building a tidal oil-jetty on the foreshore of the River Severn upstream of the North Pier.

125 TIDAL OIL-JETTY. Upstream of North Pier, Royal Edward Dock, Avonmouth. Photo: 3 September 1978.

126 U.S. OIL-TANKER *Amtank* (14,209 g.r.t.). Reputedly the World's largest all-welded tanker at that time, arriving at Avonmouth Oil Jetty. 19 July 1945.

Recommendations to build the jetty, which was designed by Oleg Kerensky, were first made in 1939, but it was not until 1943 that it became operational. Strange to relate, the entrance to the R. E. Dock escaped enemy damage, whereas the jetty received a direct hit by a bomb on 17 April 1942. In consequence a section of the jetty had to be rebuilt, and this delayed somewhat the completion of it. The cost to build the oil-jetty was £354,000, towards which the Government made a 75% grant, and assumed overall control.

The oil-tankers berthed at six buoys which were 70 feet from the jetty-head, and discharged their cargoes by flexible hoses held in position by a crane, connected in turn to the fixed pipeline on the jetty itself. The first ship to use the jetty was the *s.s. Pan Maryland* on 23 May 1943. In all, seventeen ships used the tidal jetty, including the *s.s. Amtank* in July 1945, which was reported as being the world's largest all welded tanker.

Unfortunately, the oil-jetty was not an easy place for ships to manoeuvre, and it became the cause of many collisions. After the war, the jetty fell into disuse, and the remains of it have now become a sanctuary for wild birds.

Footnote:

Doctor Oleg Kerensky, O.B.E., was son of Alexander Kerensky, Russia's last Prime Minister before the Revolution in October 1917. He joined Freeman Fox & Partners, and became largely responsible for designing the Severn Bridge, and many other important British bridges, besides the Ganga Bridge in India. He died in June 1984, aged 79.

Pan Massachusetts

Oil-tankers were priority targets for Hitler's U-boats because of their special importance to the War Effort, and the numbers of Allied tankers sent to the bottom, alas, with many of their crews, was astronomical. In many theatres of action, the availability of oil, or lack of it, had an underlying effect on events as Rommel found to his cost in the North Africa campaign.

To make good the heavy tanker losses being inflicted on Allied fleets, the United States embarked on a high speed building programme, using the revolutionary welding methods in place of the usual riveting method in building ships. The Americans began to build tankers at amazing speeds, and women found themselves welding alongside the men. In some cases ships were completed in only fifty days, but *Phoenix*, at that time said to be the world's largest tanker, took a little longer – 103 days. About 500 standard-type tankers were made, of which there were several variations, but all had a dead weight of about 16,400 tons, and most were capable of a speed of around

15 knots. In addition to their full cargo of oil, they were fitted with spar decks to carry deck cargoes, such as aeroplanes, assault craft and aircraft machinery parts, etc.

The American *Pan Massachusetts* (11,015 g.r.t.) was built in 1943 by the Welding Shipyards Inc., Norfolk, Virginia, for owners National Bulk Carriers Inc. She was electrically welded, and fitted to carry petroleum in bulk. No doubt this ship bore an unlucky name, replacing as she did an earlier riveted *Pan Massachusetts* sunk by U-128 just off the Florida coast on 19 February 1942, and was explosion prone throughout her life.

On Thursday, 25 May 1944, *Pan Massachusetts* was lying at 'X' berth, West Wharf in the Royal Edward Dock at Avonmouth, when she was the cause of the only disaster which took place here during the build-up to D-Day, when the port was going through its most hectic times. 'Remember the *Pan Massachusetts*?' . . . 'Yes, not 'arf, her decks opened up like an orange', explained one of those who worked on the Docks at the time. 'Her decks were prised open just like a tin of sardines having been opened by a tin-opener', described another. It is in this manner that local folk who worked on Avonmouth Docks during the war thereafter recalled the visit of *Pan Massachusetts*.

The time was about 4.30 p.m., and I recall we typists were preparing to finish for the day, when we heard a terrific explosion, which shook the office building like an earthquake, and immediately we saw clouds and clouds of

127 U.S. OIL-TANKER *Pan Massachusetts* (11,015 g.r.t.). An explosion whilst discharging at West Wharf, R.E. Dock, Avonmouth 25 May 1944, was the only disaster to befall Avonmouth during build-up to D-Day.

thick black smoke billowing into the sky. Very soon we heard the noise of fire-engines as they raced to the scene. A note in my diary records the event as, 'Saw a fire on the Docks – probably a tanker'. For security reasons the incident was not talked about and it was hushed up so we had to wait until the war was over to learn the full facts of the explosion, published as under.

It transpired that the *Pan Massachusetts* had discharged about half her cargo of 16,600 tons petrol, when, due to a concentration of petrol vapour, an explosion occurred in her pump-room killing three crew members. The force of the explosion ripped open a large section of her decks, and the ship was immediately set on fire. Flames spread to her magazine, and several cases of small arms ammunition exploded, but fortunately before the fire reached the larger ammunition, four N.F.S. fire-boats arrived on the scene and flooded the magazine. The fire-boats were the only means by which foam and water could be directed on to the blazing tanker from the port side, and in this position they were exposed to extreme danger. Special appliances were rushed to Avonmouth from as far away as Taunton and Swindon, and in about two hours the fire was brought under control. Two fire-boats and ten pumps poured three million gallons of foam in eight hours of the most strenuous fire-fighting imaginable before the fire was extinguished. But by the following morning the fire was completely extinguished, and so much water had been pumped into the ship, that she settled on an even keel and rested on the bottom of the Dock.

An eye-witness to the disaster was the late Mr. Harper Brayley, who recalling his experiences some 30 years after the event, wrote:

'I was asked to go aboard the American Oil-tanker *Pan Massachusetts* to deliver fresh water, and as soon as I got aboard I knew that there was something wrong. The Chief Engineer came up to me and said, "For goodness sake fill up the cofferdam first," meaning the tank between the engine-room and the ship's cargo tank, but it was too late to save the ship and she blew up. At the time Mr. C. Mathison, the man who was working with me, was standing on deck at the top of the gangway, talking to the watchman, and the force of the explosion blew them both off the deck, and landed them on the quay wall. The remarkable thing was that neither suffered broken bones.'

For a time there was the possibility that petrol spillage might spread over the water and ignite, endangering other vessels which also carried combustible materials in nearby berths. A floating boom was placed across the Docks as a precautionary measure, which prevented this from happening. Only slight damage was caused to the Dock itself, and it was not long before the *Pan Massachusetts* was refloated and taken across to Barry for repairs. Due to the danger of petrol fumes, work in nearby railway sidings and wharves was suspended for some days, and three berths were immobilised for about six weeks. The thing about this disaster was that it happened to be an accident, and was in no way the result of enemy action.

The greatest oil blaze during the whole of the blitzes on Britain, occurred on 19 August 1940, when an air attack was made on the Royal Navy oil depot at Pembroke Dock. The fire burned for seventeen days – the longest fire ever recorded in Britain. It is fitting to mention this disaster because over 100 local firemen defied immense dangers to help fight the blaze there, and thirteen of them were injured by a bomb which hit a building in which they were sheltering. Seven members of the Police, Fire Brigade, and the A.F.S., subsequently received George Medals for their gallantry – the Awards being amongst the first in the Country. When the Avonmouth tug *John King* (Captain William Bevan) returned from helping at the Pembroke Dock fire, her decks were found to be riddled with bullet holes, the tug having been the target of a Nazi bomber.

Footnote:

In June 1953 *Pan Massachusetts* was curiously enough in collision with a tanker named *Phoenix* in the Delaware River. Both ships caught fire, and explosions ripped both. *Phoenix* was run aground, and declared a total loss and broken up. The fire on *Pan Massachusetts* was extinguished, and she was beached, but refloated and later sent to Japan for rebuilding. She was lengthened and then sailed under several Companies, flags and names, going eventually for scrap in 1968 at Hong Kong. Whilst being broken up, an explosion occurred in some of her tanks still with oil in them, ripping open her shell plating for about 100 feet, and also setting on fire another tanker lying alongside. So unfortunate *Pan Massachusetts* was explosion-prone right to the very end.

SPLENDID SHIPS

As Bristol's Whitchurch Airport was a vital link in the Allied war set-up, so was the Port of Bristol, which includes Avonmouth and Portishead. Avonmouth, being the largest of the Bristol Docks complex, shouldered the lion's share of the thousands of ships which brought in vital cargoes, as rail transport and road convoys bore witness. The largest ship to enter the port was the *Orion* (23,371 g.r.t.) and ships between 10,000 and 20,000 g.r.t. were common. Furthermore, numerous men-o'-war were refitted in the Docks, and many others were built in the City's shipyards.

In the past, Bristol's shipbuilding traditions earned worldwide renown, and the corvettes, frigates, etc., which came from Bristol's shipyards during the war, maintained that fine tradition. The Albion Dockyard of Messrs. Charles Hill & Sons at Bristol, despite suffering heavy bombing during the blitzes, turned out during the six war years no fewer than eight *Flower* class corvettes, two boom defence vessels, seven *River* class frigates, one tank-loading craft, three *Loch* class frigates, three *Bay* class frigates and thirteen mechanised landing-craft, all constructed for the British Admiralty, together with six *Bird* class barges for the Ministry of War Transport. The *Loch* class frigate *H.M.S. Loch Scavaig* was graciously launched by Her Majesty Queen Mary, at the Albion Dockyard on 9 September 1944.

At Avonmouth the drydock facilities were in continuous use, day and night working throughout the war, and the ship repairing establishments of J. Jefferies & Sons and Mountstuart Ltd., with their workshops alongside the Port Authority's graving dock were kept flat out dealing with the flood of ship conversions, including arming of merchant ships, refits and making good repairs to war-damaged vessels.

At sea, mines were an ever-present menace, and the Bristol Channel was no exception. Many times Avonmouth tugs went to the aid of ships which had fallen victim of mines. On 17 January 1941 the tug *Bristolian* (Captain Bevan) with the *Merrimac* (Captain Trott) assisted the mined tanker *Athelduke* (8,966 g.r.t.) and brought her safely into Avonmouth. (The *Athelduke* was later torpedoed by a submarine 16 April 1945 and sunk.) On 28 January 1941 the *s.s. Tafelberg* (13,640 g.r.t.) was blown up within earshot of Captain Bevan on passage to Barry in the tug *Bristolian.* He immediately went to her aid, and helped beach her. (The *Tafelberg* was reconstructed as an oil-tanker and renamed *Empire Heritage,* only to be sunk by a torpedo from a submarine 8 September 1944.) The *Jamaica Planter* and the Belgian *Henri Jaspar* were two other war casualties whose owners had cause to be grateful to Avonmouth tugs. The *Jamaica Planter* (4,098 g.r.t.) was mined 22 January 1941 only 2,500 yards from Nell's Point, Barry Island, and was bombed by enemy aircraft a few months later on 1 July 1941, but survived. Salvage of this kind frequently led to litigation, and the outcome of one such case was reported in the Daily Telegraph as under:

'*From All Quarters.* Tugs and Pilots awarded £3,975. Salvage awards of £3,975 were made by Mr. Justice Bucknill in the Admiralty Court yesterday to five tugs, two pilot cutters of the Bristol Channel and six pilots for services rendered to a Belgian steamer, after she had struck a mine last February. The Judge said the tugs were expeditiously on the scene after the explosion, and put the vessel on a safe beach. She was carrying property of the British Government worth £118,000, which was more than the damage value of the ship – £85,000.'

Mines were no respecter of ships, and on 14 January 1942, whilst towing barges, the tug *Mercia* struck a mine in Redcliffe Bay and sank. The Chief Engineer, Alfred Henry Parsons, lost his life. As mines were dropped from aircraft by parachute, it was generally believed that parachute mines which fell in and around the vicinity of Bristol, for instance at Shirehampton, Bedminster and Winford, etc., were really intended for the Bristol Channel as a hazard to shipping, but were dropped off course.

The new German magnetic mines laid by aircraft from the outset of the war became a serious menace to British shipping, especially in shallow waters.

128   *H.M.S. Rockrose*. Flower-class corvette built at Charles Hill's Albion Dockyard, Bristol. Launched 26 July 1941. Seen leaving Royal Edward Dock, Avonmouth on maiden voyage in November 1941.

129   AFT GUN *Queen Adelaide* (4,933 g.r.t.). Pictured at 'O' Shed, Royal Edward Dock, Avonmouth, 21 March 1945.

They lay on the sea bed until approaching ships actuated their firing mechanism. At first there seemed no means of sweeping magnetic mines, until a magnetic ring was devised fitted to aircraft, to explode them harmlessly. The degaussing mantle was also conceived to protect ships from magnetic mines, and fitting these was carried out on a large scale in Avonmouth.

In the early days degaussing was done by hand, taking 30 to 40 men several days to fit the necessary cable around the vessels, often 900 feet long, and protected with two layers of canvas, tape and coating of marline. However, Mr. E. F. Rowley of Avon Villa, 245 Avonmouth Road, Avonmouth, Foreman Electrician at J. Jefferies & Sons Avonmouth, devised the idea of a machine that would do the job just as efficiently, reduce man–power, and also speed up the work of rendering ships safe. He was given a free hand by his firm, and the machine was made in three weeks. It was then possible to bunch cables together of varying sizes, and automatically tape and marling them at a rate of 400 feet per hour. Mr. Rowley was complimented by Admiralty Officials for his invention, in recognition of which he was awarded the British Empire Medal. This he received at the hand of King George VI at Buckingham Palace in November 1944. Mr. Rowley was aged 71 at the time.

130 BRITISH EMPIRE MEDAL awarded to Mr. E. F. Rowley. One of many accolades bestowed in recognition of Avonmouth's contribution to Victory. Photo: by Teresa Momber.

131 *Esperance Bay* (14,176 g.r.t.). Sailed from Avonmouth as a troopship in October 1942.

Troopships

For hundreds of servicemen, Avonmouth Dock was their last memory of Old Blighty when they sailed in troopships for service overseas. Avonmouth was used extensively for the embarkation of troops, and shipment of supplies, to the B.E.F. in France at the start of the war, and later to South Africa en route to the Middle East and Mediterranean theatres of war. In all, twenty-six British and American troopships embarked and disembarked men here. According to Flight-Lieutenant C. P. Stephenson, an R.A.F. pilot, who sailed in one of the troopships from Avonmouth, recalls having seen, in all, three such ships in Avonmouth at the same time.

More than forty years after the event, F/Lt. Stephenson wrote he could remember the *Largs Bay* (14,182 g.r.t.) in which he sailed, *Orontes* (20,186 g.r.t.) and *Esperance Bay* (14,176 g.r.t.) in Avonmouth Docks. The date was 25 October 1942, and before slipping out of the docks at around midnight he remembered seeing the grey upperworks of these ships towering above the roof-lines of the dock-side warehouses. *Largs Bay* and *Esperance Bay* formed part of the troop convoy bound for Southern Rhodesia. After rounding Northern Ireland this convoy ran into a full North Atlantic hurricane force gale, with mountainous seas for almost a week, rendering the troops wet, sea-sick, miserable and 'wish we could die now' feeling, but the weather was a blessing in disguise. It later transpired that the German U-boat 'wolf-packs' were fully aware of this precious troop convoy, but were kept at bay by the bad weather, and the convoy was afforded a safe voyage. Incidentally, *Largs Bay* took twelve weeks in passage from Avonmouth to Durban.

The speed of convoys was dictated by the slowest of the merchant ships, and was frustrating to the crews of the faster vessels, to say the least. At the same time, convoys had a comforting element of seamen being in company with a number of ships all moving at the same pace – besides which, help could be at hand for picking up survivors should the need arise. Stragglers and unescorted ships going it alone were particularly vulnerable to U-boat attack.

For security reasons, troop trains were required to travel with the carriage blinds down, so for the most part, when arriving at the port of sailing it was a case of servicemen asking, 'Where are we?'. F/Lt. Stephensons' train had come from Blackpool, and when enquiring of Railway and Dock staff, 'Where is this?', he was met with silence, or simply 'Dunno's'. However, in the case of Mr. Albert McGrath, now residing at Jutland Road, Avonmouth, when arriving from Wiltshire on a troop train, as a soldier for service overseas, was amazed when allowed to let up the blinds, to find the train emerging from Clifton Down Tunnel. As a Bristolian, it was a case of sailing from down the 'Mouth, and no need to ask anyone, 'Where is this?' for he knew the area like the back of his hand.

For some ladies of Avonmouth, their war work entailed going aboard troopships and hospital ships to make them 'Shipshape and Bristol Fashion', before they departed on their next assignment. Mrs. Edith (Edie) Ward, nee Male in 1984 recalled those wartime days, as follows:

'I remember those days with great pleasure. It was a most rewarding job, and the sight of ships sailing with their decks obscured by the mass of khaki or air-force blue uniforms of their passengers, brought a lump to the throat. The ladies were often so engrossed in their work that sometimes the ship would be moved without their realising it, and when they had finished would find themselves with a long walk home from the north wall of the Royal Edward Dock, or some other far distant spot'.

It was not always a case of troops departing *from* Avonmouth – sometimes they *arrived*. On 7 November 1943 welfare workers waited from before dawn until after dusk with piles of clothing for some 300 seamen survivors expected to arrive home, after having lost their ships in the South Atlantic, only to find that when the men did arrive they had been supplied with clothes in South America, and, due to Britain's wartime clothes rationing, were better dressed than they were! The W.V.S. also gave valuable assistance to the American Red Cross when American troops arrived at Avonmouth.

132 HOSPITAL SHIP *Somersetshire* (9,716 g.r.t.) arriving at Royal Edward Dock, Avonmouth 3 March 1944, bringing home wounded servicemen from theatres of war.

Hospital Ships

From time to time hospital ships put into Avonmouth, bringing home the wounded from the theatres of war. These ships, always painted white with large red crosses on their sides and funnels, and fully lit up at night, stood out in sharp contrast to the other ships in port in wartime grey. Everyone had a special regard and affection for the hospital ships on their errands of mercy. Those known to have visited Avonmouth during the war were *Letitia, Aba, Somersetshire, Lady Nelson* and *Oranje*. There must have been others.

The hospital ships always berthed at 'S' Shed in the Royal Edward Dock, where the wounded were transferred to very long ambulance trains (also painted with large red crosses, and with blinds drawn) waiting for them on the quayside to be transported to Military hospitals.

A very kindly local gesture paid to the hospital ships which came into Avonmouth was recalled in 1981 by Mrs. B. A. Francis, who was a telephonist at the Avonmouth Post Office Exchange at the time, when she wrote:

'When the first hospital ship came into Avonmouth, nurses from the ship were seen gathering a few wild flowers from the dockside to use for decorating the wards. This news got around, and local firms decided to provide flowers for every hospital ship

133 AMBULANCE TRAIN departing Royal Edward Dock, Avonmouth with wounded from Hospital Ship *Somersetshire* berthed at 'S' Shed, 3 March 1944.

134 HOSPITAL SHIP *Letitia* (13,595 g.r.t.) at 'S' Shed, Royal Edward Dock, Avonmouth, viewed from No. 3 Granary in June 1945. This liner was later renamed *s.s. Empire Brent*.

that docked here thereafter. The Post Office joined with the Petroleum Board to provide flowers for the *Letitia*. Two girls from the Petroleum Board and two from the Post Office went on a lorry provided by the Petroleum Board to deliver the flowers. We were taken aboard, and shown around the ship, and the procedures taken with the patients in the event of the ship meeting trouble was explained to us.'

The liner *Letitia* (13,595 g.r.t.) was built in 1925 for Donaldson Atlantic Line for their passenger service from Glasgow to Canada. When the war broke out she became an armed merchant cruiser, and then a hospital ship in 1944. She was later re-named *Empire Brent,* and served as a troopship. After the war from 1952 until broken up in 1960 when named *Captain Cook* she carried 27,000 emigration settlers out to Australia and New Zealand. *Letitia* was sister ship to the *Athenia,* which was sunk by a German U-boat on the very day that war broke out – details of which are given in chapter 'Evacuation'.

According to the Geneva Convention, red crosses on a ship should guarantee them immunity from enemy attack. But it happened in the Second World War as in the Great War when the Germans had no qualms about attacking hospital ships, and trying to sink them. Indeed they were successful in sinking the *Newfoundland* in September 1943, and the hospital carrier *St. David* in January 1944.

The liner *Aba* (7,938 g.r.t.) was built in 1918 and bought by Elder Dempster Line in 1921. She served as a hospital ship from 1940 until 1944

135 HOSPITAL SHIP *Lady Nelson* (7,970 g.r.t.) berthed at 'S' Shed, Royal Edward Dock, Avonmouth, 16 July 1945.

136   U.S. AMBULANCES leaving Avonmouth Docks via Gloucester Road Main Gate 19 April 1945. *Left:* Brick surface air raid shelters. *Right:* Air raid siren on roof of C. J. King (Stevedores) Pay Office.

during which time she was attacked twice. On 17 May 1941 she was bombed by German and Italian aircraft at a point 50 miles south of Crete, but not too seriously damaged. On 15 March 1944 *Aba* was heavily bombed in Naples. When she arrived in Avonmouth she was bomb-damaged, and her blood-stained decks were dealt with by the cleaning ladies. After extensive repairs *Aba* was later converted to a troopship, was sold in 1947 to Greek interests and re-named *Matrona*.

Somersetshire (9,716 g.r.t.) came to Avonmouth on 3 March 1944. She was built in 1921 with three decks by Harland & Wolff Ltd., at Belfast for the Bibby Line. On 7 April 1942 she was torpedoed by a submarine at position 32° 13′ N 26° 34′ E, but not lost.

The *Lady Nelson* (7,970 g.r.t.) was built in 1928 by Cammell Laird & Co. Ltd. at Birkenhead. She was damaged by a torpedo on 9 March 1942 whilst in Castries Harbour, St. Lucia in the West Indies, and survived. She came into Avonmouth on 16 July 1945.

The largest of the hospital ships to put into Avonmouth during the war was the Dutch luxury liner *Oranje* (20,017 g.r.t.) which arrived on 14 March 1944. Details of this really beautiful ship are given on page 5.

Banana Ships

The importing of bananas was once a firmly established Avonmouth trade from 1901 when the very first shipment to arrive in Britain came into Avonmouth Dock. The fleet of Elders & Fyffes banana ships was held in high regard by the Avonmouth and Bristol Dockers, who dubbed them the 'plum boats', meaning a plum-of-a-job which gave them three days guaranteed work, an important factor during the depression years of the 1930's.

Banana ships arrived regularly at Avonmouth, weekly in summer and fortnightly in winter, and millions of stems were received annually – representing a quarter of Britain's total import. At 'N' Shed in the Old Dock an electrical elevator plant was installed for discharging the fruit, and a special layout of railway sidings permitted circular shunting of the steam-heated vans for easier loading and despatching. The banana ships also operated a first class passenger accommodation to and from the Caribbean for up to 100 persons.

At the beginning of the war, having perishable cargo, the banana ships risked crossing the Atlantic independently, with disastrous results. Of the Fyffes fleet of twenty-one ships in 1939, fourteen were lost together with

137 TWO ELDERS & FYFFES SHIPS at Avonmouth (Old) Dock *c* 1931 in their peacetime livery. *Left: R.M.S. Bayano* (6,815 g.r.t.) taking coal from barge. *Right: R.M.S. Carare* (6,878 g.r.t.) discharging bananas at 'N' Shed.

138 FYFFES LINE *Ariguani* (6,747 g.r.t.) as *H.M.S. Ariguani* serving as a Catapult Aircraft Merchant Ship in convoy 1940/41. *Note:* Fighter 'plane on bows in readiness.

many of their crews – sunk by enemy action. The most tragic loss was that of the *Matina* (Captain D. A. Jack) which went missing in the North Atlantic in October 1940 without trace. There is some doubt about the circumstances of her loss with 64 crew, including one D.B.S. (distressed British seaman) being given passage home, plus two passengers. Subsequent German records show *Matina* was probably torpedoed by U-28 on 26 October 1940, but not seen to sink. On the 29 October 1940 U-31 torpedoed a wreck in a nearby position and sank it. This was most likely the *Matina*.

With so many banana ships already lost, the Government in November 1940 declared bananas a luxury fruit, and the trade was suspended for the duration of the war. Some of the remaining ships were either used for bringing essential refrigerated foods, such as eggs, butter and bacon, or military supplies, arms, aircraft parts, etc., mostly on the dangerous transatlantic crossing, whilst other Fyffes ships were requisitioned for Royal Navy duties.

The most regular banana ships to visit Avonmouth in pre-war days, and those readily and best remembered are the 'A', 'B' and three 'C's', as they were called, that is, *Ariguani, Bayano, Cavina, Camito* and *Carare. Ariguani* (6,747 g.r.t.) or 'arry-go-ungry' in docker's jargon, was one of the three

Fyffes ships to become catapult-aircraft-merchant ships or CAM-ships. *Ariguani* was converted by J. Jefferies & Sons at Avonmouth, and served with the Royal Navy as *H.M.S Ariguani*.

A great threat to British shipping lay in the German occupation of the airfields of western France, from which the Luftwaffe's long-range Focke-Wulf 'Condor' four-engined bomber aircraft with a range of 2,210 miles – 14 flying hours – could search the Atlantic for convoys and report their positions to waiting U-boats. The Condors were a serious menace, sinking British ships and damaging many more with sticks of bombs dropped from masthead height. During the second half of 1940 losses in the Atlantic reached a dangerous level. To counter this problem a number of merchant ships acting as escorts were fitted with a catapult, which could launch a Fulmar or Hurricane fighter 'plane, when convoys sailed within range of the Condors. On sighting an enemy aircraft the fighter was catapulted into flight. After shooting down or driving off the intruder, the fighter, not being able to land on the ship from which it took off, either had to make for the nearest friendly territory, or ditch itself alongside a merchant ship so that the pilot could be picked up. In time the CAM-ships were replaced by MAC-ships (merchant-aircraft carriers) in which a full flight platform was built over the decks of the ship – usually an oil tanker, because of her length. These were known to seafarers as 'Woolworth' carriers.

In October 1941, *H.M.S. Ariguani* escorted a convoy to Gibraltar with vital supplies for the desert forces. On escort duty with a homeward-bound

139   *H.M.S. Ariguani* 26 October 1941, after being hit aft by two torpedoes. Safely towed into Gibraltar and thence back home to Britain.

convoy on 26 October 1941 she was struck aft by two torpedoes, when about 400 miles west of Cape St. Vincent. She was left dead in the water, and 'Abandon Ship' was piped. However, as she was seen to be still afloat at daylight, the crew re-boarded her and she was towed some 600 miles safely back to Gibraltar, taking five days. *Ariguani* was not used again as a CAM-ship, but returned to trading in January 1944. (Having been built in 1926, *Ariguani* was sold to breakers in 1956.)

In June 1946, Mr. Fernley Charles Tottle, Works Manager at J. Jefferies & Sons, Avonmouth, was awarded the M.B.E. (Civil) Medal for building catapults for launching aircraft from ships. Mr. Thomas Fred Hibbs, Foreman-fitter at the same firm received the B.E.M.

Bayano (6,815 g.r.t.) built in 1917, served in both World Wars, and had the distinction of emerging from both unscathed. During the Great War she was requisitioned as an armed escort vessel (1917–1918), and put to work with convoys on the North Atlantic routes.

In January 1940 *Bayano* re-enlisted, and during the next five years she made over forty voyages across the North Atlantic, bringing 160,875 tons of war materials to the United Kingdom. She again escaped damage (although she had several very narrow escapes) and during the Second World War she became known to seamen as '*Lucky Bayano*'. To be in convoy with her was regarded as a good omen for a safe voyage.

Relating his experiences in 1984 as a former member of *Bayano's* crew, Mr. Ray Buck of Pill wrote:

'I served on *Bayano* as a look-out man in the crow's-nest during the ship's wartime service. We were homeward bound from Montreal in a 74-ship convoy. It was August 1941, and the North Atlantic for some reason was very calm.

From my observation point I saw ships coming up from astern on the port quarter; they were revealed to be H.M.S. *Prince of Wales* with an escort of eight destroyers, carrying Winston Churchill back from his momentous Atlantic Charter meeting with Franklin D. Roosevelt, President of the United States. She swept up past our starboard side, and from my perch I had an exhilarating view of all her matelots, who were not at battle stations on deck, as the signal went out, "Three cheers for Winnie". (Those same sailors were to meet their final agony a few months later.) Winston ordered, "Splice the mainbrace!" At the time we wished he had left some of his escorts.'

H.M.S. *Prince of Wales* was a brand new 35,000 ton battleship completed in March 1941, and represented the ultimate in battleship design for the Royal Navy. After only nine months service she was lost on 10 December 1941, sunk by Japanese torpedo-carrying aircraft off the East Coast of Malaya.

Sequel

After the war *Bayano* resumed her cargo and passenger service to the West Indies, finishing her last voyage by discharging a cargo of bananas at Avonmouth at the end of 1955. Her record is unequalled by any of the other Fyffes Line. In thirty-eight years *Bayano* completed 280 voyages, and delivered to Britain some 3,000,000,000 bananas, before being sold to breakers in 1956.

Cavina (6,907 g.r.t.) was converted to an Ocean Boarding Vessel at Avonmouth in 1940, and she came through the War safely. One of her pleasant wartime assignments was to ferry wives of R.A.F. Personnel stationed in Canada to join their husbands. In October 1945, sailing from Avonmouth, she carried British brides of Canadian servicemen to Canada and their new homes. *Cavina,* built in 1924, was sold to Barkstone Shipping Co. Ltd. in 1957.

140　FYFFES LINE *Cavina* (6,907 g.r.t.) serving as an Ocean Boarding Vessel, *c* 1942.

Camito (6,833 g.r.t.) was built in 1915, and served with the Royal Navy as an escort vessel during the Great War, from February 1918 until March 1919. During the Second World War she was requisitioned for Naval duties in 1940, and became an ocean boarding vessel. On 6 May 1941 *Camito* was torpedoed by a U-boat in the North Atlantic and sunk.

When the news leaked back to Avonmouth in 1940 that *Carare* (6,878 g.r.t.) had struck a mine and sank in the Bristol Channel, the Parish was stunned. It was as if the Germans had sunk one of 'our very own' ships on our very doorstep!

Sailing from Avonmouth Dock on Monday, 27 May 1940, she was bound for Kingston, Jamaica (Captain D. A. Jack, R.N.R.) with 98 crew and 29 passengers. She left on the night tide but, due to fog, anchored off Walton

141 FYFFES LINE *Carare* (6,878 g.r.t.) 28 May 1940. Mined in Bristol Channel off Countisbury Head between Lynton and Minehead.

Bay over night, and proceeded the following morning. At about 9.20 a.m., 28 May 1940, *Carare* struck a mine in the Bristol Channel off Countisbury Head at position 51°28'N 03°45'W between Lynton and Minehead. The mine struck at No. 1 hold near the bow, and the ship took about 25 minutes to sink.

The water, fortunately, being calm and warm, and in sight of land, most survivors were able to take to the lifeboats and were later picked up by a naval sloop. Three passengers were lost, Miss E. Edwards, Miss V. Lawrence and Mr. W. R. Sims – the two girls being coloured nurses returning home after receiving training in this Country. Of the seven crew who were lost one was the ship's surgeon, Mr. W. F. Roach, M.D. Chief Refrigeration Engineer, Charles Robert Barker was later buried at Canford Cemetery, and Barkeeper George Victor Bathe at St. Peter's Churchyard, Filton.

In recent times the members of Ilfracombe Sub-Aqua Club have begun diving expeditions to the *Carare* wreck, but report it is not an easy one to explore. At 32 metres it is quite deep and the visibility in the water is often nil, to say nothing of the strong currents prevailing for which the Bristol Channel is renowned. Nevertheless, local fishermen claim on having a goodly catch when fishing in the vicinity of the old *Carare* wreck.

As soon as the war was over Messrs. Elders & Fyffes lost no time in returning to their pre-war trading. History was made on Sunday, 30 December 1945, when *Tilapa* (5,392 g.r.t.) in glistening white paint replacing her wartime grey, and dressed overall, proudly sailed into Avonmouth, bringing to Britain the first consignment of bananas following the war. She received a Civic reception, and made front-page news throughout the Country. Avonmouth was back in the banana trade once again. At first though, bananas were on points rationing for sale to under 18-year-olds only. It was the first time that children under five had seen bananas, although they may have partaken of mashed parsnips flavoured with banana essence in sandwiches, served as substitute for the real thing during the war.

142 FYFFES LINE *Tilapa* (5,392 g.r.t.) entering Royal Edward Dock, Avonmouth, dressed overall 29 December 1945, bringing the first post-war cargo of bananas to Britain.

143 CIVIC RECEPTION afforded *Tilapa* at 'N' Shed, Avonmouth (Old) Dock, 29 December 1945. *Right:* Lord Mayor of Bristol (Ald. James Owen). *Left:* Daphne Richards (daughter of Elders & Fyffes Manager) enjoying a first taste.

144 *R.M.S. Queen Mary* in wartime camouflage at anchor in the Clyde off Gourock.
After carrying U.S. troops across the Atlantic they disembarked here into L.M.S. pleasure
steamers for transferring to shore bases. *N.B.* Compare size of *Queen Mary* with aircraft
carrier on left.

145 *R.M.S. Queen Mary.* Upper deck during a calm summer crossing. American troops
getting some fresh air. Lifejackets worn at all times. Not much room for exercise!

XIII. AMERICANS OVER HERE

In referring to the United States during the dark days of the war, Mr. Churchill confidently quoted lines from an Arthur Clough poem, 'But westward, look, the land is bright'. In truth, there was no other direction for Britain and the Empire to look for help when standing alone, against an overwhelming enemy. In September 1940, to bridge the gap in sorely needed escort vessels, fifty old U.S. destroyers were traded for certain British bases in the West Indies and Newfoundland.

'Give us the tools, and we will finish the job', implored Mr. Churchill addressing the United States President in a radio broadcast 9 February 1941. Although sympathetic to the cause of freedom, Franklin D. Roosevelt, the unprecedented three-times-elected President of the United States, strove hard to ward off war, and adopted a Lend-Lease policy to supply arms and foodstuffs to Britain. But the rub was, in her quest to remain 'neutral', America refused to provide convoy cover, and Britain had no option but to fetch the war supplies she so desperately needed across the U-boat infested Atlantic herself.

When America at last entered the war, she was pitch-forked into it on Sunday, 7 December 1941, by the surprise Japanese attack on her Battle Fleet at anchor in Pearl Harbour. In typical Axis fashion, they struck first, and declared war afterwards. It was a crippling naval loss, a devastation for the American people, and a black day in history. German armies at that time stood at the gates of Moscow and Leningrad, and the Japanese were now supreme in the Pacific.

But with America in the war, Russia and the U.S. had become Allies of Great Britain, and we no longer stood alone. The war had extended to both hemispheres, and had become world-wide.

The United States brought conscription into immediate effect upon entering the war, and after initial training, U.S. servicemen began arriving in Britain. They came in such large numbers as to represent a mini-invasion of this country, earning themselves an 'overseas' medal, and quickly the reputation of being 'over-paid, over-sexed, and over-here'.

The American troops were shuttled across the Atlantic from New York to Scotland in Britain's great and splendid luxury liners, *Queen Mary* and *Queen*

Elizabeth. These ships representing a nation's hopes when built during the depression years of the 1930's were now, by their unique contribution to the war effort, accredited to having shortened the build-up to D-Day and the war by some twelve months.

Stripped of all luxury fittings, and painted in wartime grey, both ships were converted into troopships. With bunks fitted wherever there was space available (even in the bars and swimming pools), and meals and sleep taken in shifts, they transported between them 810,730 troops, prisoners, politicians and G.I. brides whilst on war service. On one occasion, *Queen Mary* carried the incredible number of 15,125 troops and 863 crew, being equal to an entire army division.

The *Queens* plied the Atlantic un-convoyed, taking about five days, relying on their exceptional high speed and following a zig-zag course to confuse German U-boats. This strategy proved extremely successful. The only serious incident occurred on 2 October 1942 when the *Queen Mary* was off Ireland, zig-zagging towards Scotland with a full complement of servicemen aboard, escorted by six destroyers and a cruiser, *H.M.S. Curacoa*. The cruiser manoeuvred in too closely to the great liner, with the result she was rammed and cut in two, both halves sank quickly with the loss of 331 lives. *Queen Mary* hardly felt the bump, and limped safely into port with a damaged bow.

The G.I.'s were disembarked into pleasure steamers at Gourock on the Clyde, and thence taken by troop-trains to the numerous camps which had sprung up throughout Britain to accommodate them.

Before landing, the U.S. soldiers were given a leaflet welcoming them to this country, assuring them that the British people were glad to see them. At the same time, any supposed myths they might have about Britain, white cliffs, thatched cottages, etc. were dispelled. It was emphasised they had arrived in Britain in wartime having to cope with black-out, besides restrictions in food and clothing. The phrase 'There's a war on' was used then to cover a multitude of short-comings and inadequacies, one which they would become heartily sick of hearing, as the rest of us were.

Although Britain and the United States shared the English language, there were many words with different meanings on each side of the Atlantic. Some were listed. For instance, apartment meant a flat, automobile a car, gasoline – petrol, sidewalk – pavement, etc., and a host more. British girls soon got used to the American jargon, as did the G.I.'s having to drive on the left side of the road, instead of the right. Another major difference to be overcome by these visitors was what they called our 'quaint' currency. At that time, roughly speaking, one U.S. cent was equal to one British half-penny, one dollar to five shillings, and four dollars to one pound.

Differences, however, were quickly accepted on both sides in favour of the common task of winning the war.

Footnote:

The term 'G.I.' originally applied to United States infantry-men, and meant 'General Issue' – everything they wore having been provided by the U.S. Government. 'G.I.' as a name stuck in this country, and applied to American servicemen in general – thus, a girl who married an American serviceman was called a 'G.I. bride'. U.S. servicemen were also referred to as 'dough-boys' due to their being paid nearly four times as much as British servicemen.

'DOUGH-BOYS' IN BRISTOL

With Avonmouth the main port for the U.S. Army, it was understandable Bristol should become highly involved in American affairs, and the arrival of the 'dough-boys' was just another milestone in the city's wartime history. In August 1942 the first transport and constructional troops came, quickly followed by many G.I.'s.

The buildings of Clifton College (the school having been evacuated to Bude in Cornwall in February 1941) became the American Headquarters, and in due course other premises such as Muller's Orphanage in Ashley Down Road, and the West of England College of Art were taken over by them for various purposes. Many U.S. troops were billeted on private residents, and houses in Stoke Bishop and Sneyd Park became home for high-ranking Officers.

American Generals were often in Bristol, and many Bristolians must have seen Eisenhower, or Omar Bradley, and others, without realising it. Many notable visitors came to see the Americans whilst they were stationed in Bristol, including Mrs. Eleanor Roosevelt (the U.S. President's wife), who came on Friday 6 November 1942, when crowds gathered to see her. Equally famous in his own sphere was Joe Louis, the world heavyweight boxing champion who visited in 1944.

General Omar Nelson Bradley, fresh from commanding the U.S. 2nd Corps in Tunisia and Sicily, set up his war room in the Clifton College Council Chamber, and it was here that meticulous plans for Operation Overlord (D-Day) were made. Everything in Bradley's war room was classified 'top-secret'. An elaborate telephone system was installed linking the College with U.S. Army Headquarters in London, then a three hour car trip away. Another top-secret spot was the Wilson Tower, which became a signals room to which all intercepted German coded messages were sent. Classrooms were converted to offices, and the Close, famous for its hallowed cricket pitches, was used for baseball matches. Queen Mary took a keen interest in G.I.'s staying in this country, and one day, accompanied by Princess Marina (Duchess of Kent), she saw her first baseball match at Clifton College between two U.S. Army teams. Two soldiers were stationed each side of Her Majesty, immaculately uniformed, but wearing 'catchers' gloves to intercept any stray balls! From Clifton College it was only a stone's throw across the Suspension Bridge to Lady Smyth's Ashton Court Estate, where the Americans set up a 'secret' airstrip for the use of high-ranking Officers and other V.I.P.'s coming or going in light aircraft. A gap was made in the familiar high wall surrounding the Estate for easy access into Beggars Bush Lane. Ashton Court Park was used by the Americans for parking tanks, lorries and guns etc. during the build-up to D-Day.

Omar Bradley himself lived in a large house called 'The Holmes' near the Downs, now the property of Bristol University. He recorded later:

'The house had been tentatively ear-marked as a Home for wayward girls. When the first American truck rolled up the drive, the neighbours were said to have shrugged with resignation, if not relief.'

Large American Army camps were set up at Bedminster (to guard mountains of foodstuffs and other stores), Failand, Flax Bourton, Backwell and Shirehampton. American hospitals were established at Tortworth, Tyntesfield and Frenchay. The U.S. actually *gave* Frenchay Hospital to the United Kingdom in October 1944, including equipment, and even dressing gowns.

The Americans were so impressed by the exceptional natural beauty of Shirehampton Park where their army huts were erected beneath the trees, that they promised to restore the Park to its former state on departure. This pledge they faithfully carried out. Shirehampton Golf Course was thus reduced to nine holes during the war, and was not restored to the full eighteen holes until 1952. To this day, the fifth hole is called the 'America' as a lasting tribute to the American servicemen who were once stationed in Shirehampton Park.

We local folks found it pleasant on Sunday afternoons to watch the G.I.'s parading on Shirehampton Cricket Ground. To our ears their military band had an unusual 'tinkling' sound, made by the glockenspiels and whistles . . . not at all like civilized military music we thought, more like a jazz band! The 'dough-boys' appeared smartly turned out when compared with the British Tommies, wearing uniforms with collar and tie. We called them the 'silent' Army, marching quietly in brown rubber-soled boots, instead of the heavy black hob-nailed variety worn by British soldiers, which gave a distinctive marching clatter. The orders given by U.S. sergeants gave the impression of *playing* at soldiers, with their 'Hip . . . Hap . . . etc.' commands, instead of the British usual 'left . . . right . . . etc.' Mrs. Violet Maund noted in her diary:

'*4 February 1944* – Walked on the Downs and watched American soldiers playing a team game, but could not make anything out of it. They were then drilled and had to march up and down several times, when one soldier cried out from the file: "Have a heart, Sarge," and the Sarge said: "All right then, stand easy."'

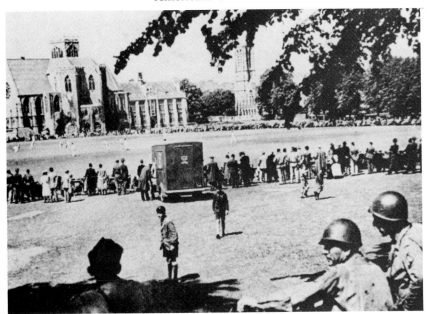

146 CLIFTON COLLEGE 1943/44. Cricket on the Close with American servicemen
bewildered spectators. Y.M.C.A. canteen van in attendance.

147 SHIREHAMPTON PARK GOLF COURSE. Site of American Army Camp 1942/44.
View towards Shirehampton from the Park Gates. Photo: June 1982.

If Bristolians found the American method of soldiering somewhat strange, they found their sporting pursuits even more perplexing. When out for a walk again on the Downs, Mrs. Maund watched several American sailors in uniform riding horses which made a queer scene, after which she wrote:

'21 October 1943 – I was surprised to see one horse collapse under a very tall sailor, and when I went over to see it, people around said it was dead. If these American sailors are used to the Wild West steeds one sees on the films, it must be strange to them to find that a canter over the Downs, kills our horses. No doubt the amount of animal food allowed is greatly reduced these days.'

On another occasion Mrs. Maund attended a baseball match, and afterwards entered in her diary:

'3 June 1944 – Went to the Rovers' Memorial Ground to see an American Baseball Match, Reversible Commando's versus All Black Star. The All Blacks won. I was amused to see how childish the Americans seem, decrying the opposition when it is their turn to hold the bat, and openly arguing with the umpire (who on this occasion was 'Holy Joe' their Padre) on his decisions. One man threw down his gloves and sulked away into another part of the field, when his chums came round and put their arms over his shoulders and tried to persuade him to carry on. Play was held up for some time while both Padre and players, the white side, argued together. As I was new to the game I could not judge if the decision was wrong, but the conduct of all was childish.'

148   AMERICAN SOLDIERS with air raid orphaned children before attending a circus performance at Bristol Hippodrome, 16 February 1943.

There were mixed feelings regarding the American troops being over here, and all was not sweetness and light. The main problem was due to the colour-bar adopted in the United States, and frowned upon by the British. The white American soldiers were the first to occupy the camp at Shirehampton, and later on came the coloured G.I.'s, but not together or at the same time! The U.S. Army were obliged to observe the segregation laws practised in many of their States at that time.

The Organiser of Bristol's Hospitality Committee had been previously warned to provide separate entertainments for coloured and whites. The Lyndale Hotel was transformed into a club for white Americans, and when that became too small they moved to the Royal West of England Academy in Queen's Road, Clifton. A club for coloured American servicemen was opened in the vacant building of the Clergy Daughters' School in Great George Street, and when large numbers of American Merchant Seamen arrived, a special club was opened for them on 1 November 1943 at the Hamilton Rooms in Park Street, Bristol.

Despite their apparently relaxed methods of soldiering, the G.I.'s, though resident in Britain, were subject to the Law of their own country, and harsh penalties were meted out to those who stepped out of line. For instance, a court martial in Bristol sent a soldier to prison for four years for crashing a Jeep whilst out joy-riding with two girls, and a coloured G.I. was sentenced to death at Bath for rape.

The black Americans were subjected to some of the most wicked rumours whilst they were in Britain. The most persistent story claimed that Southmead Hospital had become a Maternity Hospital for girls who had been seduced by black soldiers. This rumour was scotched only when an official denial by Dr. R. H. Parry, the Medical Officer of Health, was published in the Press on 10 March 1943. This must have been the only time the G.I.'s were mentioned in the local newspapers, whose editors drew a veil over the entire subject of the American 'occupation'. Reading the old newspapers now, one could gather that they had never been here. Any photographs taken during the G.I. stay were firmly marked 'STRICTLY SECRET' by the censor, and then relegated to the files, undated, and to be forgotten.

But in spite of all the Americans' strange ways, they were a very friendly lot, irrespective of rank, many had pleasant manners, and all were most generous with presents. Not least with children, who quickly discovered that pleas such as, 'Got any gum, chum?', brought forth immediate gifts of chewing gum, candies or sweets. The G.I.'s appeared to suffer no shortages of other luxuries either, like the rest of us. When a friend was thrown an orange by a coloured soldier, she promptly scrubbed it, and divided it round the office staff, one segment per person as a special treat. Very soon, too, Bristolians were smoking cigarettes with unfamiliar brand-names, such as

149   U.S. STANDARD-BEARERS with *Stars and Stripes* on College Green, Bristol. 1942 or 1943. This photo was withheld from publication by the censor, who marked the print *Strictly Secret*!

150   AMERICAN TROOPS, Park Street, Bristol. 1942 or 1943. On parade for a visiting General who was not named. Another censored picture – occasion as plate 149.

Lucky Strike, Camel, Philip Morris, Sweet Caporal, Pall Mall, Chesterfield, etc. The devastating fire at the Colston Hall (5 February 1945) which reduced the building to a burnt out shell was widely attributed to an American G.I.'s burning cigar butt.

Christmas-time was the American Season *par excellence* in entertaining thousands of Bristol's children, more particularly those from its poorer and bomb-damaged districts. At Shirehampton Camp a party was held for children of Avonmouth's dock workers, and is still remembered for the delicious jellies served – unknown in wartime Britain. On the occasion of a party advertised to take place at Clifton College, twice as many children turned up as had been invited – but all were made welcome, and had a rousing good time in company with General Omar Bradley and the Lord Mayor, Alderman H. A. Wall.

American entertainers, known to British people until then only as Hollywood stars, put on shows in Bristol. Irving Berlin brought a company to the Victoria Rooms, and it raised £5,000 for British war charities. American Army bands performed at local football grounds, and Bristol Cathedral and the Pro-Cathedral were taken over by Americans for their special services on Independence Day and Thanksgiving Day, conducted by their own Padres.

The Americans always seemed to have plenty of money, being higher paid than the British Tommies, and were not known as 'dough-boys' for nothing. With most young men serving away from home, the G.I.'s with their generous gifts of nylons and cosmetics, proved very popular with local lasses, and many lasting relationships were formed. Some 60,000 British girls married G.I.'s, including some Bristolians, and at least two Shirehampton girls, whose weddings I attended. After the war the G.I. brides emigrated to the United States to start a new life there. Countless local families now have family links with the U.S.A., which are a matter of pride, and rightly so. But alas, not all wartime liaisons ended happily. In 1945 the Ministry of Information issued a circular advising procedures for single girls who had babies by American soldiers.

As more and more Americans poured into Bristol during the build-up to D-Day, the need to find billets for them became acute, and even compulsory methods resorted to. A letter from the Lord Mayor to every householder appealing for assistance and co-operation did not help much, due to gossip and rumours which caused many misgivings, but most fears were groundless. Many columns of servicemen passed straight from Avonmouth to be trained for the Normandy landings on Slapton Sands in Devon, where a whole village was evacuated to make room for them. Two days following D-Day, a journalist in the Western Daily Press wrote:

'Not long ago some residents on the west side of Bristol were bewailing the fact that they had to have American billetees. Now there is real sorrow in many homes. The young men came, they conquered, and they are gone – literally vanished in a single night . . .'

The fact was that half a million Americans had left the West Country to storm the Normandy invasion beaches.

Before General Omar Bradley exchanged his war room at Clifton College for the bridge of the invasion ship *Augusta,* he left his Stars & Stripes flag as a lasting memento of his 'occupation' of the College, and hoped that it might be flown from the flag-pole on every Independence Day. It is now kept in a special glass case at the entrance to the school.

D-DAY-OPERATION 'OVERLORD'

On D-Day, 6 June 1944, one of the greatest military operations in history began when Allied troops landed in Normandy. It was the moment for which countless millions of oppressed peoples throughout Europe had been waiting and praying. The Allies had amassed more than 2,000,000 men and over 4,000 ships for Operation 'Overlord', the greatest amphibious assault of World War II. Under the command of General Omar Bradley, American Divisions captured Utah and Omaha invasion beaches, whilst the British and Canadian Divisions captured Gold, Juno and Sword. It was the second front

151   WALL MAP at U.S. Cemetery, Cambridge, showing where U.S. Camps existed and ports from which G.I.'s embarked for Normandy Landings on D-Day, Avonmouth being one of them.   Photo: May 1964.

for which the Russians had been pressing since 1941, and it marked the beginning of the end for Nazi Germany.

The part Clifton College played as a venue for the planning of this greatest combined operation of all time, was later confirmed by General Bradley himself in a letter dated March 1945 which he addressed to the scholars, as follows:

'It is a great pleasure for me to send you the attached photograph for Clifton College, to help commemorate our planning activities during the winter and spring of 1944. It may be of interest to you to know that most of the actual command planning for the assault of American Forces on the beaches of Normandy was carried on in the School House of Clifton College.

We held several very important conferences there with the Allied Commanders of the assault forces. Two weeks before D-Day, Commanders of our American assault divisions and brigades met in Clifton for a last minute review, and briefing of the plan. Many of them left from there to the ports where they loaded their troops into crafts for the invasion.

Clifton College will always occupy a very favoured spot in our memories. We like to recall the pleasant days we spent with your people of Bristol in the valued buildings of your institution. You compliment us greatly in associating our activities in this war to those accomplishments of your own Field Marshal Haig in the last. Certainly the associations of America and British troops in this war will contribute heavily to the fine understanding that unites our nations in peace as well as in war.

Sincerely,
OMAR N. BRADLEY.'

152   G.I. SENTRY at Junction Cut, Royal Edward Dock, Avonmouth 16 November 1943. *Foreground:* Landing craft later used in D-Day Normandy Landings. *Background:* Armed merchant ship *Empire Grace* (unnamed) lying at 'O' Shed.

The Normandy invasion was quite unlike any military operation ever staged before. In the past, any landing made in strength against an enemy coast had always necessitated the capture of a port. Even with the amazing advances in the use of amphibious landing craft for getting men, vehicles and tanks ashore, no adequate build-up of supplies could have been obtained without the Mulberry prefabricated Harbours which the Allies took with them. The Mulberries were not only a marvellous piece of engineering, but were also one of the best kept secrets of the war, and enabled the Allied Commanders to choose their landing places to create the greatest surprise to the enemy, and meet the least opposition.

As a result of an appeal made by the Admiralty for the loan of European topographical views, and holiday snap-shots of the French Coast, etc., masses of material were collected from the British public, and carefully scrutinized. This unique aspect of D-Day planning was referred to by Mrs. Maund in her diary, as follows:

'26 November 1943: Sent off a parcel of photographs, guide-books, maps, etc., of our several Continental holidays to the Admiralty, London as they requested. Somehow this action goes against the grain, as I feel I was a guest in these countries, but then, I think of our boys who will be landing in a strange place, and I feel I must give any help I can to push them on.'

Attacking in atrocious weather conditions, and with Rommel, the German Commander of Nazi Land Forces in Northern France away on leave, the Allies assault caught the enemy off guard.

It was probably in the industrial field that Bristol played her biggest part in winning the war. Factories, garages and many other business premises were pressed into war service. Some ten local firms built parts of the Mulberry Harbours, which, assembled in the sea off the coast of France just after D-Day, ensured the successful outcome of the Normandy campaign.

The Mulberry Harbours were designed by Admiralty boffins quartered during the war at Kingswood School on Landsdown, Bath. Together with the Empire Hotel and other schools in Bath, all had been requisitioned by the Admiralty during their evacuation to Bath from London. The code-name for the artificial harbours was taken from the only Mulberry Tree growing in the grounds of Kingswood School. (The Admiralty clearly still has a soft spot for the old mulberry tree, because when it was storm-damaged in 1978 Naval officials agreed to help towards the cost of tree surgery to preserve it.) These harbours were estimated to be equivalent in size to the port of Dover, two miles in length and one mile wide, consisting of huge breakwaters, steel caissons, old ships, and so on, with floating piers rising and falling with the tide. They were towed across the English Channel by eighty-five tugs, one to Arrowmanches, and the other to St. Laurent. The latter, unfortunately, was soon destroyed by a great storm and rendered useless.

153 MULBERRY TREE at Kingswood School, Lansdown, Bath. Photo: July 1988. This aged tree gave its name to the prefabricated harbours used for the Normandy landings in June 1944.

Having played a part in the withdrawal from Dunkirk four years earlier, Bristol's fleet of P. & A. Campbell paddle-steamers now had a role in the Allies' return to Normandy. *Glen Avon* and *Glen Usk* both as anti-aircraft ships, patrolled the Channel acting as guide-ships, marshalling the troopships and landing craft. Unfortunately *Glen Avon* was lost on 2 September 1944 at anchor in the Bay of Seine, Normandy, when she became overwhelmed in a gale and foundered. The Campbell's flagship *Britannia* (which served as *H.M.S. Skiddaw* A.A. ship during the war), was assigned as escort for part of the Mulberry Harbours on its way to France, and while laying off the beaches her galleys supplied some 14,000 meals for troops taking part in the operation. This task, although considered mundane, was essential all the same.

Two further examples of the engineering marvels of the Second World War were P.L.U.T.O. (Pipe Line Under the Ocean) by which petrol was pumped direct to the Allied invasion Forces in Normandy, and the other was a special cable laid under the English Channel for direct communication links

P.L.U.T.O. (Pipe Line under the Ocean), one of the
Engineering Marvels of the last World War, by which Petrol
was pumped by Pipe Line direct to the Allied Invasion Forces
in Normandy, passed through the Chine at the end of its long
journey across the Country. From the Pumping Station
on the Esplanade it commenced its last journey across the
bed of the Channel.

154   P.L.U.T.O. (Pipe-Line Under the Ocean) Notice pictured at The Chine, Shanklin,
Isle of Wight in July 1955.

155   MRS. BERYL FAWCUS at her
Cheltenham home in June 1984. As
W.A.A.F. Corporal Beryl McLeish
she received the first 'phone call from
the Normandy beach-head in June
1944.

with the front lines. It fell to an Avonmouth girl to take the first telephone call from the Normandy beach-head. She was Corporal Beryl McLeish (now Mrs. Freddie Fawcus), then serving with the Women's Auxiliary Air Force as a telephonist.

Corporal McLeish was on duty during those vital days of the war, at the underground switchboard, Fighter Command Headquarters in Middlesex, handling many hundreds of calls conveying orders to R.A.F. airfields throughout England. Noticing one of the little coloured signal lights on the switchboard in front of her twinkling more vigorously than usual, she plugged in to answer, and was told to stand by for a call coming through from an R.A.F. base in Normandy. The caller at the other end wanted to speak to Air Chief-Marshal Sir Trafford Leigh-Mallory, Commander of Allied Expeditionary Air Force. 'It came through so clearly,' said Corporal McLeish, 'that it might have been an ordinary local call. I knew the person who was making the call, and he told me where he was phoning from'. The R.A.F. Publicity Officer latched on to the story of the first call home, and it appeared both in the National and in the Local newspapers.

Corporal Beryl McLeish was the youngest daughter of Mr. and Mrs. D. McLeish of 9 Jutland Road, Avonmouth. Of her six brothers, five served in the Forces during the war, and all volunteered.

After the Normandy Landings it became clear that the Allies were going to win the war. Even so, people in Britain were by now exhausted after such a long struggle, and it was harder to bear the dangers and disasters. Hopes rose on D-Day, but the Germans had a 'secret' weapon. On 13 June 1944 the first pilotless 'plane (or flying-bomb) known as V.1 (Vergeltungswaffe or revenge weapon) fell on London. These could be heard coming – then their engines cut out, there was a moment's silence, and they fell. It was at this stage in the war that Avonmouth had to say good-bye to the barrage balloon crews who had helped so faithfully to defend the Parish from aerial attacks over the previous five years. All available barrage balloons were now posted to sites on the East Coast of England to combat Hitler's revenge weapons. Luckily, Allied Forces soon captured the V.1 launching sites near Calais in Northern France.

But worse was to follow. On 8 September 1944 the first flying-rockets were directed against Britain (V.2's) fired from bases in occupied Holland, and these had to be endured until March 1945 when the Allied Armies hurled the Germans back over the Rhine and out of Holland. Bristol, being out of range, was spared the horrors of the V.1's and V.2's. They caused much damage, and many casualties – 6,184 people were killed by the bombs, and 2,754 by the rockets.

For three years after Peace was signed, one of Avonmouth's tugs was still employed in war-work. During the summers of 1946, 1947 and 1948 *Sea*

Queen (Captain W. H. Bevan) helped in the mammoth task of clearing blockships from the invasion coast of Normandy.

Footnote:

Why should 6 June 1944 always be known as D-Day? The Imperial War Museum supplied the answer with a simple explanation – 'D' stands for 'Decision'. The term D-Day has frequently been used by the military to refer to a day of action and as Operation 'Overlord' was an event of such magnitude it has come to be most closely associated with that name, D-Day.

The 4 June 1944 could have been D-Day, but the weather was so bad that the invasion had to be delayed for 24 hours. On the 5th, though conditions were still pretty terrible there was some slight hope of improvement. Appalled by the chaos which would ensue if there were further delays, General Eisenhower (Supreme Commander of 'Overlord') decided that the risk must be taken, and the 6 June 1944 became D-Day.

XIV. RATIONING

High prices and very long queues sum up Britain's food situation during the Great War. After depending on huge supplies of food being imported from overseas countries, serious shortages were suffered as the enemy submarine campaign got under way. Some alarmists predicted that the British people would starve, but this did not happen. Instead, they resorted to growing their own food, and allotments were in great demand. In order to provide sufficient land to meet allotment requirements, Bristol Corporation even commandeered tennis courts, cricket and football grounds.

Housewives spent most of their time queueing for one item of food and then another. On one occasion when margarine was put on sale at the Corn Exchange in Bristol, an enormous queue formed through St. Nicholas Street, High Street and Corn Street to St. Stephen's Street, when in about the space of one hour approximately 6,000 half-pound packets were sold. And a pretty horrible commodity it was at that, and most unlike the highly refined margarine obtainable today. My Mother could only eat it after Grandmother had cooked the meat with it which made it more palatable.

The Great War had entered its final year before food rationing was introduced. Initially, it was on a regional basis, when in January 1918 Bristol rationed sugar to 8oz, meat (including bacon) 12oz, butter and margarine 4oz

156 RATION BOOK. One of the most important documents issued in wartime Britain, which enabled everyone to get a fair share of the limited food available.

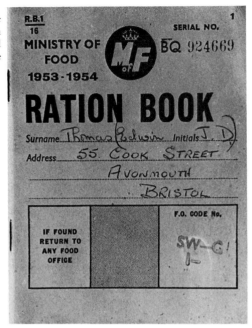

and tea 2oz per head per week. By July 1918 the rationing of these commodities had extended to the whole of the Country.

It never became necessary to actually ration bread during the Great War, but appeals were made to the citizens to economise in its use. Potatoes were added to flour to make it go further. The slogan 'Eat Less Bread' appeared in large letters on the steep cliff-face of Avon Gorge, which remained for many years following the war. To some Bristolians that particular great 'slide' is known as 'Eat-less-bread' to this day.

Come the Armistice, Britain was in the throes of a very severe influenza epidemic, which carried off the population in their hundreds. This was generally attributed to the wartime diet. In the week ending 2 November 1918 no less than 197 Bristolians died from its effects, and this figure did not include fatal cases of pneumonia following influenza.

When it came to the Second World War, with the experiences of the Great War in mind, expecting the enemy once again to try and cut off food supplies to bring Britain to her knees, food rationing was accepted and welcomed as a way of ensuring a fair share for all of the limited supplies available. The Ration Book became one of the most important documents issued in wartime Britain, and the war was only five months old when on 8 January 1940 rationing of bacon, sugar and butter was introduced. The rationing of meat came next in March 1940, followed by tea, fats and margarine in July 1940.

The amount per head fluctuated according to stocks being available. No matter how clever or rich you were, you had to try and make your rations last a week, and not surprisingly everyone thought a lot about food – in fact it was high up on the topic of wartime conversation.

It was not realised at the time, that not only were the U-boats responsible for the shortages of food, but the air raids also contributed. During Bristol's first blitz 24 November 1940, large quantities of foodstuffs were destroyed, particularly sugar and tinned stuffs. A granary with 8,000 tons of grain was destroyed near Prince Street Bridge during the blitz of 3 January 1941, to name but two incidents.

Whereas the rations went by weight, meat was the exception, being based on price. When introduced, the weekly meat ration per person was ten-pence worth (4p) plus four-pence worth (1½) of corned beef. It must be difficult indeed for today's generation to appreciate that even at those low limits, families were still able to buy a weekend joint. Sausages, offal and rabbits remained off-ration – sausages became objects of fun being referred to as 'breadcrumbs-in-battle-dress', which summed up the general opinion as to their main ingredient. Liver or hearts were 'under-the-counter' depending on how well customers fared with their butchers.

Queues formed during the Second War, as they did during the Great War, not for essentials this time, but for extras and luxuries, like cakes and biscuits. As non-rationed foods became scarce, people found it increasingly more difficult to stretch their food supply to feed their family. There was no such thing in those days as frozen foods and convenience foods, and housewives had to learn to bake without eggs and little or no fat.

Liquid paraffin was used in cakes as a substitute for fat, and egg powder as substitute for eggs, adding custard powder for colour. My Mother considered herself extremely fortunate if the butcher spared her a marrow bone, which she boiled for hours to extract the fat. This she clarified when cold, and used it for making pastry. Icing sugar and ground almonds were unobtainable, and wedding cakes had decorated cardboard to represent traditional royal icing. Marzipan icing was made with soya bean flour and flavoured with almond essence. Birthday cakes were topped with melted chocolate from the precious sweets ration.

During the Second War the Government became very health conscious, and endless advice on sensible eating habits, vitamins and balanced diets was issued by the Ministry of Food. Furthermore they churned out recipes *ad infinitum* giving housewives plenty of suggestions on wartime cooking. These appeared in leaflets, besides daily in newspapers and magazines, and not least in programmes broadcast by the B.B.C. 'On the Kitchen Front' was one such programme, with popular variety artistes of the day taking part, Mabel Constanduras with Grandma, and Molly Weir, for instance. As potatoes remained off-ration, there were numerous recipes for their use, such as Chocolate Potato Cake, Potato and Jam Pudding, or Potato Scone Sandwiches!

In November 1941, Lord Woolton, the Minister of Food, disclosed that at the time complaints were being made by the public about the astronomically high price of tomatoes, there was only ten days' supply of meat in the Country. At the same time butter, milk and eggs were in short supply, and Points Ration books were being issued for certain classes of tinned meats and fish, etc.

For the sweet-toothed amongst us, having to cope with the meagre sugar ration was always a great trial. Honey or saccharin could be used to sweeten tea or coffee, but were not very nice. When the fruit season came round, the preserves ration could be exchanged for extra sugar for home jam-making. It seemed a final blow when sweets and chocolate were put on ration in April 1942 to only 2oz per week. The sweets ration remained in force until April 1949, but was re-imposed the following August, and was not finally abolished until February 1953.

With shortages of fresh fruit and vegetables, Cod Liver Oil and pure orange juice were issued to expectant mothers and children under five. The scientists, to their credit, discovered new sources of Vitamin 'C' in blackcurrants with the introduction of Ribena, and wild rose hips were gathered to make rosehip syrup.

It was a real boon to appetites when in June 1942 supplies of dried eggs and dried milk arrived from America and were not rationed. The dried eggs, hitherto unknown, had been perfected in the United States by a new process.

157 MILK AND EGGS were in short supply during the war years. Dried milk and dried eggs were sent from America. David Ireland's photo shows the equivalent of milk and eggs represented by the tins kept in reserve by Mrs Ethel Brown of Shirehampton (Author's Mother).

158   BASIC WEEKLY RATION FOR ONE in 1944 . . . 8oz sugar, 2oz butter, 4oz margarine, 2oz cheese, 4oz bacon or ham, 2oz lard, 2oz tea, one egg, 1/3d (6p) worth meat and 2oz sweets/chocolate. Photo: by Teresa Momber.

159   ANIMAL FEEDING STUFFS FLOAT entered by Spillers Ltd., Avonmouth in the Bristol procession Wings for Victory Week, April 1943. Aimed to raise £4 million to buy 100 four-engined Lancaster bombers. By mid-week Avonmouth and Shirehampton had reached their target figure of £25,000, then set out to double it.

A 5oz tin of dried eggs was equal to 12 eggs and cost 1/9d. It could be whisked up, with an added spoonful of dried milk, to make delicious omelettes, served as scrambled eggs, or used in cakes etc. Another Godsend from America was tinned SPAM (Supply Pressed American Meat).

The basic ration per person per week in 1944 was 8oz sugar, 2oz butter, 4oz margarine, 2oz cheese, 4oz bacon or ham, 2oz lard, 2oz tea, one egg, 1/3d (6p) worth meat and 2oz sweets or chocolate.

During the Second War great efforts were made to really make Britain self-sufficient in feeding herself, so as not to rely on food from abroad. Farmers, who had had a raw deal in the years between the wars, now came into their own as the National drive for more home-grown food got under way, and extra acres were ploughed up and put under crops. 'Dig for Victory' became the order of the day, and once again allotments were in great demand. Whereas in 1939 Bristol had 7,782 allotment holders, in 1943 they had increased to 13,364. The price of milk was fixed long-term to farmers by the Government, to ensure there was a plentiful supply of this vital commodity. Forty years after the war the Government were still guaranteeing the price of milk to farmers.

Animals, like humans, were subjected to food rationing. Maize, which came across the Atlantic, was a very popular animal feed in pre-war days, but came to be meted out during the war like gold dust. One lady I knew

160 WARTIME PIG BIN (or pig-pails) were issued to all households for saving table scraps etc., to feed pigs and hens. Photo: November 1987.

exchanged her egg ration for feeding stuffs coupons, and thence kept in the basement of her Clifton Down home a couple of hens which she named Gert and Daisy after the music-hall stars, Elsie and Doris Waters.

No food was wasted. Table scraps and potato peelings etc., were collected by Bristol Corporation for feeding pigs and hens. Pig bins were placed at lamp-posts in the streets at first, but were eventually replaced by individual household pig-pails which were put out and emptied twice weekly. The Scheme started in August 1940. In 1951 it was reported that Bristol Corporation received £50,000 per year for our kitchen waste, and scraps fed to hens produced 16,000,000 eggs each year. Over 6,000 bacon pigs were being fed with kitchen waste, and householders were being urged to still make full use of their pail or street bins. The pig bin scheme was eventually abandoned during the middle 1950's.

As a means to supplement rations, eating out became a habit during the war, especially for those who could afford it. Even so, normal restaurant facilities were insufficient to meet demand. In July 1941 Bristol's first British Restaurant was opened by the Corporation in the unfinished Council House premises on College Green. Before the war ended Bristol had thirteen of these excellent eating places, including one in Avonmouth Park, where one could get a good meal with 'afters'. Mrs. Maund in September 1941 recorded having had a meal for only one shilling (5p) plus three-pence (1½p) for coffee. This was the start of the self-service style of eating out, as in the present-day Motorway Restaurants. Bristol's main British Restaurants were at the bottom of Park Street (College Green), Peter Street (Castle Green) and Belgrave Road (corner of Whiteladies Road) Clifton.

Following the war the British Restaurant buildings in Avonmouth Park were used as an over-spill for Avonmouth School, and then in 1963 for St. Andrew's Church Hall meetings while the old hall was being taken down and the present hall was being built.

The Docks and many factories had their own Canteens where excellent meals were served to keep the workers going. Extra cheese rations were allowed to shift-workers and other workers for whom canteen facilities were not available.

It is not always appreciated that the School dinner service, which nowadays is taken so much for granted and as a *right,* was, in the first instance, started as a wartime measure, following a Scheme introduced by Lord Woolton in October 1941 to ensure that children did not suffer through an inadequate diet. He made it possible for all children at School to have one excellent nourishing meal a day, in addition to the cheap milk (one-third pint bottles started in the 1930's at the cost of one half-penny) already supplied. Heads of local Schools were summoned to a meting at Bristol University on 28 February 1942 to discuss the start of School dinners in Bristol. At that time the cost of School meals throughout the Country varied from one area to another, but they rarely exceeded fourpence (2p) each. Avonmouth School dinners service commenced on 11 October 1943.

In February 1942 rationing was extended to soap – although shaving soap was not included. This led to some neighbourly sharing. After finishing her weekly wash, it was the practice of Mrs. Edith Room to pass her soapy water to the lady next door to use, who with small children, found it difficult to make her soap ration last. Harsh ingredients in wartime washing powders were the cause of my Mother having a severe rash on hands and arms, which the Doctor diagnosed 'Persilitis'. The wooden floors of St. Mary's Church at Shirehampton were not neglected, despite soap rationing. The band of valiant ladies scrubbed them clean using unrationed Glitto (scouring powder) with cold water.

The advent of Victory, did not alas, bring an immediate end to rationing. Tea rationing continued until October 1952, cheese and fats until May 1954, and meat and bacon until July 1954. On the whole the Ministry of Food did an excellent job in organising Britain's wartime food supplies – the diet was monotonous, but we did not go hungry. The restrictions came about gradually, and as Mrs. H. Yeates wrote in 1979, 'Things were bleak, but spirits were high, and there were many laughable incidents, in spite of the war'.

161   BRITISH RESTAURANT in Avonmouth Park. Photo: May 1963. In post-war years these Nissen huts were used as emergency School classrooms. Eventually removed in August 1971.

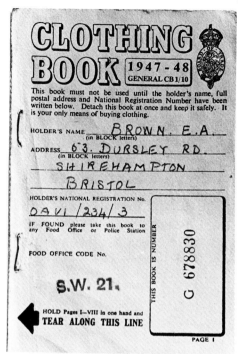

162 CLOTHING BOOK. Clothes besides food were rationed during the Second World War, and everyone was issued with a book of clothing coupons.

CLOTHES RATIONING

When clothes rationing was announced on Whit-Sunday, 1 June 1941, to take immediate effect, it was an unexpected move, and came as a complete surprise. To begin with, the allowance per person was 66 coupons to last a year, enough to ensure one could remain decently clothed – but only just – as can be judged from the following list of coupon values:

Women

Coat or Raincoat	14 coupons	Vest	3 coupons
Dress	11 ,,	Trousers	8 ,,
Pyjamas	8 ,,	Briefs	2 ,,
Nightdress	6 ,,	Stockings	2 per pair
Skirt	7 ,,	Shoes	5 ,, ,,

Men

Overcoat or Raincoat	16 coupons	Shirt	8 coupons
Blazer	13 ,,	Underpants	4 ,,
Trousers	8 ,,	Shoes	7 per pair

Everyone was issued with a special Clothing Book, which, with the Identity Cards, and Food Ration Books became an essential part of life in wartime Britain. The clothes rationing scheme included boots and shoes, knitting wools, all textiles and even handkerchiefs (½ coupon each). Coupons could be spent at any shop, and we soon got used to price tags on clothes also showing the number of coupons required.

After the first year of clothes rationing, Mr. Hugh Dalton, the President of the Board of Trade, announced that more than a quarter of a million tons of shipping space had been saved in textiles alone, and nearly four hundred thousand men and women released from making cloth and clothing for civilians, who had gone into the Forces or on to war production. After congratulating Britain on these results through clothes rationing, he then promptly reduced the following year's allocation of coupons to 48.

It was a heavy blow for the generation of teenagers leaving school, putting aside school uniform and anxious to get into adult fashions. Grown-ups were able to wear their clothes for as long as possible, and 'Make do and Mend' became the wartime slogan, but not having any adult clothes to start with was an impossible situation to be in.

As with the Ministry of Food with their wartime recipes, the Board of Trade issued 'Make do and Mend' hints by 'Mrs. Sew-and-Sew' in pamphlets, newspapers and magazines. For instance, two suggestions were that mothers could cut up their old dresses to make into blouses for a small daughter, and a skirt for her from father's old grey flannels. Woollen jumpers could be unpicked and re-knitted in a different style. Also advice on how to make clothes last longer and how to make new clothes from old was given.

Special arrangements were made for people with special needs. For example, mothers were given an allowance of 50 coupons for a new baby, and just as well, because each nappy required one coupon. There were problems for workers too. Sixty extra coupons were issued to underground miners in the coal Industry to meet their need for boots, and manual workers were allowed an additional ten coupons per year for working clothes. Other workers were allowed coupons for overalls, but *not* office workers.

Prices of clothes had escalated during the first twelve months of the war, and it was to counter this profiteering problem which led the Government to introduce 'Utility' clothing. These were price-controlled and therefore cheaper to buy, though at the the time, young people did not think them very glamorous. The Utility symbol denoted standard quality, but simple styles to save material and with minimum trimmings. On the whole, men-folk

163 UTILITY SYMBOL was the sign of price controlled quality, but austerity goods, displayed on clothes, household linen and even furniture. Clothing which bore a *utility* label was of standard quality with minimum trimmings.

164 SHEILA BROWN (Author's Sister) pictured in 1946, wearing turquoise linen two-piece dress, trimmed with *broderie Anglaise,* made herself from flour bags.

seemed indifferent to clothes rationing but were roused when it came to Utility suits being without turn-ups on trousers, single breasted coats, and with false pockets. Drastic changes indeed after the 1930's Oxford bags with their very wide trousers!

There was no alternative but to look for other supplies of materials. Flour bags, previously known only to those who worked in the Mills, now became a most sought after commodity, and smuggling them out of the Docks unnoticed by the Policeman on the Dock gates was a problem solved by fair means and foul (even beneath ladies 'unmentionables' we were led to believe!). After being washed, boiled, and dyed, flour bags were made into curtains, pyjamas, and even a smart linen two-piece dress, as I can vouch for. A friend had an excellent warm winter coat made by her mother from an unrationed grey/blue Army blanket. Sometimes too, off-cut pieces of parachute silk became available in the shops off-ration, which was real silkworm silk, and made beautiful blouses and underwear. To my mind, not to have owned a real silk blouse, being so warm and comfortable to wear, is not to have lived. Although materials by the yard were also rationed and required coupons, people who could make their own clothes found their coupons could be made to go further.

But no one could make their own stockings, and this was when women first began to discard them in the summer months. In those days ladies stockings were manufactured from cotton (lyle) rayon, artificial silk, or silkworm silk. It was not until after 1940 when the world's very first nylon factory was opened in the United States for commercial use, that nylon stockings came on to the market. Such was this revolution that it became the longing of every girl to own a pair of nylons, even willingly surrendering two coupons for the pleasure.

Due to the wartime shortage of leather, shoes appeared in the shops with wooden soles, which were hinged to assist walking. Elastic disappeared altogether from the market, but occasionally local shops received a small quota, and it was amazing how quickly the news got around on these occasions. Non-regular customers then thought up all kinds of pretences in order to purchase a yard or two of precious elastic. Make-up was also in extremely short supply. If one happened to hear that such-and-such a shop had a few lipsticks or some face powder in stock, off we flew whether or not it was the right shade to suit us.

A very ancient custom which was rescinded during the war, and has not so far been reinstated, is that of hatless women in Church. In November 1942 a statement was issued by the Archbishops of Canterbury and York as follows:

'Questions are frequently asked these days concerning the old customary rule that women should not enter a Church building with their heads uncovered. The Scriptural Authority behind this rule is St. Paul's regulation, but this required that they should be veiled. That has long ago fallen out of use, and after consultation with the Bishops generally, we wish it to be known that no woman or girl should hesitate to enter a Church with head uncovered, nor should any objection to their doing so be raised.'

St. Paul's regulation, to which this statement referred is found in I Corinthians XI v 4–6. But *not all* Clergy, it seems, agreed with the Archbishops new ruling. The Revd. C. W. Dixon wrote in Shirehampton Parish Magazine:

'If it is a case of a girl in the Services here on leave able to bring civilian clothes but not a hat-box, who, but for this relaxation would be barred from attending Services – in a case of emergency – it is right and proper for women to appear in God's House without their heads covered, but not as a general rule, and I would commend the carrying out of this new relaxation in the spirit but not the letter.'

Hats, in fact, were not rationed. It is quite interesting to note very often these days that Bishops wearing their mitres find themselves in the company of a very few women who are still accustomed to wearing hats in Church! Scarves as head-gear became in vogue during the war (even though head-scarves required one clothing coupon) and have remained the trend, no doubt, due to our present Queen favouring the fashion.

Clothes rationing meant that most wartime brides had to forego traditional long white dresses, and this was the start of beg, borrow or hire bridal gowns. Most wartime brides (and bridesmaids too) wore knee length day dresses or suits with small fashionable hats, swathed in veiling, and a corsage of flowers in place of bouquets. Even so, there was no mistaking who the *bride* was. A certain Plymouth bride wore a dress made from non-rationed net curtaining, as did her bridesmaids! The Women's Royal Naval Service were renowned for their collection of white bridal gowns which they had on hand to loan to their members for their weddings.

Some families who found they had clothing coupons to spare (and even if they did not) sold them on the black market, the usual price being about one shilling (5p) per coupon. Although this was strictly illegal, clothing coupons became an accepted form of currency to the buyers and sellers.

The 14 March 1949 was a Monday, and I remember it well. This was the day Mr. Harold Wilson, then President of the Board of Trade, announced that after eight years there was an immediate end to rationing of clothes and textiles, and complete abolition of clothing coupons. The author mounted her bicycle and headed for the nearest Ladies Outfitters, where she treated herself to a complete new set of underwear, and felt highly gratified in doing so. A little earlier, on 31 July 1948, boots and shoes had been taken off ration.

165 WARTIME WEDDING. August 1941. When Avonmouth couple Gwen Evans of Cook Street and Arthur Pinnock (Royal Navy) of Catherine Street were married at the Avonmouth Congregational Church, the bride was helped by her mother and sister in providing some of the required clothing coupons. The bride wore a silk afternoon dress in burgundy, with matching frothy hat.

XV. YEAR OF VICTORY

The year 1945 proved one of great and significant events, following upon each other in quick succession. The New Year saw the liberation of the Low Countries, and German invaders pushed back across the River Rhine, with Allied Armies in hot pursuit.

From 4 to 11 February, Mr. Churchill, President Roosevelt of the U.S.A. and Marshal Stalin of Russia, all met at Yalta in the Crimea, to complete plans for the final defeat and control of Germany. At the same time they laid the foundations of the United Nations Organisation. It was to be the last occasion that the 'Big Three' great War Leaders would meet. With Victory almost in sight, President Roosevelt quite unexpectedly passed away on 12 April 1945, his place being taken by Vice-President Harry S. Truman.

During the final weeks of the war in Europe there developed a mighty and all important race to Berlin. Who would arrive there first, we wondered? The Allied Armies advancing from the west, or the Russians advancing from the east? The front-line United States and Russian patrols first met up with each other and joined forces in the heart of Germany on 26 April 1945, amid celebrations and pledges of greater understandings between their two great peoples in future.

In the event, the final capture of Berlin was a privilege which went to the Russian Armies, but it proved a hollow victory. On arriving at Hitler's underground Chancellery bunker, he was not there, and it was revealed he and his mistress, Eva Braun, had already committed suicide on 30 April 1945; their bodies were never found, however, purported to having been burned. With the death of Hitler, came the collapse of Germany. The Nazi Leaders were now either dead or fugitives, and the war in the west was at last over.

At 3.0 p.m. on Tuesday 8 May 1945, Prime Minister Churchill made a historic broadcast, in which he announced that the new German Leaders had signed a pact of unconditional surrender to the Allied Expeditionary Force. Cessation of hostilities in Europe ended officially at one minute after midnight on that same day. 'Our dear Channel Islands are also to be freed to-day', the Prime Minister added. Tuesday and Wednesday, 8 & 9 May were declared VE-Days, and a General Holiday for all. The air raid sirens sounded the *All Clear* for the last time.

Mrs. Maund noted in her diary:

'Thank God! Thank God! How few bells can ring from their church towers in Bristol to-day? We are a sad City of ruins. The young lads will have noise to celebrate, so they have taken the lids of the pig-bins clashing them together as cymbals, as they

166   VE-DAY, LONDON. The excitement and happiness prevailing on 8 May 1945 brought these sailors and civilians together in an unrehearsed song-and-dance group. This scene was typical of many others throughout Britain on that day.

pass this house on their way towards the City Centre. I stand on the veranda to-day and look towards Bath. I can see red glows in the sky and am grateful they are not the result of a blitz. Bonfires are lit and from the Centre comes the hum of a City rejoicing. My one regret is that somewhere in the far distant East, some fine young English or American boy may be dying or killed to-night. They are *not* the forgotten Army, for I, with many a mother, wife and sweetheart, pray, "Please God, may that far distant war, too, soon cease".'

With this final entry in her wartime diary, Mrs. Maund had expressed the feelings of us all, mindful that the war was not yet completely over. There was still Japan with all her treachery and greed to be subdued. Even so, with the German war now at an end we could allow ourselves a brief period of rejoicing.

In Shirehampton, as at the end of the Great War, street after street organised their own tea parties, with sports, fancy dress parades, dancing and bonfires held in the flag bedecked streets, with great determination to make it a day the children would always remember. The Vicar of Shirehampton, the Revd. C. W. Dixon, after visiting a number of street parties, recorded that:

'The food provided at the teas almost surpassed belief, for it seemed incredible such generous quantities of cakes, with sugar tops, and other dainties could have been produced in these hard rationed days. A tremendous amount of self-sacrifice lay behind it all.'

It was obvious that folks had been saving up their food rations for the long awaited VE-day celebrations.

The flag decorations of Dursley Road, Shirehampton surpassed all others. A supply of ships' flags having been obtained via courtesy of J. Jefferies & Sons were strung from one side of the street to the other, and remained a vivid and lasting memory of VE-Day to those who lived in that road. Others may recall VE-Day as the time when Shirehampton's 'locals' were *the pubs with no beer!* With deliveries of beer on wartime quotas, and the population in jovial mood wishing to celebrate, pub cellars were very quickly drunk dry. A both frustrating and annoying position for Landlords to find themselves in.

At the close of the war in Europe, the Labour Party Ministers in Government decided that there was no further need for a Coalition Government in Britain, and agitated for normal Party Government to be reinstated forthwith. On 23 May 1945, therefore, after serving the nation so admirably for five years as Prime Minister, Winston Churchill tendered the resignation of one of the greatest and most successful Governments that Britain has ever known. The General Election took place on 5 July, but the results were not known until 26 July 1945, when voting papers from all the British servicemen and women the world over had been returned. The Labour Party gained a landslide victory, and Mr. Clement Attlee became Britain's new Prime Minister.

167   WAR CABINET of Britain's All-Party Government with the King at Buckingham Palace on VE-Day prior to dissolution. *Left to right:* Herbert Morrison, Lord Woolton, Sir John Anderson, Clement Attlee, H.M. King George VI, Winston Churchill, Anthony Eden, Oliver Lyttelton and Ernest Bevin.

The Allies now lost no time in turning their attention towards Japan, and were intent on the invasion of that country sometime in November '45. For this operation, code-named 'Olympic', a mighty armada was being amassed to do in the Pacific what D-Day had previously done in Europe. The loss of lives for such an operation was estimated to be astronomical, which, in the event was averted.

The scientists with their atomic bombs stepped in and brought the war to a climax and unexpected conclusion. The first was dropped at Hiroshima on the 6 August 1945, and the second at Nagasaki three days later. The decision to use atomic bombs was made by President Truman, but in retrospect, it was not so much a decision as *fait accompli*. No one at that time knew for sure what the terrifying and devastating results would be, and no doubt the rights and wrongs of it will be debated until the end of time. Even so, the atomic bombs brought the war to a speedy conclusion, and shortened it by some estimated 18 months. American servicemen were demobbed in a matter of six weeks.

Prime Minister Attlee announced after the midnight news on Tuesday, 14 August 1945, that Japan had surrendered. It took everyone by surprise, and we could hardly believe that the war was indeed completely over at long last. We all got out of bed and dressed, and went out into the street to spread the good news. There was impromptu dancing in Dursley Road, and a bonfire in the early hours; besides the flags being hastily hung across the road once again. In Shirehampton Village celebrations of a slightly different kind were taking place, best explained by the Vicar, the Revd. C. W. Dixon:

'Shortly after the Prime Minister's announcement, our dogs began to bark furiously. On getting out of bed to investigate, I found the two brothers Neale (one in uniform) desiring to ring the Church bells. I gave them the key of St. Mary's, and off they went to spread the good news in the quickest of all ways. I put my outer clothes over my pyjamas, a scarf around my neck (an old air-raid habit), and followed without the slightest thought of the possibility of holding a service.

On arrival, however, I saw there were already a few people at prayer in the unlighted Church, and others were converging upon St. Mary's from all directions. Obviously a service was indicated, and mercifully a young person, here on holiday, was able and ready to play the organ. So the way was clear. All the lights were switched on, hymn books dug out of the cupboard, and a short and in many ways inadequate but heartfelt impromptu service was held. Before its close, according to various estimates, there were close on 300 people in Church, and in most cases their costumes were as bizarre as that of the conductor of the service.'

During the VJ-Days that followed (Wednesday and Thursday, 15/16 August 1945) there were bonfires galore, the chief one being on Penpole Point, attended by the Lord Mayor and Lady Mayoress of Bristol, with teas, sports and games for the children in a number of streets. On the morning of the 15th King George VI and Queen Elizabeth drove in State from

Buckingham Palace to open the first session of the new Parliament, and in the evening His Majesty broadcast to his Peoples. The following Sunday, 19 August 1945, was the day of National Thanksgiving, when places of worship were crammed to overflowing with worshippers giving thanks to Almighty God, the only Giver of Victory, and for those He used to carry out His purposes.

Although spontaneous celebrations and jubilations took place on VE-Day and VJ-Day, the Ceremonial Victory Day was delayed until the following summer. Victory Day was celebrated on 8 June 1946, and in London a great Parade was held with majestic pageantry. Twenty-one thousand troops and civilians took part in the Victory Parade – the largest ever held in Britain – H.M. King George VI taking the salute from the saluting base in The Mall.

ERNEST BEVIN – STATESMAN

No history of the Second World War, especially regarding Avonmouth, would be complete without mention of Ernest Bevin. Generals and Admirals directed the battles, but it was Bevin who organised the workers at home to provide the war machines necessary for Victory. 'Our parents always told us he would go far', are the kind of remarks Avonmothians remember about the great Statesman, when recalling his early years in Avonmouth, and his struggles on behalf of the dockers.

168   ERNEST BEVIN – STATESMAN.
Born: 7 March 1881.
Died: 14 April 1951.

169 BIRTH PLACE OF ERNEST BEVIN at the small Exmoor Village of Winsford in Somerset. *Inset:* Commemorative plaque. Photo: July 1988.

Although being proudly claimed as one of the most remarkable 'sons of Bristol', he was, in fact, born on 7 March 1881 at the picturesque Exmoor village of Winsford in Somerset. His mother, Diana Mercy Bevin, was aged forty, separated from her husband, and Ernest never knew the identity of his father. His mother died when he was only eight, and he left school at eleven to start work as a farmer's boy at sixpence per week.

Ernest Bevin came to Bristol when only thirteen to work as a kitchen boy at a restaurant for a shilling per day, plus meals. Later, as a mineral water salesman, he found himself his own master in a job with ample scope for a man with energy and initiative – of which he had plenty. He married a Bristolian, Florence Anne Townley, and his connections with Manor Hall Baptist Mission, and study and discussion classes at Quaker Adult School developed his gifts of oratory and leadership.

The dockers' strike at Avonmouth in 1910, which spread to Bristol, was to mark a turning point in Bevin's career. The dockers were members of the Dock Wharf, Riverside & General Workers' Union, but the carters who drove to and from the docks were not Union men. Bevin was a carter himself. In August 1910 a carmen's branch of the Dockers' Union was formed with Bevin as Chairman, and in less than a year he had become a full-time official of the Dockers' Union. His masterly advocacy of the London dockers' case in 1920 earned him the title of 'the dockers' K.C.'. This led to his creating Britain's largest Trades Union, the Transport & General Workers with headquarters at Transport House, Smith Square, London, also the headquarters of the Labour Party.

Ernest Bevin became one of Britain's important wartime leaders when as Minister of Labour & National Service in Mr. Churchill's Coalition Government, he controlled the Nation's entire labour force throughout five years of war. Besides his measures to make dockers mobile, he not only directed large numbers of women into the munitions industries, but also ensured that they had decent working conditions. On his orders working women with husbands in the Forces were granted time off to coincide with their husbands' leave. The famous wartime radio programme 'Workers Playtime' was Mr. Bevin's idea, and with the Country badly needed coal in 1943 it was his scheme in sending young men, by ballot, down the mines, instead of serving in the armed forces, who came to be known as 'Bevin Boys'.

Mr. Bevin visited Bristol in 1941, and assured the workers and the Germans, 'You can knock down our buildings, but you cannot break our hearts. Before the war is over we shall pay Hitler back, two, three and four times,' he said. And so it came to pass. When the war was over, a telling tribute to Mr. Bevin's achievements came from his opposite number, Albert Speer, Hitler's Minister for Armaments, who said, 'You defeated us because you made *total* war, and we did not.' As Chancellor of Bristol University, Mr. Winston Churchill conferred an honorary degree Doctor of Laws on Mr. Bevin on 21 April 1945. (Mr. A. V. Alexander, First Lord of the Admiralty, also a Somerset man, born at Weston-super-Mare, received a Doctor of Laws honorary degree at the same time.)

When the Labour Government, headed by Mr. Attlee, was formed just three months later, Ernest Bevin became Foreign Secretary, which appointment he received during the historic three-power conference at Potsdam outside Berlin. In the role of Foreign Secretary Mr. Bevin proved himself a great and forceful Statesman. He was instrumental in 1949 in the establishment of the North Atlantic Treaty Organisation (N.A.T.O.), which still to this day determines the fundamental outlines of Britain's defence and foreign policy.

At the time of his death on 14 April 1951, aged 70, Ernest Bevin was Lord Privy Seal, and his ashes were interred in Westminster Abbey. History can now see Mr. Bevin as having been a truly great man, who, apart from Winston Churchill, had the most intellectual understanding of his time.

170   AVONMOUTH VILLAGE in 1945, viewed from Royal Edward Dock, showing bombed
Richmond Terrace and Richmond Villas. *Left background:* Army Embarkation huts in King

XVI. WINNING THE PEACE

Road. *Centre:* Burnt out shell of St. Andrew's Church. *Foreground:* Brick surface air raid shelters. *Background:* Open fields soon to become Lawrence Weston Housing Estate.

Despite Parliament's six years preoccupation with the task of winning the War, they nevertheless found time to consider plans for what Britain was going to be when the War was over.

In 1942 the Uthwatt Report put some control on the use of land, and from it emerged the Town and Country Planning Act of 1944 – the first great barrier against ribbon development and irresponsible spread of bricks and mortar.

The important Education Act of 1944 created the Ministry of Education, and generally laid down the principle that education was not an exclusive entitlement for the rich, but was a right for everyone, and should be freely available to all.

Britain was never to be the same again after 1942 when the Economist W. H. Beveridge drew up his plan for National wellbeing 'cradle to the grave' insurance coverage. The revolutionary ideas of the Beveridge Report were highly favoured by nine out of ten of the population. That Parliament should adopt the plan led to petitions being drawn up and thousands of signatures being collected – including Avonmothians. The Beveridge Report eventually formed the basis of our present Social Welfare State.

POST-WAR HOUSING

The housing shortage experienced in the Avonmouth and Shirehampton area at the end of the Great War, was in the main due to the new factories engaged on war work which had sprung up in the district attracting a large workforce. One of these was the National Smelting Company which had come to stay.

In the years between the wars, Bristol Corporation continued to have a housing problem, after embarking on a slum clearance programme, which was far from completion when the Second World War broke out and of necessity all building operations were brought to a halt. No new houses were therefore built between 1939 and 1945 despite the fact that Bristol lost over 3,000 houses in the air raids, either being totally destroyed by bombs, or being so badly damaged they had to be demolished. In November 1943 it was reported that 4,308 names were on the Corporation waiting list for houses, and by 1945 the situation was both acute and urgent.

Some distraught families needing a house at this time became desperate and attempted to solve their problem themselves by moving into empty huts on ack-ack and other military sites throughout Britain which were left abandoned after servicemen and women had been demobbed. In Shirehampton the vacant army barrack huts remaining on Penpole were taken over by unauthorised civilians, and the 'squatters', once established, raised even more problems for the Authorities.

171   AIROH HOUSE at Henleaze Road, Henleaze in June 1979 prior to removal. Similar in design to that of 125 Nibley Road, Shirehampton, Britain's first ever prefabricated home. Officially opened 18 July 1945.

As the war drew to a close it became obvious to everyone that houses had to be built quickly, and the dire situation produced many new ideas and one revolutionary invention, i.e., the factory-built prefabricated bungalow called the 'Airoh' house. The original name for this new kind of housing was soon dropped, in favour of the abbreviation 'prefab', and Shirehampton can be justly proud that the very first prefab to be erected and occupied in the Country was No. 125 Nibley Road on the then uncompleted Cotswold Estate. The first prefab was also a product of Bristol having been made by Bristol Aeroplane Company Ltd.

With all due credit to it being only ten weeks after VE-Day, Wednesday 18 July 1945 was a red letter day for both Bristol and Shirehampton, when the Lord Mayor, Councillor W. F. Cottrell officially opened No. 125 Nibley Road. General Sir Frederick Pile (Director General of Temporary Housing of the Ministry of Works) flew to Bristol in order to be present at the opening ceremony. Mr. W. R. Verdon Smith (Director of Bristol Aeroplane Company) handed the key of the Airoh house to the Lord Mayor, and it was made known that Mr. Churchill had visited Filton in April that year in order to see an Airoh house for himself. It was announced the rent for the prefabs on the Shirehampton site would be about 14/- or 15/- (70p or 75p) per week.

172 COTSWOLD ESTATE, SHIREHAMPTON. Prefabs at Dursley Road and Nibley Road viewed from Woodwell Road in October 1966.

Fifty Airoh houses were erected on this first site, followed by forty on a site at Filton.

The Cotswold Estate at Dursley Road and Nibley Road was a natural and very convenient site to house the first prefabs. The Estate, a private housing development of three-bedroomed houses, had been started in 1938, replacing the allotments which formerly extended from the original part of Dursley Road to Woodwell Lane. The houses were priced between £450 and £500, according to size of garden. Building had progressed as far as Hung Road when the War broke out and all operations were brought to a halt, although the concrete roads and drains for the Estate had been laid as far as Woodwell Lane.

The first prefabs were made of aluminium salvaged from crashed aircraft and melted down, and were built by B.A.C. at their Weston-super-Mare works. Their design was the most modern in housing, having central heating, up-to-date kitchens, built-in cupboards including an airing cupboard, and were even fitted with a 'fridge, a very rare feature in those days. The Airoh houses were transported from factory to site on very large lorries, then lifted by crane on to brick foundations. The prefabs sprang up like mushrooms almost overnight. Intended as only temporary

173   PREFAB AT MARKHAM CLOSE, SHIREHAMPTON. Compare design with plate 171 with front door at centre instead at side.   Photo: April 1979.

174   THE PORTWAY, SHIREHAMPTON viewed from the M.5 Avonmouth Bridge, showing in foreground the prefabs at Markham Close soon to be removed.   Photo: January 1979.

accommodation, they were given a ten year tenure, but in actual fact they became the foundations of many permanent happy homes. Nearly 5,400 prefab houses of six different types were erected in Bristol, and throughout the Country there were 150,000 of them erected in urban districts on all available sites, on waste plots and sometimes even on bomb sites.

At Shirehampton, Markham Close and Valerian Close came into being, whilst vacant sites in St. Mary's Road, Old Barrow Hill and Walton Road were soon occupied by prefabs. Two Curates lived in prefabs on the Cotswold Estate whilst serving on the staff of St. Mary's Parish Church, Shirehampton – the Revd. John Burnett 1949–1953 and the Revd. Terence Simper 1959–1961.

After their 25 year life-span it was decided in the early 1970's that due to deterioration the prefabs on the Cotswold Estate should be demolished and replaced by permanent brick houses. The tenants were offered alternative accommodation and had to move out by the deadline 17 October 1972. It is quite interesting to note that the majority of those tenants involved opted to move back to live in that area when the permanent houses were completed. Although having outlived their original tenure by some thirty years, the prefabs in Old Barrow Hill, Walton Road and Valerian Close still remain in 1988, whilst those in Markham Close were all demolished during 1979 and have not so far been replaced. In some cases remaining prefabs have been

175 AVONMOUTH PARISH viewed from M.5 Avonmouth Bridge, showing in foreground some of the steel houses built during 1947, and now become a permanent feature. Photo: June 1973

purchased by the tenants from the Corporation. Many Parishes in Bristol accommodated a complement of prefabs, including Stoke Bishop, but for some unexplained reason Avonmouth missed out on prefabs. Instead, Avonmouth became host in 1947 to steel houses, another quickly erected new kind of dwelling. These two-storey houses were built on open fields which separated Catherine Street and West Town Road, and five new streets came into being, viz: Akeman Way, Leeming Way, Maiden Way, Pilgrims Way and Stane Way. Avonmouth's steel houses were completed and first occupied between July and December 1947. At the time of writing some are still occupied by their original tenants. They have proved very warm and comfortable homes, some being purchased by the tenants from the Corporation – one having privately changed hands recently for the sum of £30,000. Steel houses were erected in Shirehampton to make an entirely new road named Watling Way, and also in St. Mary's Road and West Town Road.

RECONCILIATION

After six gruelling years the Second World War was over at last, leaving behind it a torn and battered Europe, with great cities and towns in ruins, with millions of starving and destitute people; with homeless children who had forgotten the days when they had homes and parents, now wandering in bands with only the urge to find food and shelter in the ruined lands. There were, too, the helpless victims of the concentration camps, and the prisoners of war, some of whom now had no country of their own. Looking back, one can only marvel at the wonderful work which was accomplished by Organisations speedily set up, mainly by Anglo-American co-operation, to help restore some kind of order out of the chaos, and to give new hope to the displaced persons.

The Lend-Lease arrangement signed in 1941 terminated abruptly with the ending of hostilities, and Great Britain and other war torn countries suddenly found themselves without the means of paying in dollars for indispensable American supplies, including foodstuffs, materials and capital goods, needed for economic reconstruction. Eventually, in 1947, the Marshall Aid Plan came into being (named after the American General, George Catlett Marshall) through which help was given to the destitute, and miracles were accomplished. Slowly but surely the world returned to sanity – the horrors of war banished, food and the implements of peace were brought from across the seas, the desolate fields were ploughed again, and the rehabilitation of the homeless went steadily on until all was accomplished.

For Britain, the dollar crisis continued for some years. In January 1950 Queen Mary surprised the world by producing the carpet upon which she had been working since 1942, and which had occupied a great deal of the time she spent at Badminton House as an evacuee. This enormous piece of embroidery, measuring 12 ft. by 7 ft., consists of twelve panels of old English flower designs worked in petit-point. Queen Mary offered the carpet to the nation for sale in America to raise dollars. In the event, Canada out-bid the United States for the carpet, which was purchased by the Imperial Order of Daughters of the Empire at a price of 100,000 dollars, for presentation to the Canadian people. But first, it was taken on exhibition to a number of cities in the United States. The sum of £35,354 from its sale and exhibition was passed to the Exchequer as Queen Mary's personal contribution to the National Debt.

A new Organisation, the United Nations, replaced the old League of Nations formerly wound up in 1946. The hate inspired by war was at least balanced by the goodwill and patient efforts of both statesmen and the common people to re-establish the reign of peace and friendship throughout the world.

Britain at that time was in no position herself to materially help a great deal towards the recovery of Europe, but she contributed in other ways particularly in implementing the great resolve that Britain would not go to war with Germany ever again! 'Getting to know you' was the underlying purpose of the twinning schemes which have proved so successful in the succeeding years in promoting goodwill and friendships between our two countries. Bristol became twinned with Hannover, the capital of Lower Saxony in West Germany, on the grounds that both cities had much in common, and that shared help in rebuilding could be of mutual benefit. Both cities suffered terrible destruction during the war, and were well-matched in size and importance. Trade and commerce had, over the centuries, given the two cities power and wealth; now the mediaeval centres of both cities were severely damaged and redevelopment was necessary. Perhaps, too, the link also owed something to the historical connections between England and Hannover.

On 30 August 1947 a goodwill mission of five people from Bristol left for Hannover. The party was led by Alderman St. John Reade, and the mission represented educational, youth and industrial interests, and was supported by Church and Trade Union organisations. As a result of this successful visit a Bristol–Hannover Council was formed, and a Working Party set up. In the Autumn of 1947 the visit from Bristol to Lower Saxony was reciprocated by Hannover when Bishop Lilje of Hannover visited Bristol, and since that time a whole range of continuing contacts and exchanges has been firmly established.

Among the regular or annual activities are exchanges between civic leaders, schools and youth, and adults and families. In addition, exchanges have taken place and continue to do so involving many different

176   GERMAN SEAMEN: German Navy Veterans of the Second World War honouring Bristol's War Dead in a wreath-laying ceremony at the Bristol cenotaph in Colston Avenue on 6 September 1987.

organisations: university and polytechnic groups, churches, police, theatres, housewives, teachers, musical groups, trade unions, businessmen, sporting and athletic organisations, besides elderly people's clubs.

The partnership reached a high point in 1983, when Bristol conferred the Honorary Freedom of the City upon Hannover – the highest honour that it could possibly bestow – thus cementing the Bristol/Hannover friendships which over the years have gone from strength to strength. No one could have possibly foreseen in 1945 that the day would come when five German Navy veterans of the Second World War would visit Bristol with their wives and families specifically to lay a wreath at the Bristol War Memorial in Colston Avenue in honour of Bristol's war dead. One of the visitors, Erwin Ruger, a former torpedo boat navigator, said that German sailors had always admired the skill and courage of the Royal Navy, even though they had been enemies. This unprecedented gesture by the German group took place in September 1987, and was after an invitation by the Royal Navy Association and the Bristol-Hannover Twinning Association – bearing out the truth of the words spoken in Washington on 26 June 1954 by Mr. Churchill . . .

'To jaw-jaw is better than to war-war'.

DIARY OF EVENTS

1914
Aug. 4   OUTBREAK OF THE GREAT WAR.
Dec. 20   First enemy air raid on Britain.

1915
January   Conscription introduced.
Apr. 22   Germany first uses gas warfare.
Aug. 13   Troopship *Royal Edward* sunk, with loss of 935 lives.
Sept. 7   George V & Queen Mary visit Shirehampton Remount Depot.

1916
May 17   First Daylight Saving Act received Royal Assent.
June 6   Battle of Jutland. Lord Kitchener drowned.
Sept. 3   First German Zeppelin brought down on British soil.
Sept. 15   Battle of the Somme. First tanks went into action.
Dec. 7   Lord George becomes Prime Minister and forms War Cabinet.

1917
Apr. 6   United States of America enters the war.
July 20   Separate Parish of Avonmouth formed.

1918
January   Britain first introduces food rationing.
Apr. 1   Royal Air Force formed.
Sept. 30   British first use of gas warfare against German troops.
Nov. 9   Kaiser William II abdicates, and escapes to Holland.
Nov. 11   ARMISTICE SIGNED BY GERMAN ARMIES.

1919
July 24   Peace Day celebrations. National Holiday.
Dec. 1   Nancy Astor (First woman M.P.) to House of Commons.

1920
Jan. 10   Birth of the League of Nations.
Nov. 11   The 'Unknown Warrior' interred in Westminster Abbey.

1921
Feb. 25   Dedication of Avonmouth Congregational War Memorial.
Sept. 4   Unveiling of Shirehampton War Memorial.
Dec. 20   Dedication of St. Andrew's Avonmouth War Memorial.

1926
July 2   Official opening of The Portway.

1932
June 26   Unveiling of Bristol's War Memorial.

1933
Jan. 30   Hitler appointed German Chancellor.

1934
Aug. 2   Hitler becomes Dictator.

1937
May 28   Neville Chamberlain becomes Prime Minister.

1938
Mar. 13   Germany annexes Austria.
Sept. 28–30   MUNICH CRISIS. Munich Agreement signed.

1939
February   Wardens call on householders to obtain sizes for gas masks.
Mar. 15   Germany over-runs Czecho-Slovakia. Hitler installed in Prague.
July   'What to do in an Air Raid' pamphlets issued.
Sept. 1   German troops invade Poland.
Sept. 2   National Service Bill enables men aged 18–41 to be called up.
Sept. 3   BRITAIN AND FRANCE DECLARE WAR ON
                  GERMANY. Black-out enforced immediately and all to carry
                  gas masks.
Sept. 16   Petrol rationing introduced.
Sept. 29   Identity Cards issued.

1940
Jan. 8   Food rationing begins.
Feb. 8   King George VI & Queen Elizabeth visit Avonmouth and
                  Bristol.
Apr. 9   Germany invades Denmark and Norway.
May 10   Germany invades Belgium, Luxemburg and Holland.
May 10   Churchill replaces Chamberlain as Prime Minister and forms
                  National Government.
May 14   L.D.V. formed – later renamed the Home Guard.
May 27   Belgium surrenders.
May 29–June 4 Dunkirk Evacuation.

June 10	Italy enters the war as Germany's allies.
June 17	Fall of France.
June 25	Avonmouth's and Bristol's first air raid.
July 23	Imposition of Purchase Tax.
Aug. 10–Sept. 15	R.A.F. win the Battle of Britain.
Sept. 23	George Cross introduced for civil acts of gallantry.
Sept. 25	First daylight raid on Filton.
Nov. 24	First great blitz on Bristol.
Dec. 16	The King visits Bristol for second time this year.

1941

Jan. 16	Great blitz on Avonmouth.
Feb. 5	Duke of Kent visits Avonmouth and Bristol.
Feb. 19	Children of Bristol and Avonmouth evacuated.
Mar. 11	U.S. Lease and Lend Bill signed.
Apr. 9	The Observer Corps. granted a 'Royal' title.
Apr. 11	*Good Friday*. Last heavy raid on Avonmouth and Bristol.
Apr. 19	First Register of women for war work.
May 10	Rudolph Hess (Hitler's Deputy) lands in Scotland.
June 1	*Whit Sunday*. Clothes rationing started.
June 4	William II, the ex-Kaiser of Germany, dies in obscurity.
June 22	Germany attacks Russia. Britain and Russia now allies.
June	The 'Utility' Scheme introduced by the Board of Trade.
Dec. 1	Points Rationing introduced to complement rations.
Dec. 6	Japanese surprise attack on U.S. Fleet at Pearl Harbour.
Dec. 8	Britain and U.S. declare War on Japan.
Dec. 11	U.S. enters the war against Germany and Italy.
Dec. 25	Hong Kong surrenders to the Japanese.

1942

January	American troops start arriving in Britain.
Feb. 9	Soap on ration. Clothing coupons reduced to 48 per year.
Feb. 15	Fall of Singapore.
Mar. 16	Supplies of flour restricted.
Mar. 29	*Palm Sunday*. National Day of Prayer.
Apr. 25	Blitz on Bath.
June 19	Dedication of partly restored St. Andrew's Church, Avonmouth.
June 28	Blitz on Weston-super-Mare.
July 26	Sweets and chocolates on ration ($\frac{1}{2}$-lb. each per month).
Aug. 25	Duke of Kent killed in an air crash in Scotland.
Sept. 6	Germans halted at Stalingrad.

Nov. 7	Allied invasion of North Africa.
Nov. 15	Church bells ring out for Victory in North Africa.
Dec	Beveridge 'Cradle to Grave' Report presented.

1943

April 12–17	Bristol's 'Wings for Victory' Week raised £4 millions.
July 10	Allied troops land in Sicily.
Sept. 3	National Day of Prayer (4th anniversary of the war).
Sept. 7	P.A.Y.E. introduced for tax payers.
Dec. 26	Germany's last battleship, *Scharnhorst,* sunk off Norway.

1944

Jan. 15	Education Act passed.
Apr. 2	Double Summer Time begins (Two hours ahead of G.M.T.).
May 13	Bristol's 'Salute the Soldier' Week.
May 15	Last air raid alert in the Battle of Bristol.
May 25	*Pan Massachusetts* disaster at Avonmouth.
June 4	Allied Forces enter Rome.
June 6	D-DAY ALLIED LANDINGS IN NORMANDY.
June 13	First flying-bomb (V-1) lands on Britain.
July 20	Unsuccessful 'Bomb plot' on the life of Hitler.
Aug. 25	Paris liberated.
Sept. 3	Special Day of Prayer (5th anniversary of the war).
Sept. 8	First German rocket (V-2) falls on Britain.
Sept. 11	First Allied crossing into Germany.
Oct. 26	Order given for Bristol's evacuees to return home.
Dec. 3	The Home Guard disbanded.

1945

Feb. 4	Yalta Conference, with Churchill, Stalin and Roosevelt.
Feb. 5	Colston Hall burnt down.
Apr. 12	Death of Franklin D. Roosevelt – three times elected President of U.S.A. Succeeded by Harry S. Truman.
Apr. 20	Russians reach Berlin.
Apr. 21	Winston Churchill visits Bristol and honours Ernest Bevin.
Apr. 30	Hitler commits suicide in Berlin.
May 7	Germany surrenders unconditionally.
May 8	V.E. DAY (VICTORY IN EUROPE) GENERAL HOLIDAY.
May 13	Thanksgiving Sunday.
July 5	General Election. Clement Attlee (Labour) forms new Government.

July 18	Britain's first prefab officially opened at Shirehampton.
Aug. 6	U.S. drops first atomic bomb on Hiroshima.
Aug. 9	Second atomic bomb on Nagasaki.
Aug. 14	Japan surrenders.
Aug. 15 & 16	V-J DAYS. (VICTORY IN JAPAN) GENERAL HOLIDAY.
Aug. 17	U.S. Lease and Lend Agreement terminates.

END OF SECOND WORLD WAR.

Data from Author's Personal Diaries

1942

Apr. 8	Took part in 'Aid to Russia' Concert at Groveleaze Youth Club.
Apr. 25	Registered under Youth Act (16/17 yr. olds) at Labour Exchange.
May 1	Received two shillings (10p) per week rise War Bonus.
Dec. 12	My first hair perm, cost 10/6d (52½p) at Westlake's, Avonmouth.

1943

May 18	Balcony seats at Savoy Cinema gone up to 2/9d (14p).
June 12	Attended my first American wedding. Service at Shirehampton Baptist Church. G.I. Bride was Betty Derrick.

1944

Jan. 15	Had to register at Avonmouth Labour Exchange for calling-up.
Mar. 26	Watched U.S. baseball match on Shirehampton Cricket Ground.

1945

June 15	Received 6/– (30p) per week rise. Paid 4/– (20p) Income Tax!
Aug. 26	Dad dug up our Anderson air raid shelter to relay the lawn.

BIBLIOGRAPHY

Bristol and the Great War 1914–1919. C. Wells & G. F. Stone. 1920
Bristol Under Blitz. Alderman T. H. J. Underdown. 1942
Roof Over Britain. War Office & Ministry of Information. 1943
Bristol Siren Nights. Revd. S. Paul Shipley. 1943
Bristol Bombed. F. G. Warne. 1943
Bristol's Bombed Churches. Revd. S. Paul Shipley. 1945
The L.M.S. At War. George C. Nash. 1946
The Diary of a Bristol Woman. Violet A. Maund. 1950
The House of Kings. 1950
The Defence of the United Kingdom. Basil Collier. 1957
Bristol At War. Professor C. M. MacInnes. 1962
Life in Wartime Britain, E. R. Chamberlin. 1976
British Vessels Lost At Sea 1939–1945. H.M. Stationery Office. 1976
Yes! We Have Some. Patrick Beaver. 1976
Scourge of the Atlantic. Kenneth Poolman. 1978
Gloucestershire at War 1939–1945. Derek Archer Editor. 1979
The Luftwaffe in the Battle of Britain. Armand van Ishoven. 1980
Duke of Beaufort Memoirs. The 10th Duke of Beaufort. 1981

Newspapers and Magazines

The Times
Western Daily Press & Bristol Mirror
Bristol Evening Post
Bristol Evening World
Clifton Chronicle & Directory
Parish of Avonmouth Monthly Magazines
Shirehampton Parish Monthly Magazines
Purnell's History of the Second World War 1981
Avon Conservation News January 1981
Gloucestershire & Avon Life Magazine June 1984

INDEX